TRADITIONAL PAPERMAKING
AND PAPER CULT FIGURES OF MEXICO

TRADITIONAL PAPERMAKING AND PAPER CULT FIGURES OF MEXICO

BY ALAN R. SANDSTROM
AND PAMELA EFFREIN SANDSTROM

UNIVERSITY OF OKLAHOMA PRESS : NORMAN AND LONDON

Library of Congress Cataloging-in-Publication Data

Sandstrom, Alan R.
  Traditional papermaking and paper cult figures of Mexico.

  Bibliography: p. 304
  Includes index.
  1. Indians of Mexico—Papermaking.   2. Indians of
Mexico—Religion and mythology.   I. Sandstrom, Pamela Effrein.
II. Title.
F1219.3.P3S26   1986   299'.74   85-40947
ISBN 0-8061-1972-1

Publication of this book has been made possible in part by grants
from the Andrew Mellon Foundation and the Indiana University
President's Council on the Social Sciences.

The paper in this book meets the guidelines for permanence and
durability of the Committee on Production Guidelines for Book
Longevity of the Council on Library Resources, Inc.

Dedicated with affection to
Carlos and Cristina Boilès

CONTENTS

vii

ILLUSTRATIONS

ix

MAPS AND DIAGRAMS

PREFACE

PAPER hardly seems a promising subject for a work about Mexican Indian religion. Yet we hope to show that this unassuming substance plays an important role in the religious life of some of the most traditional Indians in Middle America. We will also show that paper has been an important part of religious rituals since pre-Hispanic times. But it is not the paper that interests us so much as what people do with it, and thus what it reveals about their culture. In one remote region in east-central Mexico, Indian shamans cut remarkable figures from paper for use during sacred ceremonies. This region has been little studied by anthropologists, and few outsiders have witnessed the rituals in which the figures are used. The paper figures depict spirits that the shamans are able to summon and influence for the benefit (or harm) of humanity. The figures are the central features of rituals, and thus they provide a key for gaining insight into the religious beliefs and world view of the people who use them.

The main body of this work is a catalog of more than two hundred drawings of the figures with information about each spirit that is portrayed. The descriptions of the paper images and the ethnographic and historical information accompanying the catalog are written from an anthropological perspective for the interested nonspecialist. The purpose of the work is to inform people about a little-known aspect of Mesoamerican Indian history and culture and to provide information on the paper images, some of which are now for sale in tourist markets in Mexico and elsewhere throughout the world.

We first became interested in this subject in 1972, during an anthropological expedition into the remote regions of the southern Huasteca, in the state of Veracruz. There the Indians, isolated from the influences of urban Mexico, have been left to follow their traditions. After living four or five months in a Nahua (modern Aztec) village, we were permitted to witness a remarkable ritual dedicated to a pre-Hispanic fertility deity. At one point during the proceedings the shaman took out a bundle of tissue papers of various colors and, using a pair of scissors, began to cut fantastic shapes from individual sheets. We had seen the small "paper doll" figures cut from parchment-like bark paper, which Otomí Indians from the state of Puebla offered for sale in tourist markets and shops specializing in folk arts. But at the time we were not aware that other Indians also cut them, nor that the paper images are part of a living religious tradition. We learned that, besides Nahuas and Otomís, Tepehua Indians from the same region also cut and use paper images in their rituals.

Early in the research we realized that to understand principles of Nahua world view, religion, cosmology, and disease etiology we had to obtain a representative collection of the paper images. As our research continued, it became clear that the ideal strategy would be to gather a sample of paper cuttings from neighboring groups as well. Nahuas, Otomís, and Tepehuas share aspects of their religious beliefs and myths, and the enlarged collection would help delineate the system of spirits in the whole culture area. We reasoned that through the systematic comparison of all three groups it should be possible to gain greater insight into the pantheon of any single group. For example, Señor de la Noche (Lord of the Night) seemed to be an undefined, ambiguous spirit among the Nahuas, associated with the underworld and the spirit Tlauelilo (Devil). We wondered why Nahua shamans do not cut a paper image of Señor de la Noche. The Otomís, by contrast, do cut an image of Señor de la Noche, and we know that one aspect of the spirit's role is to serve as gatekeeper of the underworld. Thus the Nahuas appear to be in the process of blending Señor de la Noche with Tlauelilo, and the status of this spirit among the Nahuas becomes clearer.

Since paper images are usually destroyed during rituals and the inexpensive tissue paper favored by most shamans disintegrates after a few months, we decided to make color photographic transparencies of each specimen. Transparencies are durable and lend themselves to exact reproduction of the ritual figures because they can be fitted into a microfilm reader and the images projected and traced onto paper. At first we included only specimens that we collected ourselves, but later we added examples from private collections, from the few published sources on the cultures of the area, and from shops specializing in folk art. All available ethnographic information on the figures is recorded on edge-notched data cards, which are catalogued and indexed for easy retrieval. At present we have more than one thousand specimens in the archives, of which the examples in chapters 4 to 6 are representative. We have made the drawings of the paper images from the original slides by tracing them and then reducing the traces by means of a grid scale; they are accurate to the smallest detail. Sometimes the shamans make errors in cutting, which result in slight asymmetries. In the interest of accuracy even these small mistakes have been preserved in the drawings.

The chapters which follow provide the background necessary for an understanding of the paper images. Chapter 1 is a brief history of paper manufacture and use among pre-Hispanic Indian civilizations. It also includes an account of the scholarly debate over the source of the fibers the Indian craftsmen used for the paper—a debate which led to the discovery, at the turn of the century, of the papermaking Indians who live in the southern Huasteca and its border regions. Chapter 2 is a description and analysis of a Nahua-Otomí seed ritual which illustrates how the paper images are actually used by contemporary shamans. In chapter 3 a discussion of the history, geography, and Indian cultures of the paper-using region is presented. Chapter 4 is an outline of Nahua religion, followed by a catalog of fifty-nine paper figures with annotations. Chapter 5 is an outline of Otomí religion, followed by a catalog of ninety-seven paper images, fifty-nine of which were cut from traditional bark paper. Many of these figures are available commercially, and this chapter can be especially useful to those interested in identifying examples they have purchased. In chapter 6 a description of Tepehua religion is followed by a catalog of forty-four paper images used in Tepehua rituals. Chapters 4 to 6 include lists of the major rituals held by each group. After the concluding chapter is a bibliography of published works relating to the cultural use of paper among Indians of Mexico.

In the pages that follow, we present a descriptive treatment of one aspect of Nahua, Otomí, and Tepehua religion. What little ethnographic work has been done on the paper-using cultures is scattered, difficult to find, and published in a variety of languages. The first step in any scientific analysis is description, and toward that end we have attempted to organize what is known about the paper cult while adding findings from our own research. We do not yet have a full understanding of how the religions are integrated with other aspects of the sociocultural systems of which they are a part. Furthermore, we lack comprehensive data on native cosmologies and myths, the systems of logic whereby the various spirits can be related to each other, and the ecological dimensions of ritual performance. Despite these gaps in knowledge enough is known to allow us to make suggestions for interpreting the paper-cult religions. We have reserved these suggestions for the concluding chapter. Our fundamental purpose in writing the work, however, is to stimulate an interest in this most fascinating and at the same time neglected area of Mesoamerican research.

The catalogs contain all the available information about each cutting. The name of the paper figure, when known, is given in three languages: Indian, Spanish, and finally English translation. Also included is information on the material from which the image is cut. Figures cut from traditional bark paper are labeled as such, while those made from industrially manufactured paper are indicated simply by identifying the color of paper used. Next the dimensions of the original are given in centimeters. Certain of the seed figures cut by Otomí Indians living in the village of San Pablito are made from layers of tissue paper that have been sewn together. The top layer is cut in such a way that differently colored layers underneath are revealed. These are indicated by crosshatching, and the colors of both the first and the second layers of paper are given. Questionable information has been omitted from the catalogs.

The terminology used throughout the book requires some explanation. When they are speaking Spanish, the Indians call the paper images *muñecos de papel* ("paper dolls"). Although some other researchers use this phrase, we decided to avoid it, for several reasons. First, shamans cut more forms than just the doll-like anthropomorphic images. Second, to people of Western European cultural heritage the phrase "paper doll" brings to mind children's games. We use the terms "paper figure" or "paper image" throughout this work. Another term used here is "shaman." This refers to any part-time religious specialist who is considered by his or her peers to possess extraordinary knowledge about religious myths and beliefs and who has the ability to summon and manipulate the spirits. The word "ritual" is used throughout the book in its nontechnical sense of any series of symbolic acts, usually under the direction of a shaman, designed to influence spirit entities. "Cult" is used to mean a system of ritual practices surrounding a particular symbolic form or material. The title of the book has two meanings and is intended to emphasize the importance of paper in Indian ritual life. Finally, the term "spirit" itself is problematic. The Indians often use the Spanish word *espíritu* when describing the unseen forces depicted in the paper figures. Evidence suggests, however, that what they mean by "spirit" is something like a life-force or nonpersonalized shadow soul (see chapters 4 to 6). They do not, for example, believe that the human personality survives death, but rather that the essence or life-force of the person goes to the afterlife (Provost 1981). The term "spirit" is used throughout the work in preference to "deity," "god," "soul," or "life-force" simply because it seems to be the closest English equivalent to the Indians' concept as expressed in the paper images.

Information on the seed ritual (chapter 2), the Huasteca culture area (chapter 3), and the Nahua religion (chapter 4) comes largely from our own fieldwork. Chapters 5 and 6, which contain descriptions of Otomí and Tepehua religion, along with catalogs of their paper images, are based on information from published and unpublished works of ethnographers and travelers. All publications consulted in the writing of this work are cited throughout and listed in the bibliography. We wish to thank Paul Jean Provost, James Dow, and the late Charles Boilès for allowing us to use specimens along with ethnographic data from their private collections. Other specimens were taken from our own archives and from the published works of Bodo Spranz, Bodil Christensen, Roberto Williams García, and Robert Gessain.

We have translated into English the Spanish names of the spirits found in the catalogs and have provided translations for many of the quotations from ethnohistorical sources. We would like to thank David Oberstar for his help in deciphering some of the more ambiguous sixteenth-century Spanish phrases. Additional editorial help was provided by John A. Mead, Steven Hollander, Paul Jean Provost, and Steven Harroff, all of whom have our gratitude. We would like to extend our gratitude to Evon Z. Vogt for making the resources of Harvard University available to us while we were writing the final draft of the manuscript. We would also like to thank Nancy Schmidt, former librarian of the Tozzer Library of the Peabody Museum of Archaeology and Ethnology, for carrel space and for permission to use the partial translation of Schwede's report of 1912 (catalogued in the unpublished "Miscellaneous Mexican and Central American Pamphlets," vol. 3, no. 8). At Indiana University–Purdue University at Fort Wayne we particularly appreciate the bibliographic skills of Ruth Harrod, who obtained for us many of the obscure sources consulted during the writing of the book. We are also grateful to Guy Stresser-Péan, head of the French scientific mission in Mexico, who read the manuscript and made many valuable suggestions. Finally, thanks go to Marci Irey, who typed the manuscript, and to John A. Mead, who provided invaluable assistance.

Significant collections of paper figures are found in the Mathers Museum of Anthropology at Indiana University, Bloomington, Indiana, and the National Museum of Anthropology and History, Mexico City.

ALAN R. SANDSTROM
PAMELA EFFREIN SANDSTROM

Municipio of Ixhuatlán de Madero,
Veracruz, Mexico

TRADITIONAL PAPERMAKING
AND PAPER CULT FIGURES OF MEXICO

CHAPTER 1

PAPER AND THE
INDIANS OF MIDDLE AMERICA

In 1900 an American anthropologist named Frederick Starr made a remarkable discovery in a remote mountainous area in east-central Mexico. Starr was leading a small expedition that had been searching for traditional Indians in the Mexico outback. He was intrigued by information he had received that some Indians in the region continued to produce handmade bark paper for use in their religious rituals. Up to that time it was thought that papermaking had died out hundreds of years earlier under the repressive rule of the Spaniards.

Starr's search for papermaking was unsuccessful until he entered the Otomí village San Pablito, in the state of Puebla. There, after asking repeatedly, he was shown a small packet of paper made from the inner bark of certain trees. Later he was able to witness women pounding the bark fibers into thin sheets, which were then placed in the sun to dry. Starr had discovered that in remote mountain villages the ancient craft of papermaking survived. He was the first outsider to witness and describe the technique since the sixteenth century.

After collecting sheets of bark paper to take with him, he discovered quite by accident what the paper was used for. In neighboring villages he had seen small statuettes, which, he was told, were venerated during elaborate rites. He was curious whether the people of San Pablito also used statuettes in their rituals. While searching through a small shrine, he found large numbers of cut-paper images covering an altar. He wrote about them that "the most curious was cut into groups of human figures, some of which had crowns and horns, or tufts of hair, upon the top of their heads. These were said to be decorations for Montezuma, in whose honor [a] feast was given" (Starr

3

1978 [1908], p. 260). Thus not only papermaking survived but also apparently many of the beliefs and rituals associated with the craft. In fact, what Starr had discovered was an entire religious complex, shared by neighboring Indian groups, in which paper was used as a medium to portray and communicate with important spirits. In these religions paper was the most important symbolic medium employed in rituals.

Since Starr's discovery anthropologists and other interested people have begun gathering information on the Indian cultures that continue to flourish in the region. The research is still incomplete, leaving us with a fragmentary idea of the nature and structure of religious beliefs and rituals and other aspects of culture. In this book we attempt to show how paper cutouts are used and to uncover some of the key ideas they express. The pages that follow include a catalog of more than two hundred selected cutouts, along with descriptions of four of the rituals in which they are used.

Paper figures are central features of rituals, and thus knowing what the figures mean gives us insight into what the rituals are about. We are not always able to provide as much religious and cultural context as we would like, but each figure we discuss, either as an individual specimen or because it completes a series of figures that are used together, increases what is known about the total religious complex.

The idea that paper has sacred qualities seems strange to people living in modern societies of the Western European tradition. Paper so surrounds us that it has become background material, scarcely noticed by most of us. And yet hours that are not spent reading from it are often spent writing on it. Babies are wrapped in it; the most important or trivial information is recorded on it; it cleans windshields and serves as money. Paper is sometimes even a focus of our frustrations with modern life. Bureaucrats are called paper pushers, and workers often say they like their jobs except for the paperwork. It has become associated with the insubstantial, leading fiscal conservatives, for example, to rail against paper money. The fact is, however, that anything produced in such abundance

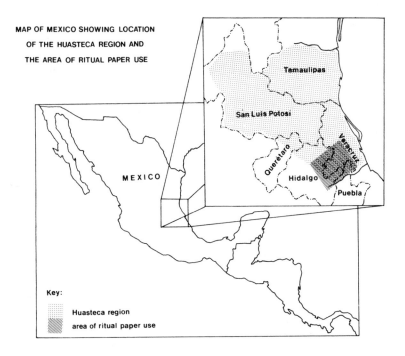

MAP OF MEXICO SHOWING LOCATION
OF THE HUASTECA REGION AND
THE AREA OF RITUAL PAPER USE

Tamaulipas

San Luis Potosi

MEXICO

Querétaro

Veracruz

Hidalgo

Puebla

Key:

Huasteca region
area of ritual paper use

and available so widely at such low prices surely has far greater importance to the society than our indifference or even hostility to it implies. For better or for worse, and computers notwithstanding, paper is fundamental to the development and continuance of modern society.

The Indians of Middle America, by contrast, have long valued paper as an important commodity. For them it was and still is a substance of dignity and beauty, produced by craftsmen and treated with care. At least three contemporary Indian groups continue to use cut paper as an integral part of their religious rituals and curing ceremonies. The Nahuas (modern Aztecs), Otomís, and Tepehuas of the southern Huasteca region cut paper images of important spirits whom they wish to propitiate. Of these, as far as we know, only the Otomís continue to produce the bark paper once so important to pre-Columbian civilizations.[1] In all three cultures there is an increased use of industrially manufactured paper because it is readily available and comes in a variety of colors. Despite this reliance on mass-produced paper, the use of paper in rituals by contemporary Indians traces back directly to the great pre-Columbian civilizations. In fact, many of the religious concepts that contemporary Nahua, Otomí, and Tepehua shamans express through their paper cuttings have been in existence since pre-Columbian times. To explain the use of paper by contemporary Indians and to help counteract our own tendency to undervalue this important substance, we present below a brief history of paper use among Middle American Indians. Included is an account of the people and the events that led to Starr's remarkable discovery at the turn of the century.

PAPER IN THE PRE-COLUMBIAN WORLD ·

The ancient civilizations of Middle America still fascinate the world almost five hundred years after Hernán Cortés and his fellow Spaniards landed in what is now the state of Veracruz, Mexico. By the time the Spaniards arrived in 1519, the people of Middle America had a tradition of settled life stretching back for thousands of years. Middle American civilizations had large population centers, monumental architecture, highly stratified social classes, standing armies, and written documents —features that are the hallmarks of "civilization" (literally, "city life") everywhere. There was much to be learned from these New World civilizations. Unfortunately, the mission of Cortés was to add new lands to the Spanish Empire and to accumulate personal wealth rather than knowledge. In the course of this mission he set out to replace the aboriginal system with one based on the Spanish model. Thus indigenous governments were destroyed and ·replaced with the Spanish viceroyalty system, the armies and traditional class structures of local city-states were dismantled, and the temples devoted to native gods were supplanted by Christian churches.

At the time of the Spanish invasion, the Mexica, or Aztecs, were the primary military, economic, and social power in the region. They had subjugated neighboring city-states and forged a tribute empire that included millions of people. The Spaniards under Cortés hit upon a plan to defeat the Aztecs and thereby gain control of the entire region. Almost immediately upon arriving, they set about winning allies among the subject states of the empire; less than three years later the Spaniards controlled most of Mesoamerica. The cities that had been the seats of Middle American civilization came under Spanish dominion, and the transformation of Indian culture followed shortly thereafter. Because the Aztecs were the supreme power in sixteenth-century Mexico, most of what we know about Middle American civilizations is based upon them. Our understanding of the history and culture of civilizations that declined before the arrival of the Spaniards comes largely from archaeology.

As the Aztec empire grew and prospered, the demand for raw materials and luxury goods increased significantly. In addition to precious stones and metals, feathers, and decorative clothing, one of the most sought-after items in ancient Mexico was handmade paper. It was of special importance to the Aztecs, who valued it as almost a sacred substance. Local craftsmen in the Aztec capital and traveling merchants were unable to meet the demand for paper, and it thus became a primary object of tribute. Paper was not only an article of tribute but also a medium for keeping tribute records. Aztec scholars had developed a partly phonetic picture writing that was used to record the exact amounts of various goods owed by each of the conquered provinces. In fact, the followers of Cortés used these records to direct their military campaigns so that they could recover the maximum plunder (Díaz del Castillo 1944 [1568–84], 2:314). An early viceroy of New Spain (Mexico), Don Antonio de Mendoza, ordered one of the tribute lists to be copied and sent to the Spanish court, probably to show the wealth of the new colony. The document, which has come down to us as the *Codex Mendoza*, has proved to be an invaluable early historical record. It names forty-two cities and towns in which paper was made and specifies that 480,000 sheets of paper were to be collected each year from just two of the named places (Lenz 1946, p. 695; and Martí 1971, p. 53). The *Codex Mendoza* gives us at least some idea of the immense quantities of paper that flowed into the Aztec capital each year.

Paper was eagerly sought by the Aztecs, who put it to a variety of uses. Besides employing it as a medium for the keeping of tribute records, they used it in the manufacture of books (although sometimes animal parchment was used instead). Only a few of these books, called codices, survive today. They were made by folding a single long sheet of material accordian-style, like a screen or a fan. Decorated slabs of wood or leather were glued on each end as covers or binders. Both the front and the back of the folded strip were filled with the colorful picture writing of the Indian scribes. We know that, in addition to the Aztecs, the Mayas, Mixtecs, Zapotecs, and Toltecs produced books. In fact, probably all major groups in Middle America made and kept books. The word for book in Nahuatl, the Aztec language, is *amoxtli;* books were housed in libraries called *amoxcalli, amoxpialoyan,* or *amoxtlatiloyan* (Molina 1944 [1571], p. 5). Probably the largest library was in the city of Texcoco, an Aztec ally in the Valley of Mexico. The library building at Texcoco was constructed of stone and is said to have contained thousands of manuscripts (Von Hagen 1977 [1944], p. 22). The libraries at Cholula and the Aztec capital of Tenochtitlán followed that of Texcoco in importance (Lenz 1973 [1948], p. 40).

Since so few of the codices have survived, it is difficult to say with certainty what they contained. The sixteenth-century Franciscan cleric Fray Toribio Benavente, known as Motolinía, wrote concerning the codices:

> There were, among these people five [types of] books, as I said, of figures and characters: the first speaks of the years and time; the second of the days and celebrations they held throughout the year; the third speaks of dreams and auguries, illusions and vanities in which they believed; the fourth is of baptism and names they gave children; the fifth is on the rites, ceremonies and auguries related to matrimony. . . . they had various orders and ways of counting the same time periods and years, celebrations and days. . . . at the same time they wrote and recorded the deeds and

stories of war (and also) the succession of the principal lords, of tempests and plagues, and at which time and under which ruler these happened, and all those who ruled and dominated this land until the Spanish arrived. All this they have in characters and figures.

This book I speak of is called in the Indian language *xihutonal amatl*, which means book of the count of the years. [Motolinía 1971 [1536-41?], p. 5][2]

Other books contained methods of divination, cures for diseases, histories of ancient times, genealogies, methods for learning to read the codices, information on plants and animals, maps, paintings recording land ownership, poetry, songs, and agricultural calendars (Peterson 1962, p. 235). Many pre-Columbian books were of a sacred character and probably dealt with the complex magico-religious system that was connected with the calendar and astronomical observations. The Aztecs called these sacred books *teoamoxtli*.

Thus, among the peoples of Middle America a connection was made between the books, most of which were made from paper, and the religious system. It was primarily upon paper that records of the sacred rites, prayers, and calendar were written. Books were probably kept in each temple so that the priests could consult them regularly. Only the priests, nobles, and a few scribes had the knowledge to decipher the writing, a skill learned in an institution of higher learning called the *calmecac*. To the ordinary person the books undoubtedly had a semisacred status, and the paper from which they were made was held in some reverence.

Evidence for the sacred nature of paper can be seen in its use during religious rituals. Virtually every Aztec rite included the adorning of statues or sacred objects with paper. Called *amatetéhuitl*, these paper adornments were cut to the proper shape and were usually decorated with drops of latex before being used. Often they were dyed or painted to correspond to the symbolic colors of a particular deity (Lenz 1973 [1948], pp. 14ff.).

We owe much of our knowledge of the details of Aztec

rituals to the sixteenth-century Franciscan monk Fray Bernardino de Sahagún, who produced a multivolume archive of information called *Historia General de las Cosas de Nueva España (General History of the Things of New Spain;* 1950–69 [1575–80?]). Sahagún devotes one entire volume to the calendrical observances of the Aztecs, all of which involved the use of paper in some way. Statues were adorned with paper headdresses *(amacopilli,* or *amacalli),* while other images of deities were given paper helmets *(amatzoncalli;* Molina 1944 [1571], p. 4). Papers were carefully arranged and placed with the dead to facilitate the soul's journey through the nine levels of the underworld (Sahagún 1950–69 [1575–80?], pt. 4, bk. 3, pp. 41ff.). Latex-spotted paper was the common offering to the *tlalocs,* or rain deities (Thompson 1941, p. 64), and sacrificial victims were often dressed in paper regalia before they were killed. During certain holy days houses were adorned with latex-spotted paper streamers or flags called *amapantli* in honor of the deities (Lenz 1973 [1948], p. 30). In addition, the priests were often dressed in elaborate paper costumes during rituals, particularly when they were impersonating deities.

One of the more remarkable rituals recorded by Sahagún was held in the fifth month, *toxcatl,* and was dedicated to the sun god Huitzilopochtli:

> They made still another ornament to honor this god, and which consisted of an enormous piece of paper, twenty fathoms (six feet each) long by one in width, and one finger thick. This paper was carried by a number of strong young men in front of the image [of Huitzilopochtli]. . . . [T]he image . . . was raised onto the shoulders of a number of captains and warriors who, grouped on either side, carried it like a litter with the long paper always in front. Thus they proceeded in a procession, singing the songs to the god and dancing before him in a solemn dance. Arriving at the foot of the temple steps, . . . [t]hose who carried the large paper again mounted ahead of the statue, and to prevent tearing it, those who climbed first at once began rolling the paper up with great care. . . . As soon as the statue had reached the top they placed it where it belonged on its throne or chair, and they laid in front of the platform the roll of paper securely tied, to prevent its unrolling. [Sahagún 1932 [1575–80?], bk. 2, pp. 85–86]

Sahagún and other sixteenth-century observers recorded scores of rituals which featured the use of paper. Many of the smaller rites involved the sacrifice of paper, usually by burning:

> Those who, through the advice of their astrologers, were able to ward off a disease, chose a very lucky day, and on that day burned, in the hearth of their homes, a great many papers on which the astrologer had painted with *ulli* (gum) the images of all those gods who, they guessed, . . . had helped them to ward off that illness. The astrologer (after thus painting them) handed them to the man who made the offering, telling him (the name of) the god painted thereon; the man then burned all the papers; they gathered the ashes and buried them in the courtyard of the home. [Sahagún 1932 [1575-80?], bk. 2, app., pp. 159-60]

It is difficult to exaggerate the importance of paper to the pre-Columbian peoples of Middle America. Examples of how it was used could be listed almost indefinitely. Two more recorded uses of paper will help draw the connection between how paper was used in pre-Columbian times and how it is employed among contemporary Indians. Excavations at the great pre-Aztec city of Teotihuacán and at certain Maya sites have uncovered strange anthropomorphic statues with well-sculptured heads but amorphous bodies (Lenz 1973 [1948], pp. 35-36). Archaeologists have interpreted these statues as images of messenger spirits used by the devout to communicate with more powerful and distant deities. It is thought that the bodies were wrapped in paper by devotees wishing their prayers to be heard (Heyden 1975, pp. 346-47).

Another interesting use of paper is recorded by Sahagún. In a section called "The Merchants," the great sixteenth-century ethnographer records the ritual performed by the *pochtecas* (traveling merchants) before they left on one of their dangerous missions. On the night preceding their departure they cut a series of papers to propitiate various protector deities. First they cut a banner-shaped length of paper with forked ends to represent the fire god. They then decorate the paper with melted latex:

> And thus they did paint the paper: they gave it lips, nose, eyes.

It resembled a man. Thus they did make a representation of the fire (god).

Then they cut the (paper) which pertained to the earth (god), whom they called *tlaltecutli.* He was bound about the chest with paper; also with the liquid rubber they gave him lips, nose, eyes. He also resembled a man. [Sahagún 1950–69 [1575–80?], pt. 10, bk. 9, pp. 9–11]

The ritual continues as the *pochtecas* paint several more deities on paper. When the paintings are completed, they lay them out in the courtyard. Then, standing before the fire, they behead sacrificial quails and draw their own blood by piercing their ears and tongues. They offer the blood to the fire and then scatter it upon the papers. Finally they cast the papers into the fire to see how they burn; if the papers crackle and do not burn well, it is considered a bad sign. Afterward the paper ashes are buried in the courtyard of the sponsoring merchant.

We have, then, in Middle American civilizations a pattern in which paper is closely associated with the religious system. Theology and instructions for carrying out rituals were painted in sacred books. Paper was used to adorn statues and priests when they dressed as deities. It was also used to dress sacrificial victims, and, when burned, it became a direct offering to the gods. Paper played a significant role in medical practices, being part of rituals held to ward off disease. In the ritual just described, it was used as a medium for portraying deities so that they would protect the traveling merchants. The same ritual also contained a sequence in which paper was burned as a technique for divining the future. Slips of paper accompanied the dead on their journey to the underworld and were sacrificed in appeals for rain. They were offered to deities to avoid bad luck or to counteract the harmful effects of a birth on an astrologically unfortunate day. In sum, paper acted as a kind of messenger or go-between, providing a medium of communication between the human and spirit worlds.

THE INVENTION OF PAPERMAKING IN MIDDLE AMERICA

It is not known exactly when the Middle American Indians

invented the technique of papermaking. The historical records we have suggest that paper manufacture and use were widespread throughout the region by the time the Spaniards arrived in 1519. This suggests that the invention of paper may have been ancient. Most authorities are convinced that the Mayas of the Yucatan were the first to produce paper (Lenz 1946, p. 694; Von Hagen 1977 [1944], p. 10). Early in their history the Mayas produced a kind of tapa cloth from the inner bark of certain trees; several Indian groups in the region and farther down into Central America still make tunics from this material. Bark-cloth manufacture apparently evolved into papermaking, although when this occurred is not known. The Mayas call their paper *huun,* and it is possible that when the Toltecs or pre-Toltec peoples made contact with the Mayas they carried the papermaking techniques back to the central plateau. Toltec history is extremely sketchy, but it appears that by A.D. 660 pre-Toltec peoples possessed a sacred book, which included a "History of Heaven and Earth" (Von Hagen 1977 [1944], pp. 11–12). Also, the Mayas stopped erecting dated stone stelae at the end of the ninth century, a fact which has led one authority to suggest that this is the period when they began to keep records exclusively on paper (Von Hagen 1977 [1944], p. 69). This suggestion is little more than a guess, however, since there is no evidence that the pre-Toltecs or earliest Mayas were using paper as a writing surface.

Archaeology can throw some light on the question of the antiquity of papermaking in Middle America. While paper disintegrates unless it is carefully stored and preserved, some of the tools used to manufacture it are made of durable stone. Most traditional paper used in Middle America was made either from the inner bark of trees belonging to the family Moraceae, which includes the figs *(Ficus)* and mulberry plants *(Morus),* or from the leaves of species of maguey, a succulent. The Aztec word for paper is *amatl,* the same word used for the trees from which it is made. Preparation of the paper required that the loose fibers be felted together with a beater, called an *amauitequini* in Nahuatl (Molina 1944 [1571], p. 4), which was typically made from a grooved stone. These stones are found in archaeological sites throughout the zone in Middle America where the plants used in papermaking grow. An early site where beaters have been found and dated is the prehistoric city of Teotihuacán. The stones at this site have been dated to the sixth century A.D., which gives an approximate time for the appearance of papermaking in the highlands (Cook de Leonard 1971, p. 221; Johnson 1971, pp. 316–17; Lenz 1973 [1948], pp. 9, 36; Tolstoy 1971, p. 292).

Most anthropologists interested in Middle America believe that virtually all culture traits found there developed independently. Suggestions that specific traits may derive from the Near East or Asia typically are met with derision. Poorly researched theories of early culture contact have hardened the case against such diffusionist explanations. A few scholars (e.g., Meggers 1975; Schneider 1977), however, have presented more sophisticated evidence to suggest contact between the New and Old Worlds. Among these Paul Tolstoy (1963) has examined the remarkable similarities in the manufacture of bark cloth and bark paper in Mesoamerica and Southeast Asia. He notes that the earliest documented paper beater found in Mesoamerica comes from Pacific Coast Guatemala and is dated to approximately 1000 B.C. This is later than similar artifacts found in Southeast Asia, pointing to an older industry there. After presenting a detailed comparison of bark-cloth and bark-paper manufacturing techniques, Tolstoy concludes that his findings appear to

> justify a strong case for the introduction from Asia of the Meso-american bark cloth and paper complex into the area of upper Central America and the isthmus of Tehuantepec toward the beginning of the 1st millenium B.C. Its most likely source appears to have been some part of eastern Southeast Asia, on the periphery of Chinese cultural influence. [Tolstoy 1963, p. 661]

This conclusion is controversial, however, and the issue of the origin of papermaking in Mesoamerica remains a subject of debate.

One legacy of the ancient importance of paper is found in present-day place-names. Many villages, towns, and cities in

Mexico have retained their Indian names, although typically the sounds have been hispanicized. The pre-Columbian Indians often named a place for a historical or mythical event, a product for which the area was renowned, or some major activity of the people (Dávila Garibi 1942, pp. 8–9). Many towns in central Mexico preserve their original Nahuatl names. Some were named for scribes, writing, or the painting of hieroglyphics: Amaculi, in the state of Durango, from *amatl*, "paper," and *cuiloa*, "to paint"; Cuilco, in Chiapas, meaning "place where they write"; Tlacuiloca, in Tlaxcala, meaning "place where there are writers or painters"; and Tlacuilotépec, in Puebla, meaning "town of scribes" (Lenz 1973 [1948], p. 39). Other places in Mexico were named for paper trees and the paper-making activities of their inhabitants: Amatitán-caz, in Puebla, meaning "place where paper is made"; Amatitlán, in Morelos, "place of many paper trees" or "much paper"; Amayuca (Ama-yocan), in Morelos, "place where paper is made"; Amazonco (Amatzonco), also in Morelos, meaning "place of papermaking fibers"; Amecameca (Amaquemecan), in the state of Mexico, meaning "place where they wear paper tunics"; and Amapala (Amatlapala), in Sinaloa, meaning "place of paper sheets" or "place where manufactured paper abounds" (Lenz 1973 [1948], pp. 64–66). The wide distribution of paper-related activities gives further evidence of the antiquity and importance of this substance to the peoples of Middle America.

THE DESTRUCTION OF INDIAN PAPER
AND THE DECLINE OF PAPERMAKING

With the emphasis placed on paper, an emphasis so great that Von Hagen has called sixteenth-century Mexican society the "paper world of the Aztecs" (Von Hagen 1977 [1944], pp. 77ff.), it is legitimate to ask why so little has survived to modern times. The pitifully few codices and loose sheets that remain must represent an infinitesimal percentage of the holdings of a single library. It also appears that none of the papers used for adornment or sacrifice have survived. One would think that souvenirs, at least, would have been collected by the Spanish soldiers or newly arriving colonists. Undoubtedly much paper was destroyed during the wars waged by Cortés and his soldiers. Of far greater importance, however, is the attitude of the conquerors toward the subjugated natives of Mexico. Part of the ideology of conquest was that the Indians had fallen in league with the devil and that all vestiges of the traditional culture must be rooted out. This policy was particularly applied to anything connected with the native religion. Thus one of the first official acts was to dismantle the temples and disperse the worshipers. The European invaders smashed the statues, destroyed the altars, and killed the priests.

Paper was so closely connected to Aztec and Maya religious practices that it too was systematically destroyed. Two sixteenth-century clerics, Fray Juan de Zumárraga and Fray Diego de Landa, played a major role in the destruction of native libraries. Soon after 1529, Zumárraga, bishop of Mexico, ordered the Aztec libraries emptied and the books brought to the town of Tlatelolco. "He then caused them to be piled up in a 'mountain-heap'—as it is called by the Spanish writers themselves—in the market-place of Tlatelolco, and reduced them all to ashes!" (Prescott 1843, 1:90). Diego de Landa arrived in 1549 and was assigned to work among the Mayas. He destroyed temples and searched out the sacred books. Finally in 1561 he located a great archive of sacred texts. He wrote:

> These people also used certain characters or letters with which they wrote in their books concerning ancient things and their sciences. With these figures and certain signs of the same type, they understood their things and explained and taught them. We found a great number of books of these letters and because they contained nothing but superstitions and falsehoods of the devil, we burned them all, which the people felt most deeply and which gave them much sorrow. [Landa 1938 [1566?], p. 207][3]

The sorrow is felt to this day; we will never know the extent of our loss.

After the defeat of the Aztec armies by Cortés and his Indian allies, the ancient tradition of papermaking began to decline. The Spaniards who took over the tribute empire saw no profit in continuing the flow of native paper into the capital. They concentrated on stamping out all activities related to the old religion and sought forcibly to convert the Indians to Christianity. Many people were killed during the inquisition that followed, and countless others died from dislocation, disease, and forced labor. Huge areas of Mexico were almost depopulated by the colonial policies. Town after town and village after village ceased making the paper that was so intimately a part of traditional ritual observances. But the greatest culture loss occurred in the urban centers and towns. There the Spanish colonial authorities had their seats of power, and there policies could be carried out most efficiently. Life in the small, isolated villages, while greatly affected, was far more difficult to control, even though missionaries were sent into the remotest regions to exterminate the old religion. Many Indians hid their activities from the authorities and maintained the old beliefs by combining them with the outward trappings of Christian practices. To this day the greatest survival of the ancient religion is in the most remote areas.

In the centuries that followed the Aztec defeat, occasional signs hinted that the traditional religion was still vigorous in the provinces. In 1635, in the remote Tutotepec region, some Otomí "idolators" were discovered conducting a non-Christian ritual in three huts filled with ceremonial items. On the altars were incense, sacrificial fowl, and paper cut into strips called "vestments of the gods." The shrine was run, according to the Augustinian who recorded the event, by *seudoprofetas* ("false prophets"), priests, and their disciples. In the rituals the sun, the moon, air, water, harvest, and a mountain god were venerated (Lenz 1973 [1948], pp. 115–16). In the Oaxaca region in 1684 Nicholás de la Cruz Contreras and his associates were caught with sacred bundles made of paper splattered with blood and were brought to trial for idolatry. In the same area in 1700 are recorded other incidents in which blood-spotted paper was used in connection with traditional rituals. One rite involved cutting an image of the devil out of paper. In 1889, again in the same region, a priest wrote of "idolatries" practiced to cure sickness and to ask for rain, abundant harvests, and protection from lightning (Gillow 1889, pp. 82, 203ff.; app., pp. 123ff.; cited in Lenz 1973 [1948], pp. 115–19). Ten years later, in a similarly remote area, Frederick Starr made his remarkable discovery.

THE SURVIVAL OF PAPERMAKING IN MEXICO

The discovery that contemporary Indians continue to make paper and to use it in their sacred rituals is connected with a curious debate that arose among scholars interested in both pre-Columbian civilizations and modern Indian culture. For centuries the chroniclers, historians, and scholars who wrote about indigenous Middle America have known of the importance of paper in religious practices. A controversy developed, however, over the material from which the paper was made. It began with an article entitled "Mexican Paper" published by Philipp J. J. Valentini in the October 1880 *Proceedings of the American Antiquarian Society*. Valentini gave a brief review of the various references to paper in the codices, followed by a discussion of the means used to produce pre-Columbian paper. According to the early documents, paper was made primarily from two sources: the inner bark of the *amatl* tree and the leaves of the maguey plant. As previously mentioned, the Nahuatl word *amatl* generally refers to any number of trees belonging to the family Moraceae (usually members of the genus *Ficus*), although Valentini apparently misidentified the *amatl* (Valentini 1880, p. 66). Maguey refers to any of the desert plants known as agave (genus *Agave*) of the family Amaryllidaceae. Valentini noted throughout the article that the early observers are inconsistent and sometimes contradictory in their accounts of the materials from which paper is made.[4]

Was the paper made from maguey leaves or tree bark? One obvious conclusion is that both types of paper were in fact produced. While lamenting "how little information can be drawn from the writings of the chroniclers" (Valentini 1880, p. 70), Valentini indirectly suggests that perhaps the lowland Mayas used *amatl* paper while the highland Aztecs used maguey paper: "The Mayas occupied a zone of vegetation in which the amatl tree has its home, whilst the Nahoas [Aztecs] had settled on the *mesas* of the Cordillera, where the tree does not exist" (Valentini 1880, p. 68). While the contenders as the main sources of raw material used in paper manufacture are *amatl* and maguey, other minor sources of raw material have also been suggested, including the leaves of a species of palm; cotton; a substance produced by caterpillars; nettles; the juice of the banana tree; a combination of palm, yucca, and *anacahuite* fibers; and the inner bark of the rubber tree (Lenz 1973 [1948], pp. 37, 74ff., 110-11, 170, 175ff.; Lenz 1946, p. 695; Christensen 1942, pp. 111-12; Lannik, Palm, and Tatkon 1969, p. 10; Martí 1971, p. 59).

Following Valentini's work, anthropologist Frederick Starr conducted a series of expeditions throughout southern and central Mexico. The expeditions took place between 1897 and 1901 and had three major objectives: first, to collect anthropometric data on selected individuals of the various Indian groups encountered; second, to take photographs of these groups; and third, to make plaster busts of representative members of the various tribes. Starr was in search of Indian Mexico and thus was also interested in evidence of "pagan" practices. In March 1899, while in the state of Mexico, Starr met a Señor Xochihua, an Aztec Indian connected with the political authorities in the region. He informed Starr that bark paper was still being produced in the Otomí village of San Gregorio, in the state of Hidalgo, and that it might be interesting to go there. During the expedition of 1900, Starr made a point of visiting the area to gain firsthand information on this ancient craft.

The area to which Starr was directed lies just outside the Huasteca region, in the Sierra Madre Oriental (Sierra Norte de Puebla). Starr entered the area ostensibly to search for Totonac and Tepehua Indians to measure but also to collect information on local cultures and papermaking activities. While he was in the town of Pahuatlán, in Puebla, he asked a political leader about papermaking and ritual practices. He was told that paper was being made in San Pablito, a nearby village, and that it was used in witchcraft rituals: ". . . it is cut into *muñecos* ["dolls"], representing human beings and horses and other animals, and these are used to work injury to human beings and beasts, being buried in front of the house or in the *corral*" (Starr 1978 [1908], p. 246). Starr also met a judge who said that several years previously an Otomí prisoner had been brought before him for trial and that the prisoner had had on his person a cut-paper figure. The figure was sewn through the body with thread and also had the lips sewn shut. Upon being questioned, the Indian had said that the doll was an image of the judge and that the lips were sewn to prevent him from passing sentence.

In a nearby village Starr continued his inquiries about bark paper and associated religious practices. He was told by local officials that the traditional practices for which he was searching were observed only by the Otomís. The traditional rituals were called *costumbres* ("customs"), and they appeared to be dedicated to a spirit called Montezuma. They believed that Montezuma would come again, and that in the meantime he provided health, crops, and all other good things. The villagers constructed a long altar in a special shrine hidden from the view of outsiders. On this altar a feast was laid for Montezuma to win his favor for the village. The table was covered with a layer of figures cut from paper, often one or two inches deep. People sometimes slipped silver coins under the paper figures as a way of achieving religious merit. In former times only bark paper was used, but Starr learned that industrially manufactured paper was increasingly used. It was also reported that the Otomís killed turkeys and chickens in the course of their rituals and sprinkled the blood on the paper images (Starr 1978 [1908], p. 250). Starr knew that these practices survived from ancient times and that the continued use of paper in religious rituals after hundreds of years of persecution was nothing short of amazing.

The first Indians that Starr met in the region were Totonacs. He was disappointed to learn that, although the Totonacs made use of bark fibers in their rituals, they used it only to tie up small bundles of sacred sticks (Starr 1978 [1908], p. 253). He found no evidence that they cut images out of paper. As he traveled farther into the mountains, Starr learned that the Otomís of San Pablito also made use of small wooden figurines in their rituals. These figurines were dressed in tiny clothes and shoes and placed on the altar. They were hidden when the Catholic priest arrived (Starr 1978 [1908], p. 258). Starr was told that each year two to three hundred Indians made a pilgrimage to a distant sacred lake, carrying the statuettes with them. The lake, which was also visited by several other Indian groups, was the home of a water deity called La Sirena (the Siren). The Indians threw seeds and money into the water, there was dancing and feasting, and several turkeys and chickens were sacrificed to induce the Siren to send rain.

In the Tepehua town Huehuetla, Starr heard about a man who kept pre-Columbian statues on an altar. Local political leaders ordered the man to bring the figurines to a house so that Starr could see them, but the man refused, saying that the images were not toys to be shown to strangers. Starr was eventually admitted to the shrine beside the man's house, where on an altar he saw two sealed cabinets containing the statuettes. Starr was permitted to view the stone and ceramic figures, some of which were dressed in miniature clothes (Starr 1978 [1908], p. 270). The cabinets were the focus of rituals at sowing time, at the harvest, and when there was an overabundance or lack of rain.

Among Otomís near the village of Pantepec, Starr made inquiries about traditional rituals and the use of paper. He was told that specialists cut the paper into images and used them for curing purposes, mainly by holding them against the patient's body (Starr 1978 [1908], p. 268). In San Pablito, Starr finally was able to witness bark paper being made and to examine the implements used in its manufacture (Starr 1978 [1908], p. 259). He noticed that two types of paper were made, a dark, purplish variety made from the *xalama* tree and a white variety made from the bark of the *moral*. Starr was not able to identify these species with certainty, although he knew that neither was related to maguey. Later researchers have determined that *xalama* is a *Ficus* and *moral* is a species of mulberry. Both of these species belong to the Moraceae family. After purchasing seventeen dozen sheets of the paper, Starr explored the village to try to find evidence of ritual activity. He saw no paper images in the village church, which he found "mean and bare" (Starr 1978 [1908], p. 259), but inside one of the small shrines set back from the main trail he finally encountered the "curious" cut-paper figures.

By 1900, then, an expert had seen bark paper being manufactured by Otomí Indians and had learned what the paper was used for. He was able to affirm that paper was being made in at least four villages—San Gregorio (district Tenango, state of Hidalgo), Xalapa (district Zacualtipan, state of Hidalgo), San Pablito (*municipio* Pahuatlán, state of Puebla) and Ixtololoya (*municipio* Pántepec, state of Puebla)—and that it was used in several other villages. Starr's findings are of great ethnographic interest, but they cannot be used to clear up the questions surrounding the paper used in the codices. The modern Otomí craftsmen he witnessed primarily used plants from the Moraceae family as a source of fiber. His research does not, however, prove that Moraceae plants were the sole source used in pre-Hispanic times because, for one thing, maguey does not thrive in the region where papermaking has survived.

Almost as a by-product of his search for Indian papermaking, Starr obtained information on the remarkable ways in which paper was used by the Otomís. He spent several days questioning local Indians about traditional religious practices, although he was not able to witness a ritual himself. He was the first modern researcher to document that paper was cut by Otomí shamans into anthropomorphic and theriomorphic (animal-shaped) images representing certain spirits. These paper images along with small statuettes were the objects of rituals in which the Otomís sought to regulate rainfall, assure harvests, and cure disease. These religious practices seemed reminiscent of the ceremonies recorded by Sahagún and others in the sixteenth century, although they were understandably far more modest.

Paper images may have been cut since pre-Columbian times, although no sixteenth-century chronicler specifically records the practice. We know that the Aztecs painted images of spirits on paper and that they cut paper into garments and banners for rituals, but no record exists that they cut it into visual images of specific spirits. Possibly the practice was confined to rural areas that did not receive the attention of early chroniclers, or perhaps they simply failed to document the custom. As previously mentioned, court documents from the early eighteenth century record trials of accused idolators who were caught with paper images of "devils," suggesting that the practice of cutting spirit images out of paper is quite old. Another possibility is that cutting images of spirits is a post-Conquest innovation developed in response to the need for easy concealment of ritual activity after the Spaniards destroyed the sacred statues. Unfortunately, Starr treated the paper images he saw simply as curiosities of a forgotten pagan past. The craft of papermaking captured his attention, and he left it to later researchers to investigate the remarkable paper images cut by the Indians. He returned to the United States to find that an interest had developed in pre-Columbian paper.

In 1899, Walter Hough published in the *American Anthropologist* a comment on the use of maguey fibers for the manufacture of paper. He stated, "There seems to be a general impression that the ancient Mexican codices were written on paper made from the bark of the maguey (agave species), as this statement appears in the works of all the writers who have mentioned the subject" (Hough 1899, p. 789). Hough continues, "It will be seen by those familiar with the century plant that it has no bark." He concluded that the skin of the maguey leaf "is a material not suited to the codices, and it has not been used for any of those records that the writer has examined" (Hough 1899, p. 790). This note elicited an immediate response from Starr, who stated that no writer had ever claimed that pre-Columbian paper was made from the *bark* of the maguey. He said, "There can be no question that two kinds of paper were made and used by the ancient Mexicans—the maguey paper on the Plateau, the bark paper in the low country: the former would have been more common among the Aztecs, the latter among the Mayas" (Starr 1900, p. 302). Starr went on to describe how paper was being made among contemporary Otomís.

A few years after this exchange, Dard Hunter, the famed expert on paper, visited an Otomí village in the state of Hidalgo to witness traditional papermaking. Hunter had apparently discovered that paper was made in the region from reading the works of Frederick Starr. At the time Hunter visited Mexico and wrote about his findings, very little work had been done on the manufacture and use of paper in prehistoric and contemporary Mexico. Hunter himself, however, was unable to resolve the controversy of the fibers since he only witnessed paper being made from the *amatl* tree. He was struck by the incredible circumstances that allowed for the continuance of the ancient craft after so many centuries. He wrote of his "unique privilege to live among the Otomí Indians" and "the rare opportunity of watching these primitive workers fabricate their coarse, broadformed paper which, after being dried in the sun, was cut into grotesque images for use in religious rites" (Hunter in Von Hagen 1977 [1944], p. 4). Hunter first published his observations in *Primitive Papermaking* (1927), but was unable to spend enough time in Mexico to complete the research. He was gratified, therefore, shortly after the publication of this hand-printed limited edition, to receive a letter from the historian Victor W. Von Hagen expressing an interest in the subject. With Hunter's support Von Hagen began work on a major research project which resulted in his book *The Aztec and Maya Papermakers* (1944).

Soon after Hunter went to Mexico in search of traditional papermaking, research was conducted in Germany which affirmed both Valentini's and Starr's early conclusions. In 1912, Rudolph Schwede published the results of a microscopic and chemical analysis he conducted on the paper of four known Maya codices, the *Dresdensis*, the *Peresianus*, the *Troanus*, and the *Cortesianus*, and on some other fragments. He found that, contrary to prevailing opinion in Germany, the codices were made from the inner bark of various species of *Ficus* and not from the maguey leaf (Schwede 1912, p. 47). The prestigious expert on Middle America Eduard Seler asked Schwede to examine twenty-one additional fragments to verify the original findings. In 1916, Schwede published his conclusions that all but one of the fragments were made from *amatl* fiber. The one exception was made of maguey fiber (Schwede 1916, p. 54).

The evidence produced by Schwede seems conclusive: maguey was used to make paper among the ancient Mexicans, but most of the surviving pages were made from the inner bark of the *amatl* tree. It was to take over thirty years for this conclusion to be widely accepted, however. After World War I research interest focused on Starr's discovery that paper was still being made in remote areas in and around the Huasteca. Nicolas León, a senior professor in the National Museum of Archaeology, History, and Ethnography in Mexico, visited the Otomís of San Pablito to gather more information on papermaking. He was one of the first researchers to publish a picture of a paper image cut by a contemporary shaman, although he provided no information about the figure. He was also the first to reveal that bark paper was being made by Nahua (Aztec) Indians in the Chicontepec region of the southern Huasteca (León 1924, p. 103; Lenz 1973 [1948], p. 86).

But it was Von Hagen who set out to clarify the issues of papermaking and paper use in pre-Hispanic Middle America by writing the definitive work on the subject. In 1931 he visited the Otomí papermaking village of San Pablito to gather direct information on the survival of the ancient craft. In the course of his researches he consulted the ancient sources, made use of modern scientific techniques to test the fibers of traditional paper, and traveled to Honduras, where Sumus Indians still manufactured bark cloth. His book *The Aztec and Maya Papermakers* was flawed, however, by his insistence that maguey was never used a source of raw material by the ancient papermakers. In fact, a close reading of the sixteenth-century chroniclers and of Schwede's report of 1916 should have laid that issue to rest. Von Hagen's book was attacked by scholars, and its main conclusion was shown to be in error (Miranda 1946; Reko 1947; Lenz 1973 [1948]).

In the course of his work Von Hagen interested two residents of Mexico in his research project. One, Hans Lenz, owned the largest paper mill in Mexico and was particularly interested in the history and manufacture of paper. The other was Bodil Christensen, an adventurous woman who was interested in Mexican ethnography. Lenz made a series of trips into the Huasteca and its environs from 1942 to 1945 in search of the traditional papermaking. He initially followed the routes of Frederick Starr and eventually went into the Chicontepec region of northern Veracruz. He gathered information on how paper was made and on the religious rituals in which it was used. In addition he made collections of specimens of paper, some of which he donated to Von Hagen to be included as samples in a special limited edition of his book. Lenz was able to document papermaking among the Otomís and among modern Aztecs of the Chicontepec region. In 1948 he published a book entitled *El papel indígena mexicano: historia y supervivencia (Mexican Indian Paper: Its History and Survival)* which remains the definitive work on pre-Columbian papermaking and the fiber controversy.

Bodil Christensen also made trips by horseback into the remote regions where paper continued to be produced. Like Lenz, she assisted Von Hagen with his paper project, although her initial motivation for entering the area was a general interest in the local cultures. Christensen photographed papermaking among Otomís and modern Aztecs and collected samples of the plants to be sent away for botanical identification. She also obtained a great deal of information on the traditional religious systems that use paper. Beginning in the 1940s, she published a series of articles on her research, and later she was coauthor of a small book on ancient and modern uses of paper in Mexico (Christensen 1971; Martí 1971).

The mystery of the fibers will perhaps never be completely solved, but we now have a clearer picture of ancient Mexican paper. It appears that maguey was used by pre-Columbian papermakers but not to the extent that the Moraceae trees were used. Faustino Miranda, a botanist critic of Von Hagen, suggested that the Aztecs may have used Moraceae paper, obtained through trade and tribute, for books, tribute rolls, maps, and so on, while reserving the possibly cruder maguey paper for disposable adornments, banners, and vestments (Miranda 1946, p. 202). Thus, since none of these objects has survived to the present day, maguey paper may be underrepresented in remaining fragments. Interestingly, all of the almost one hundred fragments examined so far have proved to be of Moraceae, maguey, or European manufacture. Either the other sources of fiber suggested by later writers were never used or, more likely, the paper made from them has been lost.

TRADITIONAL PAPERMAKING TECHNIQUES

One of the questions most commonly asked by persons who have seen bark paper is how the paper is made. We include several descriptions of the process here, beginning with a possible technique for producing maguey paper.

The major problems faced by researchers trying to establish that maguey was used in the production of Mexican paper is that we have no firsthand description of how the fibers were extracted and reworked. Boturini Benaduci, who visited Mexico in the eighteenth century, long after the Aztecs ceased large-scale production of paper, provided one of the few descriptions of how maguey paper might have been made:

> The leaves were putrified, after which the fibers were washed. Thus softened, the fibers were extended to make thick as well as thin paper. The paper was later polished so that it could be painted upon. [Boturini Benaduci 1933 [1746], pp. 95–96][5]

This description was taken up by other writers, including the great geographer Alexander von Humboldt, and uncritically included in subsequent works on Mexico.

The only sixteenth-century chronicler to leave a written description of bark papermaking based on eyewitness observation was the naturalist Francisco Hernández. While some question exists about the precise species of tree he linked to paper manufacture (Miranda 1946, p. 197), Hernández's description is clear:

> [The *amaquauitl* tree] grows in the mountains of Tepoztlán where one can frequently see swarming multitudes of workers making paper from it. The product is not very fit for writing or drawing lines, although it does not make ink run. It is useful for wrapping and is more than adequate for use by these Western Indians in their celebrations of feast days of the gods. From this paper they make sacred vestments and funeral adornments. They cut only the thick branches, leaving the shoots, and soak them in rivers or streams overnight. On the following day they tear off the bark and, after removing the exterior cuticle, they spread out the inner bark with blows from a flat stone which has a surface furrowed with grooves. The stone is held by an unfinished willow twig doubled over in a circle like a handle. That flexible wood gives readily; later it is cut into pieces which, beaten again with another flatter stone, are easily joined together into a single sheet which is then polished. These sheets are finally divided into pieces two palms [8¼ inches each] long and approximately a palm and a half wide. The product is like our thicker and cheaper paper, although it is more compact and whiter. Theirs is inferior to our smoother paper. [Hernández 1959 [1571-76?], 1:83-84][6]

While there are differences in the methods described by Hernández and Boturini Benaduci, they are surprisingly similar, considering the different plants employed.

The description by Hernández is probably accurate because more modern descriptions of papermaking by contemporary people are similar. Frederick Starr described papermaking as follows:

> At San Pablito two kinds of bark are used: *moral* [mulberry] gives a whitish, *xalama* [*Ficus*] a purplish paper. The bark is best gathered when full of sap, but is kept after drying. A board is used for a foundation on which to beat. A stone approximately rectangular and generally with the corners grooved for convenient grasping is used for a beater. The bark is carefully washed in lyewater, taken from maize that has been prepared for *tortillas;* it

is then washed in fresh water and finally boiled until it shreds readily into slender strips. These are arranged upon the board—first a boundary line for the future sheet of paper is laid out and then strips are laid near together lengthwise within this outline. They are then beaten with the stone until the spread fibres are felted together. The sheets are dried in the air, folded, and done up in packages of a dozen, which sell for three *centavos*. The work is done by women and usually in the houses with a certain degree of secrecy. [Starr 1901, pp. 181–82]

Starr's description includes more detail, but his statements suggest that papermaking techniques have changed very little over the centuries.

Following is a description by Dard Hunter of how paper is made among the Otomís:

The bark of these trees used by the Otomís is gathered in the autumn when full of sap. After the bark is well dried it is placed in a pool of running water, which washes away the parenchyma or glutinous substance, leaving the pure fibres. These are then made into bundles and laid in a stream where the material receives a further cleansing. It is then boiled with ashes, or in the liquid *(nejayote* or *nixcómél)* in which corn tortillas (Mexican cakes) have been boiled. A large earthen pot of native construction, heated over an open fire, is used in boiling the bark. After washing, the fibres are beaten with wooden clubs or mallets until they have separated and are in a pulpy condition. When the material has been thoroughly macerated it is made into a paste and spread over a board in a thin sheet with the fingers; and then gently beaten with a small stone, which mats the fibres, forming a homogeneous sheet of paper. This sheet, still upon the board, is then dried in the sun. When it is dry it can be easily removed, the board causing the underside of the paper to be smooth, with an almost glossy appearance. [Hunter 1927, pp. 15–16]

In both Starr's and Hunter's descriptions we see that modern Indians boil the bark in lime water to soften the fibers and then form the sheet on a board. One small inaccuracy in Hunter's account is that the corn used to make tortillas is boiled before being ground but the tortillas themselves are not boiled. Hunter points out, "In all regions where paper is made in a primitive

manner, there will be seen, even within short distances, slightly
different methods of working" (Hunter 1927, p. 17).

The following is an eyewitness account of modern Otomí
papermaking by Bodil Christensen:

> The bark is peeled off the trees in the spring, preferably when
> the moon is new, as this facilitates the work and does less harm
> to the trees. The men collect the bark, and the women do the
> actual paper-making. After the peeling, the inner bark is separated
> from the outer bark and sold to the women. It may be dried and
> stored away as it is for later use; but before it is used, it must be
> boiled in ash-water, or lime water, in which corn for the *tortillas*
> has been soaked. It must boil for several hours, generally from
> three to six; then it is rinsed in clean water and is finally ready for
> use. While making the paper, the women keep the fibers in a
> wooden bowl filled with water to keep them soft. The paper is
> made on a wooden board, the size of which depends on the size
> of the paper wanted. The Otomís of San Pablito make small, thin
> sheets of paper measuring only about five by nine inches; those
> made by the [Aztec] Indians in Chicontepec are much heavier and
> twice the size. A woman spreads a layer of fibers on the board
> and beats it out with a stone until it is felted together. The stones
> are either grooved or smooth on the pounding surface with fluted
> sides. Amongst the Indians in Chicontepec, dried corn-cobs scorched
> in fire are used instead of the customary stone beaters. The boards
> with the wet fibers are placed in the sun to dry, and after a while
> the paper can be lifted off the board. [Christensen 1963, p. 363]

There seem to be minor disagreements with Hunter's account,
for example, whether the bark is best peeled in the autumn or
spring, but the basic process described is the same.

The techniques for making bark paper are quite different
from those used to produce modern industrially manufactured
paper. We can assume that the ancient Mexicans followed
similar procedures in papermaking, and, in fact, the best of
today's bark paper strongly resembles that used for the codices.
The traditional process allows paper to be made in any thick-
ness or size, depending on the amount of fiber used, the degree
to which it is pounded, and the size of the board on which
it is formed. Thus the gigantic sheet of paper used in the Aztec

ritual described earlier by Sahagún could have been made by use of techniques employed today.

Most of the paper made today is sold in various forms to tourist markets. For this purpose a rough finish on the paper is acceptable. The ancient Aztecs, however, developed the technique of ironing the paper with a hot stone to give it a better surface for painting (Von Hagen 1977 [1944], pp. 64–65). They also painted the codices on paper which had been coated with a white substance, probably bicarbonate of calcium. This coating may have served to improve the surface of the paper or perhaps to provide a uniform white background. Finally, to make it more durable, Aztec craftsmen sometimes made laminated paper composed of thin sheets held together with a vegetable glue (Christensen 1963, p. 361).

THE USES OF PAPER AMONG CONTEMPORARY INDIANS

One of the most important legacies of the interest in papermaking is that it motivated researchers to visit the remote and hitherto unstudied southern Huasteca area where paper is still produced. According to Starr, Mexico has no better region in which to study the survival of ancient beliefs and practices (Starr 1901, p. 180). The three major culture groups that occupy the area—Nahua (Aztec), Otomí, and Tepehua—have remained fairly isolated and thus have been able to retain many of their ancient traditions. The discovery of these fascinating cultures was an unforeseen event derived from the search for the origins of native paper. The early researchers Hunter and León and later ones like Von Hagen, Lenz, and Christensen were interested in discovering how paper was traditionally made. The ancient sources were lacking in reliable descriptions of the craft, and the controversy over the source of fiber added to the confusion. The only solution was to follow up Starr's discovery that paper was still being produced in the old way and to witness the techniques firsthand.

By the 1930s only a few families in the Otomí village of San Pablito appear to have been making paper, mainly to supply local shamans, who cut it into sacred images (Dow

1982, p. 630). It appears that the final blow to this ancient craft was the ready availability of cheap mass-produced paper, which had the advantage of coming in many colors. Then Nahua Indians in the state of Guerrero began painting colorful pictures on Otomí bark paper to sell to the growing numbers of tourists visiting Mexico (Eshelman 1981; Stromberg 1976). The paintings, called *amates* after the Aztec word for paper, were extremely popular, and the demand for bark paper soon became enormous. The depressed papermaking industry rapidly revitalized and transformed the economy of San Pablito. Anthropologist James Dow, who has conducted extensive field research in and around San Pablito, reports that every family in the village now produces bark paper; in 1974 between 50,000 and 60,000 pesos' worth of paper were being produced each month in the village (Dow, personal communication). The increased economic importance of bark paper, so closely associated with ritual life, seems to have had a revitalizing effect on Otomí religion as well. Dow reports that many Otomís now militantly support the native religion. Another researcher reports that Saint Martin the Lesser has been added to the list of saints in the church. This saint is known to the villagers as San Jonote, or Saint Bark Paper Fiber (Kaupp 1975, p. 169).

With the discovery that paper was still used in Otomí rituals, an interest soon developed in the traditional religion of the Otomís. Christensen and Lenz were the first to collect information on the local rituals, although they presented only vague sketches. Earlier researchers had held the local customs in disdain and thought them unworthy of study. After describing the use of paper in certain magic rites, Von Hagen said: "Such is the lamentable decadence of Mexican paper" (Von Hagen 1977 [1944], p. 58). Hunter dismissed traditional Otomí religion when he declared, "Paper among the Otomís does not concern the intellectual" (Hunter 1957, p. 47). The sale of Otomí sacred paper figures in handicraft markets produced an even greater interest in the religions that produced them. Modern researchers (see the works of Dow; Boilès; Galinier; Lannik, Palm and Tatkon; Kaupp; Fitl; and Spranz) have increased our knowledge a great deal, but the philosophical and mythological basis of Otomí religion is still only poorly understood. At least three Otomí shamans have produced written works on their religious system. In the 1960s, Santos García produced small books, handwritten on bark paper and bound by hand, in which certain rituals and associated cut-paper images are explained. Alfonso García T. and, later, Antonio López M. produced similar small books, also hand-lettered on bark paper, which attempt to explain something of traditional religious belief (see Sandstrom 1981). What has emerged is a clearer but still incomplete picture of Otomí religion. Far from the simple-mindedness attributed to it by some early researchers, Otomí religion has been found to be highly complex, sophisticated, and comprehensible on a variety of levels. Chapter 5 contains information on Otomí religion and illustrations of paper cuttings collected from Otomí shamans.

Meanwhile, work has also begun on the other cultures that make use of paper figures in their rituals, the Nahuas and Tepehuas. While neither of these groups still produces bark paper, they do use manufactured paper extensively in ritual performances. The Nahuas are probably remnants of the Aztec empire, which invaded the region sometime before the Spanish conquest (Barlow 1979 [1949], p. 55). They have been investigated by a number of researchers, and, like the Otomís, they possess a highly traditional religious system (see the works of Reyes García; Williams García; Montoya Briones; Provost; and Sandstrom). Research findings on Nahua religion along with illustrations of paper images collected from Nahua shamans are included in chapter 4.

In 1937–38, while Von Hagen was researching pre-Columbian papermaking, a French investigator named Robert Gessain entered the region of traditional papermaking. A member of a scientific exchange program between Mexico and France, he conducted anthropological research among the Tepehua Indians of Huehuetla, in the state of Hidalgo. Gessain found that the Tepehuas made extensive use of industrially manufactured paper in their religious observances. Ill health forced

Gessain to leave Mexico before his work was completed (G. B. 1938, pp. 381ff.), but he published the first systematic information on the sacred paper images used in the region, along with photographs of the several he was able to collect (Gessain 1938, pp. 343–71). Later a Mexican ethnographer, Roberto Williams García, was able to extend Gessain's work with a long-term field project in a Tepehua village in northern Veracruz (see Williams García 1963, 1972). Information on Tepehua religion along with illustrations of paper images collected by these researchers is included in chapter 6.

The Indians of today practice a religion that has meaning within their agricultural way of life and derives from the context established by their own history. Modern researchers have just begun to uncover the complex metaphysical and philosophical bases of the sacred paper images and the religious thought that underlies them. Much work remains to be done. Although many beliefs and practices among the Nahuas, Otomís, and Tepehuas have been blended or syncretized with Christian religious ideas, their systems remain essentially foreign to people of Western European culture. The use of paper to portray and represent their most powerful and sacred concepts, while particularly strange to those of us living in urban bureaucracies inundated in paperwork, has a long and well-established history among the Indians of Middle America. In a very real sense paper images are the central focus of rituals. They are symbolic of the spirits and concepts most closely connected to key areas of daily existence, and they are a physical image of what is vital to the Nahuas, Otomís, and Tepehuas who are still living traditional lives. The importance of paper as a medium of communication between human and spirit worlds is as great today as it was five hundred years ago.

CHAPTER 2

XOCHITLALIA : A NAHUA-OTOMÍ
CROP FERTILITY RITUAL

In the Nahua Indian village of Amatlán (not its real name), where we conducted most of our field research, there is a small shrine to the seed spirits, located off of the main trail and hidden from the view of passersby. After having spent several months in the village questioning people about religious beliefs and gaining little information, we were invited there to attend a ritual held to bring rain to the parched fields. Of the dozens of rituals we witnessed in the village, this was one of the most elaborate and colorful. It was also the first one in which we saw extensive use of paper images. In the following pages we describe this fertility ceremony in order to place the paper images in their context and to impart something of the flavor of *costumbre* rituals.

Including preparations, the ritual lasted about two weeks. What follows is a summary of its major events. The ritual was somewhat unusual in style and content for the Nahuas because it was conducted by an Otomí shaman. This shaman has a reputation for being an extremely effective ritual specialist. Nahua informants noted that he lives alone in the jungle, and all agreed that he conducts a powerful ritual that always brings results. Throughout the event a Nahua shaman assisted him, for example, by chanting in Nahuatl, while the Otomí chanted in his own language. In this way the ritual was rendered comprehensible to village participants. The use of an outsider for such an important occasion illustrates the degree to which religious beliefs and practices are shared among Indians of the region. Some of the mythological and cosmological principles underlying the ritual (of which we were ignorant at the time) are discussed in chapters 4, 5, and 7.

EVENTS LEADING UP TO THE RITUAL

By the middle of March the village Amatlán had been without rain for almost two months. The villagers were growing worried about the drought, especially since the winter crops were showing signs of deterioration. Winter is the dry season in the Huasteca region, and crops planted at this time always yield less than those grown during the summer rainy season. Two months without rain, however, is unusual even for this time of year. The problem greatly concerned the people of Amatlán because they are small-scale horticulturists who have no means of saving produce from previous seasons. Thus the loss of the dry-season crop would mean the month of hunger before the rainy-season crop was ready for harvest.

The usual practice in the village is to hold a ritual in late February or early March to insure the fertility of the fields. Called Xochitlalia (Flowery Earth), the ritual is designed as an offering to various spirits that are believed to influence the conditions of plant growth. Among these spirits are the seeds, whose paper images are stored in a sacred wooden cabinet kept in the special shrine. These paper figures are dressed in tiny suits of clothes and are placed in the cabinet along with miniature furniture. Other spirit entities addressed in this ritual include the Earth, Water, Fire, the Cross, and Lightning and Thunder, which, along with the seed spirits, live on twelve sacred hills in the vicinity of the village. Each hill has a name and may be visited during other ritual occasions throughout the year (see chapter 4).

Because of the drought, village leaders decided to hold a particularly elaborate Xochitlalia ritual that year. They planned the ceremony to last for twelve days, one day for each of the sacred hills. One of the wealthier Nahua families agreed to pay the substantial fee of 150 pesos (U.S. $12 at what was then the current exchange rate) to hire the Otomí shaman to cut the paper figures and organize the proceedings. Despite the fact that the observance would be Otomí in character, the villagers agreed that this ritual, observed with greater elaboration than usual, would be particularly effective at producing rain. The following is from our field notes taken as the events occurred.

A full day before the Otomí master arrives, excitement grows in the village as preparations are begun. Men and boys gather piles of marigold blossoms and palm leaves to be made into altar adornments. The Nahua shaman directs several volunteers to purchase candles and sacrificial turkeys and chickens at a distant market. Other men wash altar tables, and women begin to prepare meals for the shamans and their helpers. While preparations are being made, the Nahua shaman places lighted beeswax candles near the workers, and a guitarist and violinist begin to play the slow and highly repetitive sacred music which will be heard for the duration of the ritual. About half a dozen men squat in a circle and make several types of adornments. The most common, called *coyoles*, are wandlike strips of palm leaf to which are tied one or two marigold blossoms. They are used to decorate altars, and altogether 2,100 of them are produced for the upcoming ritual. Pinwheellike adornments are also constructed from palm leaves and marigold flowers. These symbolize guardian stars (sing. *citlali*) and are tied on leaf-covered arches over altar tables. A third type of adornment is made from varying lengths of flexible vine to which marigold blossoms are tied. This item is called *xochicostli* (or *rosario*, "rosary"), and it is used to decorate altars and to cleanse people ritually of disease-causing spirits. Finally there are various adornments made from bamboo, including *bastones* ("walking sticks" or "staffs"), which are decorated with flowers and ribbons, and *xochimapilli* ("little flower-hand"), small fork-like implements on which marigold blossoms are impaled.

As these adornments are being completed, the Otomí master arrives with a large bundle of paper. A man adds resinous copal incense to a nearby brazier while the Otomí instructs a group of men how to fold and cut the paper into uniform sheets. As the Otomí shaman works, scores of villagers enter the thatch-roofed shrine and respectfully greet the master. He takes out a pair of scissors and rapidly begins to cut paper figures from the prepared sheets. The process continues for the next several hours as hundreds of paper figures are fashioned. Finished cutouts are smoothed and separated by helpers and placed twelve at a time on decorated sheets of paper called "tortilla napkins" or "beds" (see chapter 4 for an explanation of these terms). These, in turn, are carefully stacked by the helpers, one on top of the other. The finished stacks are divided into piles of about twenty and tied with strips of bark.

The figures laid on the paper beds are symbolic representations of the various spirits to be addressed in the ritual. Many figures are cut repeatedly, and the spirits are often represented in both male and female forms. After this initial series of figures is cut from the white paper, the Otomí cuts several dozen figures from colored paper. Finally he cuts several large squarish figures with hideous claws, gaping mouths, and skeletonlike ribs. The face, claw, and rib cuts are circled with heavy black charcoal to emphasize their malevolent nature. These last two groups of images represent the disease-causing winds that threaten both people and crops.

While the figures are being cut, helpers open the sacred cabinet containing the seed spirits. One man places a smoking copal incense brazier before the cabinet as others empty it of its contents. The seed figures, dressed in sets of tiny clothes, have been stored in bunches of five or ten, neatly stacked upright in the cabinet. These, along with the miniature furnishings, are removed and placed in a shallow basket (see color plate 1). Most of the figures represent the corn plant, although other crops are also included (see figures 41–51 for a sample of the cuttings kept in the cabinet). Women and girls begin to take the clothes off the figures as male helpers thoroughly cense and clean the cabinet. The clothes are washed, dried, and placed back on the paper images during the ritual. As the women and girls wash the clothes, helpers go outside and set up a small table dedicated to the Spirit of the Cross. Other volunteers place lighted candles for the Fire Spirit on the mud and stone fire table nearby. Finally another group of helpers sets up a small altar dedicated to the Water Spirit at a nearby spring.

The Otomí shaman then instructs the growing number of helpers to decorate the main altar. They erect an arch covered with green *limonaria* leaves over the table and then tie the star adornments and bunches of flowers to the arch. An old midwife, called the *copalmitoti quetl* in Nahuatl or *copalera* in Spanish ("incense dancer"), begins to dance gracefully before the partially completed altar while holding a smoking brazier. A man places the cleaned but still empty cabinet at the center of the altar and leans the walking-stick adornments against it. A number of young girls enter and begin to sway back and forth to the sacred music while shaking rattles. Helpers line the altar with lighted candles and place a pot of water with a lighted candle sticking out of it by the cabinet. Many people now enter the shrine, and each person bows before the altar and leans an unlighted candle against the cabinet. All scraps of paper from the cuttings are carefully gathered up by nearby participants, while the small altar outside, dedicated to the Spirit of the Cross, is adorned with candles and the palm and marigold items prepared earlier.

THE CLEANSING

Work on the main altar is halted by the Otomí shaman as he instructs everyone to move outside for a general cleansing. Before any major ritual is held, harmful spirits must be removed from the participants' bodies and from the surrounding area. A danger always exists that harmful spirits will be attracted to the music and offerings and thus will gain strength. The shaman lays out beds of white and colored paper figures in a pattern on the ground (see accompanying diagram). Surrounding these, he arranges the large, square charcoal-blackened images and a number of leaf packets to which have been tied single white paper images. Helpers lay out sprigs of sacred herbs near the bottom of the array and then place bundles of palm-leaf adornments over the paper cutouts. Next they place a long vine and marigold rosary so that it completely surrounds the display. Two men arrange cups of coffee on the paper images while others place bottles of *aguardiente* (a white rum), Coca-Cola,

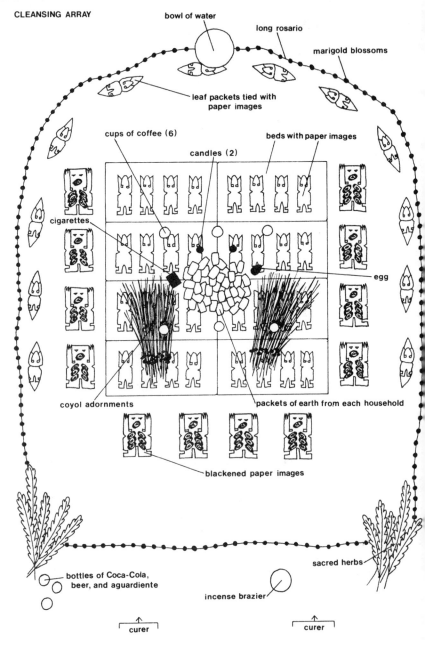

DIAGRAM OF XOCHITLALIA

CLEANSING ARRAY

bowl of water

long rosario

marigold blossoms

leaf packets tied with
paper images

cups of coffee (6)

candles (2)

beds with paper images

cigarettes

egg

coyol adornments

packets of earth from each household

blackened paper images

bottles of Coca-Cola,
beer, and aguardiente

sacred herbs

incense brazier

curer

curer

and beer at the bottom of the array near a smoking brazier. The musicians now play before the display as the shaman sticks lighted candles in the earth. Helpers pile leaf packets containing earth from each house in the village on the paper beds. A man sets a large bowl of water at the head of the display as another places an egg, a pack of cigarettes, and pieces of bread on the display itself. A woman adds bread to each cup of coffee as the two shamans kneel before the array.

The Nahua and Otomí shamans chant simultaneously in their own languages. They dedicate the display and offerings to the *malos aires* ("bad airs")—wind spirits associated with disease and death. The shamans list the offerings in their chants and implore negative spirits to keep away from the village. As the group of young girls sway and shake rattles to the music, the shamans grab handfuls of the palm-leaf adornments from the display. After parading the walking-stick adornments in front of the paper figures in the display, the shamans rub all the people with palm adornments. The incense dancer begins to cense everyone as the Otomí waves a branch cut from a sacred tree over each person's head. Next the shamans position two male helpers before the display, each holding a lighted candle in one hand and a ritual walking stick in the other. The walking-stick adornments have two major meanings: they are symbolic of travel or communication, in this case between people and the spirits, and they are the implements carried by Thunder and Lightning, dwarflike spirits who travel in the clouds and cause rain. Parading or holding the sticks communicates the offerings to the appropriate spirits and suggests that rain is needed by the village.

A woman emerges from the shrine carrying the basket with the naked seed figures in it. Helpers now place small bits of lighted white candle, symbolizing the underworld, around the display. The *malos aires*, whose images make up the display, come from the underworld; they represent the wandering spirits of people who died tragic, usually violent, deaths. A male participant brings out the stacks of cut-paper images from inside the shrine as the shamans place lighted cigarettes in the mouths of the blackened square figures surrounding the main display. The Otomí master now holds a small chicken in the smoke rising from the incense brazier. He waves the chicken over the display and exhibits it before the crowd of people. The same procedure is followed by the Nahua shaman. The two shamans then take both chickens inside to the main altar to be blessed. Returning outside, they suddenly wrench off the chickens' heads and sprinkle their blood over the display. At the same moment helpers pour the beverage offerings over all the ritual items. The shamans reserve the egg and some of each offering to be poured into the bowl of water at the head of the display.

The large marigold blossom rosary surrounding the display is removed and held by two helpers. A small group of onlookers moves into the loop of the rosary, and it is lowered to the ground. The people step out, and the rosary is raised over their heads and lowered down over them again. In all, the process is repeated seven times. Next the helpers lay the rosary on the ground and the people step into it, after which it is raised up over their heads. This procedure is also repeated seven times. The first group to be so cleansed includes those people designated to hold the cut-paper figures. As the Otomí master continues to sprinkle white rum on the display, all of the people in attendance have the loop passed over them. Finally, at the instruction of the shamans, the entire display is divided in half and formed into two tightly tied bundles. Each bundle contains half of the offerings and paper images, along with a marigold blossom rosary and one sacrificed chicken. After the shamans step back into the shrine, they parade the bundles before the altar, fireplace, cooking area, and the group of people in attendance. The bundles are then given to boys to be discarded. One bundle is placed on a bank high above a trail, while the other is thrown into a deep ravine. Because the bundles contain all of the harmful wind spirits removed during the ritual, they are disposed of carefully so they cannot be encountered accidentally.

Each step in the cleansing procedure is designed to remove dangerous spirits. The elaborate display contains paper images of the wind spirits that receive offerings and are exhorted to depart by the shamans. Spirits are believed to have appetites similar to humans, and offerings thus include luxury items such as cigarettes, white rum, beer, Coca-Cola, coffee, eggs, and bread. Unlike humans, however, they feed on blood, which is supplied by the sacrificial birds. The Nahuas want the display to be a beautiful place where the spirits can enjoy the offerings, so they surround it by lighted candles, marigold blossoms, and sacred herbs and arrange for musicians to play special music. The ritual cleansing of the packets of earth from each house placed in the center of the display symbolically cleanses each individual dwelling in the village. The bowl of water is included in the array because certain harmful spirits come from the water. Ritual participants and the remaining paper images are cleansed of dangerous spirits in a number of ways. The shamans rub each person with the sacralized palm adornments as the *copalera* dances and censes everyone. Finally each paper figure and ritual participant goes through the large marigold loop a fixed number of times to eliminate any lingering wind spirits.

THE OFFERING

In front of the main altar the *copalera* dances to the continuing sacred guitar and violin music while holding a smoking brazier. The entire shrine is filled with aromatic copal smoke. As nearly 75 people gather inside the shrine, helpers place all the paper images cut by the Otomí shaman in two piles beside the empty cabinet on the altar. These helpers then pass out bundles of palm adornments to each person in attendance as other men set out a candle, a soft drink, and a food offering under the main altar. This offering to the earth is completed as a helper places a plate holding a pair of scissors nearby. While lighted candles are distributed to everyone, the shamans position the two men holding the walking-stick adornments in front of the altar. Men now bring in several live turkeys and chickens. Every so often one of the shamans walks up and down the altar ringing a small bell to awaken attending spirits. The Otomí shaman gives the pot of water containing the burning candle to a girl to hold and then joins the Nahua shaman, who is kneeling before the altar. A helper hands each shaman half of the stack of newly cut paper figures. Four musicians play the sacred melodies as all the other people, each holding a candle and bundle of palm adormnents, face the altar and kneel.

The stacks of paper beds and figures are sacralized in incense smoke by a helper as the shamans chant in mounting cadence, each in his own language. They name the various spirits and list the offerings about to be made. Everyone in the area bows as the shamans shake rattles and ring the small bell. Next, all stand as the shamans dance energetically before the altar. The stacks of paper figures are taken from the two shamans by their assistants and folded in half. The bamboo-fork adornments and some candles are placed in the fold as all the people make a quarter turn to their left and again kneel. Helpers begin to lay out the paper beds containing the spirit figures on the altar and beside the earth offering as people rise, make another quarter turn to their left, and again kneel. Paper figures continue to be laid carefully on the altar as the people, still holding their palm adornments and candles, turn left again and kneel. Soft drinks are placed on the altar as everyone turns another quarter turn to face the main altar once again. The two shamans kneel before the altar, one ringing the bell, as they make final preparations for the sacrifice.

A chicken and a turkey are held by male assistants as the shamans continue to kneel and chant. The helpers force-feed each bird some *aguardiente* as the shamans rise to dance. The Otomí master puts aside the incense brazier with which he is dancing and cuts the birds' throats with the pair of scissors. He spreads their blood over the paper images laid out on the altar and on the earth display beneath the altar. Two more birds are brought in and killed in the same fashion. The Otomí collects some of the blood in the plate and, using a feather dipped in the blood, paints each paper figure. The people in attendance now carefully place their palm adornments on the altar over the blood-spattered paper images. Smaller altars to the spirits of Fire, the Cross, and Water also receive palm adornments. Helpers place the bamboo-fork adornments on the altar along with marigold blossom rosaries. Finally, as the incense dancer lays the naked seed figures on top of the adornments, a man returns the water pot with the burning candle to the altar. Girls in a tight group sway and shake rattles to the ongoing music while other girls smooth and prepare the miniature seed figures' clothing.

It is 9:45 A.M., and the ritual has continued all night. The shamans and a large number of villagers walk to a spring that provides water for nearby households. Here a small table has been set up and decorated like the main altar. Close to the spring the shamans place lighted candles and food offerings. Two musicians play as the *copalera* performs her dance while swirling the smoking incense brazier. Some women arrive with plates containing the cooked meat of the birds sacrificed the night before. They place some of this meat on the small altar table along with soft drinks, beer, coffee, bread and other food. At the same time, the young girls draw close together and begin swaying and shaking rattles to the music. Helpers place ceramic water jars around the spring while a woman stands before the altar holding a full water pitcher with three protruding walking-stick adornments. This juxtaposition is designed to communicate to the appropriate spirits the immediate need for rain. A woman helper places a packet of naked seed figures by the spring as each person in attendance approaches the altar and adds a coin offering to others in a dish.

After these preparations are completed, the two shamans approach the altar and begin to chant simultaneously. As they kneel, a helper gives a dish of water taken from the spring to a girl standing nearby. After a short while, the girl flings the water upon the crowd of people. Then each person, one by one, moves forward to throw water over the crowd. This act is a form of sympathetic magic designed to show the spirits what the ritual participants want. They hope that the artificial rain will call forth real rain. As this procedure continues, helpers pour all of the food offerings over the altar. Meanwhile, the seed figures having been moved beforehand, the *copalera* continuously rings a bell. Led by the shamans, the entire group proceeds back to the area of the shrine. Two additional offerings are made, one to the spirits of the Cross and Fire at each of the small altars. The procedures followed are similar to those described for the offering at the spring.

At the main altar, musicians continue to play, and the *copalera* continues to perform her dance holding the smoking incense brazier. Young girls have put freshly dried clothes back on the paper images of the seed spirits; the images are then carefully laid in a row on the altar on top of the palm adornments. At this point the major part of the ritual is over and the Otomí shaman leaves for his house. Every few hours, however, the intensity of the ritual resumes as people arrive and a new offering is made to the seeds. Between offerings, the number of people in attendance dwindles as participants go off to sleep. At 5:45 A.M. on the morning of the fourth day, a new offering is made, and as part of the procedure, the Nahua shaman performs a special cleansing for the musicians, incense dancer, and remaining participants. At the finish of the cleansings he passes out palm adornments and candles to each person in attendance. These are placed on individual home altars.

That night another offering is held, and on the next day the shaman places the seed figures back in their cabinet for another year. He makes offerings intermittently for the next several days while music and dancing go on almost continuously. On the twelfth day the final large offering is made. Helpers have cleared the altar, and all the old adornments and paper cuttings have been discarded. New adornments are placed upon the altar, and the usual complement of food, tobacco, and drink offerings are added later. Once again the ritual builds in intensity as people anticipate its conclusion. The Nahua shaman makes a final appeal in a long chant while he stands before the newly decorated altar. After he dedicates the offerings for the final time, the shaman once again faces the altar and, with everyone in attendance kneeling, prays for the life of the seeds.

Within two days a rainstorm saturated the fields. The crop was saved.

THE MEANING OF XOCHITLALIA

Even presented in outline form the symbolic richness and sophistication of this ritual is apparent. One cannot help but wonder whether Frederick Starr would have been more interested in the paper figures if he had witnessed a ritual such as this. He certainly would have noticed that it evokes the ceremonial flavor of pre-Hispanic rituals described by Sahagún and other sixteenth-century chroniclers far more than Christian practices brought in by missionaries.

No written description can completely capture and convey the powerful and moving atmosphere created by the shamans. These shamans possess forceful, charismatic personalities and an assurance of action that makes them the focus of attention and slightly frightening at the same time. These are "people of knowledge" who control forces that can kill as well as produce rain. The ambience of the ritual with its candlelight, incense smoke, repetitive sacred music, dancing, low rhythmic chanting, and blood-soaked paper images is both exciting and awe-inspiring. These reactions were felt not only by us, the ethnographers, but also by the Nahuas to whom we talked.

Interpreting a ritual such as this presents many problems. For one thing, like any ritual event it is composed of a number of layers of meaning. For the purpose of illuminating the role of the paper images, however, we adhere to a straightforward analysis of major symbols as explained by Nahua informants. The ritual is a systematic attempt to control elements that are responsible for crop fertility and growth. The Nahuas explain that many factors or conditions affecting crop success or failure are directed by spirit entities. The shaman does not try to control these spirits in a mechanical way, but rather he tries to influence their behavior using what amounts to reciprocal exchanges. Rituals are exchanges in which offerings are made to spirits so that they will feel obligated to supply the conditions necessary for crop productivity. Even the dangerous wind spirits are given offerings of the best food and drink before they are exhorted to depart. Adorned altars are designed to be beautiful places, a microcosm of the universe, with palm and marigold stars on the arch above and a display to the earth below. Human and spirit tastes are believed to overlap, except that the spirits crave blood, which the shaman supplies by sacrificing birds. The ritual, in short, is part of a social exchange between the human and spirit worlds. Spirits repay the gifts by providing the conditions leading to green and healthy fields.

For several of the symbolic components of this ritual we were unable to elicit a native interpretation. Shamans did not seem to know the meaning of certain adornments or symbolic acts and answered our questions with the statement, "This is the way we do it." We could not discover the precise meaning of the bamboo forks, for example, although it is possible that they symbolize the growing plant. When asked, the Nahua shaman could say only that they are demonstrations or "models" *(muestras)* for the spirits. Another unknown is why the people holding candles and palm adornments face the four directions. Perhaps this action is a reflection of the widespread American Indian idea that the four directions are sacred. These components may relate more strictly to the Otomí symbolic system, which would explain why the Nahuas did not seem to know their meaning.

Other elements were easily explained by our informants. Richly aromatic copal incense smoke is a universal sacralizing agent in the Huasteca area, as are candles and music, which together constitute an offering of beauty to the spirits. The pot containing water and the lighted candle is a special offering to the related spirits of Thunder, Lightning, and Water designed to achieve relief from drought. The group of young girls who sway before the altars during offerings symbolize potential fertility. They are like the seeds—unmanifested productivity—and they are seen as proper companions to the seed spirits. It is no coincidence that the majority of the paper seed images are dressed in clothes exactly like those worn by young village girls.

The four major altars were built to the seeds and associated spirits: Fire, the Cross, and Water. Fire is a manifestation of a spirit called Xauantsi or Tlixauantsi, which lives in the hearth stones of each household. It symbolizes the house and family and acts as a kind of guardian of the kin group. The cross in the form used in the ritual is probably borrowed from Christian missionaries, although there was also a cross in pre-Hispanic times that was highly charged with meaning. For contemporary Indians it has come to symbolize the sun (see chapter 4). Viewed as a whole, then, the major altars are dedicated to the seeds and entities that promote seed growth, the sun, water, and the kin group. The ritual thus both models the forces that underlie village life in the Huasteca and constitutes an attempt to interact with them.

In the background, however, is a spirit entity so encompassing and crucial that it is rarely emphasized in rituals. It is the Earth. Without the continuous presence of the Earth there can be no crops, people, or rituals. In Xochitlalia the Earth's presence is marked by the small displays placed under each of the altars to the seeds, Fire, the Cross, and Water. The location and subtlety of these displays do not diminish the importance of the Earth, but, rather, indicate that it is basic to, or symbolically prior to, all other activities.

The focus of ritual activity is clearly the paper images, both those kept permanently in the wooden cabinet and those cut by the shaman. Once sacralized in copal smoke, the figures acquire the ability to attract the life-forces of spirits they represent and, in so doing, become ritually potent in their own right. The fact that many images are cut partly reflects the large number of spirits included in the offering and, more importantly, reveals a high degree of repetition. Repetition in paper cutting, just as in chanting, is a way to emphasize or highlight something significant. Paper images are visual representations of important concepts—concrete symbols that help ritual participants center their minds and emotions on significant ideas in the religious system. The images add to the symbolic richness of the ritual while simultaneously reducing religious abstractions to a more easily understood and manipulable physical form.

The ritual event contains many of the major elements that are common to the *costumbre* complex throughout the region. These common elements include the use of paper images to represent spirits, the construction of altars, the dedication of offerings, addressing the spirits through chanting, and the general strategy of entering into exchange relations with spirits. Dozens of smaller elements are also shared among the Nahuas, Otomís, and Tepehuas, such as the use of copal incense, candles, the palm and marigold adornments, tobacco, *aguardiente*, guitar and violin music, and so on. The three additional rituals described in chapters 4 to 6 share these and many additional features. Perhaps most important is that the spirits addressed during rituals are similar throughout the region. Each village has its *malos aires*, Water, Earth, and seed spirits, and Christian-derived elements such as saints and the Roman cross. Interestingly, the paper images that represent these spirits and that are the focus of ritual behavior also share commonalities. These will be discussed in the following chapters.

Xochitlalia also reveals certain characteristics of the *costumbre* complex that are puzzling and problematic to outside observers. First, there exist multitudes of spirits, many of which seem to be simply slight variations on one another. The earth display, for example, contains dozens of different paper images, all representing aspects or perhaps alter egos of the earth spirit. Each variation, however slight, can have a different nature and often a different name. Second, subtle contradictions often exist in the spirit realm. Although the seeds, for example, are captured in the wooden cabinet, they live in a cave on a sacred hill. The ritual is intended to produce rain, yet the spirits most directly connected to rainmaking (Thunder, Lightning, and Water) play relatively minor roles. These and additional puzzles are also discussed in the following chapters.

Regardless of the ultimate meanings of symbols or their apparent inconsistencies, Xochitlalia demonstrates that paper persists as a central feature in Indian rituals even 450 years after the Spanish Conquest. It further illustrates that the paper images themselves must be examined and analyzed to understand Nahua, Otomí, and Tepehua religions and world views.

CHAPTER 3

THE HUASTECA CULTURE AREA

THROUGHOUT its history the region in which paper cult figures are found has had a reputation for being remote and difficult to traverse. Its tropical climate and mountainous terrain have impeded conquerors and discouraged settlement by Europeans. It has traditionally served as a zone of refuge where Indians might escape conquering armies, slavers, rapacious governments, and European diseases. Even the missionaries were too busy fighting among themselves to have a destructive effect on the traditional cultures. The area is far from major cities, it is too hilly for modern agriculture, and it lacks roads. Today, just as in pre-Hispanic times, it remains one of the most isolated and undeveloped areas in Mesoamerica. Thus the survival of the paper cult religions can be attributed as much to the character of this region as to any other factor.

The region lies along the borders of the states of Veracruz, Hidalgo, and Puebla on the eastern slopes of the Sierra Madre Oriental. A majority of the area lies in the states of Veracruz and Hidalgo in a region known as the Huasteca. Both scholars and local inhabitants disagree on where to place the borders of the Huasteca, although it is clear that part of the paper-using area falls outside of its southern boundary. The Huasteca is named after the Huastec Indians, a Maya-speaking group who inhabited the entire region in pre-Hispanic times. Just to the south of the Huasteca is an area known as the Totonaca-pán, where Totonac Indians lived in pre-Hispanic times and continue to live today. Both the Huastecs and the Totonacs were organized into political units that militarily opposed the highland civilizations of the Mexican plateau. Thus the area in which paper figures are cut lies on the border between the Huastecs and Totonacs and straddles the region between highland and Gulf Coast cultures.

The area of ritual paper use, which we will simply call the southern Huasteca, changes aspect as one moves from the coastal region westward. The coast has lost its traditional Indian cultures as a result of early depopulation and economic changes brought about by a highway that connects Tampico with Veracruz. From the coastal plain moving west, one soon encounters low undulating hills that mark the beginning of the foothills of the Sierra Madre Oriental. These become quite steep and soon present a barrier to travel. In the western part of the southern Huasteca the mountains reach altitudes of two thousand meters, and entire areas are approachable only by horse or on foot. There are passes through the mountain range, however, and historically one of the most important penetrates the southern Huasteca near the present-day town of Huauchinango.

Although the Huastecs traditionally occupied much of the southern Huasteca region, other groups migrated into the area in pre-Hispanic times. Between the tenth and thirteenth centuries the Toltecs moved in and perhaps built the provincial town of Castillo de Teayo (Stresser-Péan 1971, pp. 586–87). In the thirteenth and fourteenth centuries Otomís arrived in the area, and during the same period Nahuas began to move into the region in the direction of the coastal settlement of Tuxpan (Stresser-Péan 1971, pp. 585, 588). The history of the Tepehuas is sketchy, but they are thought to be related to the Totonacs, in which case they may be ancient inhabitants of the region (Williams García 1963, pp. 38ff.). In addition to these migrations and branchings, legendary histories suggest that the area was invaded numerous times by Chichimec peoples from the north (Kelly and Palerm 1952, pp. 16ff.). Indirect evidence indicates that Comanche Indians from North America also raided the area. During present-day celebrations of Carnaval, young men in the Indian villages strip to the waist, paint their bodies and faces, and wear feathers in their hair. In fun, they run around screaming and disrupting the village, demanding a small payment from each household. These performers are called "Comanches" (Provost 1975, p. 22; see also Reyes García 1960).

The Aztecs showed an interest in the southern Huasteca early in their history. Invasions were launched by the emperors Moctezuma I, Axayacatl, Tizoc, Ahuizotl, and Moctezuma II (Kelly and Palerm 1952, pp. 22–23). By the time of the Spanish invasion, the Aztecs had subdued the Totonacs and pushed the Huastecs to the northern part of their own territory. They had opened a wedge between the Huastecs and Totonacs, which they filled with new Nahua settlers (there were probably Nahua-speakers in the area before that time). The reason usually given for Aztec interest in this area is that coastal maize harvests were more reliable than those in the highlands. The Aztecs had endured periodic famine, and they wanted to ensure food production by incorporating tropical areas into the empire. This assertion has been questioned by Nigel Davies, who points out that tribute lists from the Gulf Coast do not include corn. He states that the Aztecs were after luxury items: "The coast produced finery for the nobles rather than food for the people" (1982, p. 183). One of the major items of tribute listed from the region is bark paper (Stresser-Péan 1971, p. 594).

The modern distribution of Indian peoples reflects these historical occurrences. The Huastecs live in the north, while the Totonacs are in the south. Between these groups are the "strange interminglings" of Nahuas, Otomís, and Tepehuas that Starr noted when he first entered the region (Starr 1901, p. 79). This was also the situation when Cortés landed in Veracruz in 1519. The Totonacs, suffering under the yoke of Aztec domination, allied themselves with the Spaniards and peacefully surrendered control of their territory. This included sections of the southern Huasteca; thus, parts of the region were spared war with the Spaniards (Kelly and Palerm 1952, p. 30). With his Totonac allies close by, Cortés marched to the Aztec capital, gathering additional warriors as he went. In 1522, after defeating the Aztecs, Cortés launched an expedition into the Huasteca, possibly passing through the southern region on his way to meet the Huastec army. After fierce fighting,

POPULATIONS OF INDIAN LANGUAGE
SPEAKERS (FIVE YEARS AND OLDER)
FOR THE NATION AND THE SIX
HUASTECA AREA STATES

	Nahuas	Otomís	Tepehuas
Total MEXICO	799,394	221,062	5,545
Hidalgo	115,359	82,418	1,210
Puebla	266,181	5,533	384
Querétaro	178	11,016	0
San Luis Potosí	72,495	742	0
Tamaulipas	487	126	0
Veracruz	199,435	12,078	3,951

Source: Censo general de población, 1970

he vanquished the Huastecs and brought the region under
Spanish domination (Melgarejo Vivanco 1960, p. 61).

Cortés and his followers soon lost interest in the area because it had no mineral resources they could exploit and the
Indians were not wealthy in gold (Kelly and Palerm 1952,
p. 39). The missionaries were quick to move in, however, and
as a result the southern Huasteca underwent one of the most
prolonged proselytizing efforts in the New World (Kelly and
Palerm 1952, p. 30). Franciscans arrived in 1523 to begin the
task of converting the Indians to Christianity. In 1533 the
Augustinians arrived; they eventually set up a headquarters in
Pahuatlán, Puebla. They even stationed a resident priest in
Chicontepec, Veracruz, right in the heart of the paper cult
district (Kelly and Palerm 1952, p. 32). Paradoxically, papermaking and the paper cult rituals survive in the exact area that
has experienced the greatest missionary activity. The reasons
for this apparent contradiction are important for what they

reveal about the history of the region and the nature of the paper cult religions.

One factor that accounts for the apparent failure of the missionaries is the almost continual conflict between the Franciscans and Augustinians. The struggle apparently became more important than the mission, and the Indians were spared the worst of the missionaries' zeal (Kelly and Palerm 1952, p. 32). Second, individuals or whole villages would escape the Spaniards by simply moving to remote and inaccessible mountain valleys. The Indians' form of horticulture lent itself to mobility, and they could move without great disruption. A third factor accounting for the missionaries' failure lies in the nature of the Indian religions. Pre-Hispanic religion was syncretic and flexible: deities were added or deleted according to the fortunes of war or the revelations of the priesthood. The Aztecs, for example, often placed their own deities alongside those of the people they vanquished without attempting to destroy the local religion. Thus the peoples of the southern Huasteca, like those all over Mesoamerica, were able to accept aspects of the new religion and at the same time practice their traditional rituals. This characteristic of the pre-Hispanic religions, so alien to the Spanish conquerors, will be discussed in greater detail in the concluding chapter.

A fourth factor that helps account for the failure of the missionaries relates to the arrival in 1527 of Nuño de Guzman, the newly appointed governor of the province of Pánuco. Pánuco lies in the northern part of the Huasteca, but its boundaries are vague (Chipman 1967, p. 19). It seems likely, however, that the policies of the new governor had a disastrous effect on the Indians in the southern Huasteca. Nuño de Guzman was, according to one authority, "one of those rare characters whose exclusive function seems to have been that of destroyer . . . [and] his capacity for hatred was only equaled by an apparent delight in sadistical orgies of burning, torture, and destruction" (Simpson 1967, p. 38; however, see Chipman 1967 for a revisionist view of Nuño de Guzman). Partly as a result of his policies, the population of the Huasteca area declined.

Those who did not fall prey to his slavers or forced labor policies, however, often managed to escape into the hills of the southern Huasteca. The social disorganization that must have existed, plus the physical isolation of the survivors, militated against the rapid spread of Christianity (Kelly and Palerm 1952, pp. 32, 38).

Scholars have long known that the population of Mesoamerica rapidly declined after the Conquest, but the magnitude of the decline has not been documented until recently. One authority stated that the total population of Mesoamerica in 1519 was twenty-two million and that this total had declined to less than one million by 1620. The same authority states: "In the first decades after the conquest vast numbers of Indians, probably in the millions, succumbed in the hot country behind Veracruz. . . ." (Gerhard 1972, pp. 23–24). William Sanders wrote that the population of the state of Veracruz was almost destroyed following the Conquest and that at one point the Gulf Coast population declined to 9 percent of the 1519 total (1952–53, p. 46; 1971, p. 547). Cook and Simpson, in trying to estimate pre-Conquest population totals, state that they can provide little information on the southern Huasteca simply because the population had practically vanished by the time the Spaniards began to keep records (1948, pp. 2–3). Those who had managed to escape from Nuño de Guzman's reign of terror or the European diseases that accompanied it were also unrecorded by the early census takers.

The lack of a population base in the Huasteca created a labor shortage that prevented the early Spanish settlers from developing large-scale farming on their *encomiendas*. As a result, "virtually the whole province was turned into sheep and cattle ranges: sheep in the uplands, cattle in the coastal plains" (Simpson 1952, p. 73). In fact, Nuño de Guzman, who is known as "Mexico's first rancher," was probably forced to abandon large-scale farming because of his brutal treatment of the Indian population (see Harnapp 1972, pp. 32ff.). Beginning at the end of the sixteenth century and continuing through the seventeenth, the *encomiendas* were transformed into *haciendas*. These privately owned ranches relied on hired labor and were organized around cattle raising. On several occasions the Spanish authorities tried to move the remaining Indians into "congregations" so that they could be more easily ruled. The attempts apparently failed because the Indians simply escaped into the rugged hills (Kelly and Palerm 1952, pp. 37–39). The War of Independence led to great changes in the region as *haciendas* encroached on the remote villages and the Indians were systematically dispossessed of their land holdings. Following independence there was sporadic guerrilla activity in the region, but it was only after the 1910 revolution that attention turned to the plight of the Indians (Kelly and Palerm 1952, pp. 39–44).

The Agrarian Laws of 1915 were enacted to return land to the Indians, land which had been expropriated by the *hacienda* owners. This was accomplished by establishing land-communes called *ejidos*, which were similar in organization to the pre-Hispanic land-holding village. Interestingly, the mountainous region of Veracruz is one of the few areas in Mexico where remnants of the ancient land-holding village survived into the 1920s (McBride 1923, pp. 125, 135). By the 1940s, however, most of the Indian lands had been converted to the *ejidos*, which still exist today. As might be expected, however, not all land was returned to the Indians. Under the Agrarian Laws, *hacienda* owners were allowed to retain certain of their properties. They naturally selected the most fertile and productive land for themselves, leaving the less desirable hilly tracts for the Indians.

The Indian population did not recover from the Spanish conquest until the twentieth century and the period of political stability following the revolution and the greater availability of medical care. Today the Indians of the southern Huasteca live in small village *ejidos* scattered throughout the hills, each village averaging under one thousand inhabitants. The non-Indian, mestizo-owned cattle ranches, contemporary versions of the old *haciendas*, occupy the desirable flatlands between villages. Interestingly, in pre-Hispanic times the rural population was also divided between land-holding villages and provincial estates of the Indian nobility. Thus the roots of the modern village-cattle ranch land distribution pattern can be traced to pre-Conquest Mexico (Whettan 1948, pp. 79ff.). In fact, despite all of the intervening history, pre-Hispanic "demographic and settlement-pattern data would suggest that the basic relationship of rural population to land did not differ strikingly from that of today" (Sanders 1971, p. 546).

There are several varieties of *ejidos* throughout Mexico. In the southern Huasteca region, *ejido* rules generally allow individual household heads to farm their own plots and to leave the land they work to their heirs. Land may not be sold, however, and it may not be owned by anyone who is not legally a member of the *ejido*. Thus *ejidos* are relatively closed communities. Virtually every *ejido* family supports itself through farming. In areas where the land is sufficiently flat, a horse or mule-drawn plow may be used. In hilly areas or in more traditional villages farming is done by the slash-and-burn technique. Slash-and-burn horticulture is the oldest method of cultivation in Middle America, tracing back to pre-Hispanic times. Using this method, sections of forest are cleared, dried, and burned. Seeds are then planted by dropping them in holes made with a digging stick. After two to five years of planting, depending on soil fertility and weed growth, the field is abandoned for a number of years, and a new area is cleared and prepared. Slash-and-burn horticulture is based entirely upon human labor.

Geographical factors such as rainfall, temperature, and vegetation have a direct effect on farming practices and thus on the total cultural adaptation of the people. The paper cult region lies well below the Tropic of Cancer and is therefore in the tropical zone. An important factor in climate is altitude. As indicated earlier, altitudes vary a great deal in the southern Huasteca and its border regions. Thus generalizations about cultural ecology are difficult since each village is adapted to its own microenvironment. In the east, altitudes may average 200 meters above sea level, while in the western region some peaks reach 2,000 meters.

One method of discussing geographic features of a complex area such as this is to divide it into zones. Three basic zones are recognized by geographers and by the local inhabitants alike: the *tierra caliente* ("hot country") from sea level to 800 meters; the *tierra templada* ("temperate country") from 800 to 1,600 meters; and the *tierra fría* ("cold country") above 1,600 meters (Sanders 1952–53, p. 30). Each of these vertical regions is characterized by a distinct set of ecological features that affect the societies living within them. Because nearly all the paper cult villages lie within the hot and temperate countries, discussion will be limited to these zones.

Climatic zones run parallel to the coast and change as one moves westward and gains altitude. Using the Koeppen system of climatic classification, the zone of lowest altitude (hot country) is classed as Aw': a tropical, humid climate having no month with an average temperature below 18° C with a dry season in winter and maximum rainfall in September and October. The temperate country has two climatic zones: Cfa, which is a temperate climate with the average temperature of the coldest month being higher than 0° C and that of the warmest month being greater than 22° C, with rain every month and no pronounced dry season; and Cwa, which is identical to the previous class except that there is a dry season during winter (Vivó Escoto 1964, pp. 205, 210, 212). Temperatures in the hot country average 20 to 25° C and in the temperate country 15 to 20° C (Vivó Escoto 1964, pp. 198–99, fig. 7).

Rainfall is extremely variable from one season to the next. In addition, because of the topography, areas separated by only a few miles may receive significantly different amounts of rain in a given year. On the average the region receives more than thirty thunderstorms a year (Vivó Escoto 1964, p. 196) and mean rainfall is between 1,500 and 2,000 millimeters a year (Puig 1976, map). The generally heavy rainfall gives rise to three types of forest that correspond to the three climatic zones. In the hot country there is *forêt tropicale moyenne subsempervivente*, tropical forest with about 25 percent deciduous species with a height of less than 20 meters (Puig 1976, p. 114). The temperate country has two types of forest cover: *forêt caducifoliée humide de montagne*, which is a cloud forest with mixed tropical and temperate species (Puig 1976, p. 223); and *forêt aciculifoliée*, characterized by mixed vegetation dominated by pines (Puig 1976, p. 274). In general vegetation in the southern Huasteca region has been so modified by the Indians' slash-and-burn activities and the creation of pastures by cattle ranchers that it is difficult to determine the original character of the forest cover (West 1964, p. 378).

Indians in the southern Huasteca grow maize, black beans, squash, tomatoes, chile peppers, sugar cane, bananas, coffee, and various tropical and semitropical fruits as their major crops. In many areas two crops a year can be grown, which greatly increases productivity. Most villages are fairly self-sufficient with regard to food although there is beginning to develop regional specialization. In Puebla and Hidalgo some villages grow coffee to the exclusion of other crops, and in some areas sugar cane is grown as a cash crop. At a series of weekly markets controlled by non-Indian middlemen villagers either sell their surplus produce or trade it for manufactured goods or other cultivated products. Steel machetes—the basic all-purpose tool of Indian men—cloth, modern clothing, roofing material, flashlights, and a variety of luxury items are all high on the list of desired items. For many of the more remote and traditional villages, markets are the primary contact that individuals have with urban Mexico.

Travel is extremely difficult in the region, which even today is penetrated by only a few dirt roads. Most traveling is done on foot or over unimproved trails that twist and turn among the hills. Even a brief trip may involve a dozen crossings of the numerous streams and small rivers that run from the mountains into the Gulf of Mexico. During the rainy season these often flood, preventing travel for weeks at a time. In addition the region is covered with dense secondary tropical forest growth that encroaches on the trails. Difficulty of transport and ruggedness of terrain make much of the southern Huasteca and border region undesirable for intensive modern agriculture. These factors are also responsible for the isolation of the people who inhabit the region.

In general the small villages in the paper-cult region are highly traditional. Houses are thatch-roofed, and people dress in distinctive costume: a loose-fitting white shirt and pants along with a straw hat for the men, and a long skirt and embroidered blouse for the women. Men do not have beards or moustaches, and they prefer medium-length hair. The women never cut their hair, preferring to wear it in long braids, which sometimes hang to the back of their legs. Both men and women are barefooted, although men occasionally wear sandals. When men leave the village they invariably wear their straw hats, and each man carries his machete in a leather case at all times. The advent of transistor radios and somewhat improved communications with the outside, however, has led to inevitable changes. Increasingly, younger people are seen wearing mestizo-style clothing, and houses are built with corrugated tin roofs.

To date no scholar has attempted to compare the cultures of the Nahuas, Otomís, and Tepehuas who continue to use cut paper in their rituals. The present absence of basic ethnographic research in the region makes the task nearly impossible. Because of their resemblance to one another, these groups constitute what anthropologists call a "culture area," a geographical region whose inhabitant cultures show a marked similarity.

Several factors have fostered a cultural convergence among groups that we assume were once quite distinct. For instance, all three cultures have applied identical technology to exploit their environments. Anthropologists have long known that similar technoecological bases can cause similarities in otherwise unrelated cultures. Thus it is not surprising to see many identical features among the Nahuas, Otomís, and Tepehuas. Evidence also exists that extensive borrowing has taken place among them. In addition, all three groups have shared historical experiences dating from the Conquest, and they are all lumped together at the bottom of the socioeconomic hierarchy by the more powerful urbanized Mexicans. Finally, processes of culture change, for the most part Westernization, have contributed to the erosion of cultural differences. Within the past several years, for example, the Indians' use of the Spanish language has increased markedly.

Similarities in the religious systems of the Nahuas, Otomís, and Tepehuas in the paper cult region are marked. Some of the more important of these are suggested here as a general orientation to the more detailed treatments in the chapters that follow. In all three groups the most important rituals serve to ensure crop fertility. This is understandable considering the horticultural production base of their economies. A second ritual type is the curing or cleansing ceremony, which is held to control disease and misfortune. A third type includes smaller rituals with a variety of purposes. These include love magic rituals and rites to prevent the return of the dead. Religions in this area share an animistic view of nature and the universe as a whole; important processes and events that affect humans, such as sickness, rain, and crop growth, are believed to be under the control of spirits or forces. Depending on a variety of factors, these forces may act to help or to harm people. For example, gossip, disrespect, envy, or greed may cause spirits of the dead to become angry. Some classes of spirits are inherently malevolent and may be intentionally loosed among humans by sorcerers. Most spirits in the pantheon, however, are basically salutary so long as they are not angered or neglected. In this culture area the general purpose of rituals is to maintain a balance or harmony between the human and spirit worlds. This is accomplished by making sacrificial offerings to the appropriate spirits.

The rituals themselves are very similar among the three groups, both in the structure of the performance and in the symbolic episodes and paraphernalia employed by the shaman. People in the region use the Spanish name *costumbre*, meaning "custom," to describe traditional ritual performances, although in some cases the term is used only if the ritual is elaborate and involves the use of floral adornments and music. The purpose and symbolic content of the *costumbre* may vary somewhat from village to village, but the basic structure of rituals is shared by each group. This common structure was revealed in the Xochitlalia ritual described and analyzed in the previous chapter. In the first step a shaman is called in and preparations are made. These often include cutting paper figures, constructing an altar, making adornments, and assembling offerings. Next a cleansing rite is performed to clear the area of potentially harmful spirits. The cleansing itself is highly regular in its performance and always involves making offerings before paper images of the various harmful spirits. The central feature of any ritual is the main offering, which is made on one or more altars. Paper cuttings of the various spirits are laid out, and standard offerings are spread over them.

Many ritual elements described in chapter 2 are mentioned again as additional rituals are discussed in the following chapters. Any elaborate ceremony usually includes the construction of an altar. This is commonly a table over which a leaf-covered arch is erected. About a dozen common altar adornments are used by the three cultures. These include palm and marigold wands, decorated walking sticks, palm and marigold pinwheels that stand for guardian stars, "rosaries" made from vines and marigold blossoms, and decorated paper mats used to hold the paper figures. Other ritual activities common to the three groups include the shamans' use of large quartz crystals for divination and the practice of going on pilgrimages to sacred locations such as hilltops, pre-Hispanic ruins, caves, and lakes. Sometimes the same location is visited alternately by delegations from Nahua, Otomí, and Tepehua villages.

Music also plays an important part in major rituals throughout the southern Huasteca. The predominant instruments used are violins and guitars, although drums and rattles are also common (Provost and Sandstrom 1977). In some of the more remote villages the pre-Hispanic *teponaztli* (slit drum) can still be heard. Finally, animal sacrifice is common among the Indian cultures of the area. Chickens and turkeys are the usual victims, although on occasion a pig or steer may be slaughtered as part of a ritual.

The pantheons of spirits addressed in Nahua, Otomí, and Tepehua rituals also bear striking resemblances. A spirit complex surrounding celestial bodies, specifically the sun, moon, and stars, is paramount. To this are added a number of spirits, some beneficial and others dangerous, associated with the earth. Water-related spirits are the subjects of many ritual observances concerning the control of rain, and angry spirits of the dead are thought to be responsible for disease and misfortune. There is an enormous proliferation of spirits among all three groups, and these generally are associated with one of four basic realms: sky, earth, underworld, or water. Finally, the list of saints from Spanish Catholicism has been added to each culture's pantheon. In many cases individual saints have been combined with traditional spirits; Saint John the Baptist, for example, is often associated with the local water spirit. The process whereby alien concepts are blended with local traditions is called syncretism, and it is a definite characteristic of the *costumbre* religions.

The influence of Christianity upon the Nahuas, Otomís, and Tepehuas is revealed in their ritual calendars. While elements of the pre-Hispanic calendar can still be seen in the scheduling of certain observances, the local ritual cycle is based essentially on dates taken from Christianity (Reyes García 1960, pp. 39–40). Because this work concerns the paper figures, which are used only in the most traditional rituals, we have excluded the strictly Christian celebrations from consideration.

Because the *costumbre* religions are syncretic, in a sense it is impossible to differentiate the Christian from the non-Christian practices. The Indians implicitly recognize a difference between their older rituals and those brought in by Spanish priests, however, when they take care to conceal traditional practices from itinerant missionaries. Also, shamans never cut images of Christian saints from paper, indicating that they recognize a difference between paper cult and Christian rituals. In general calendrical rituals are more Christian in orientation than the non-calendrical rituals. The latter do not have a specific celebration day; they are more traditional and involve the use of paper images. *Costumbre* practices, however, may take place in conjunction with a Christian celebration, such as when a cleansing is performed before a priest arrives in a village to say Mass. On the other hand, some Christian observances, such as All Souls, have been so influenced by Indian practices on a national level that local practices reflect this pre-Hispanic character.

In some villages a formalized set of offices called the cargo system has developed to sponsor the many celebrations of saints' days. In others, the village celebrates only the feast day of its eponymous saint. In yet others, such as the Nahua village we lived in, saints' days were recognized only by individual households. A household may burn some incense or light a candle, but no real celebration is held. Table 1 lists the most commonly celebrated holidays taken from the Christian calendar. Ethnographers who have worked in the paper cult region have not provided complete information on this aspect of Indian religious life (for an exception see Dow 1974), and thus the list is probably not exhaustive. Also, variation in village participation in the Christian feast cycle makes generalization difficult. In some cases a non-Christian observance is held on a designated Christian holiday. Examples of this practice will be noted in the discussions of traditional rituals in the chapters that follow.

TABLE 1. Christian Saints' Days and Celebrations Often Observed by Indians of the Southern Huasteca Region
(Actual observances may vary from the official dates given and may include pre-Hispanic ritual elements)

Date	Religious observances
June 13	San Antonio (Saint Anthony)
June 24	San Juan (Saint John)
June 29	San Pedro (Saint Peter)
	San Pablo (Saint Paul)
July 25	Santiago (Saint James)
August 15	Asunción (Assumption of Mary)
August 24	San Bartolo (Saint Bartholomew)
August 28	San Agustín (Saint Augustine)
August 30	Santa Rosa (Saint Rose)
September 10	San Nicolás (Saint Nicolas)
September 21	San Mateo (Saint Mathew)
September 29	San Miguel (Saint Michael)
October 4	San Francisco (Saint Francis)
October 18	San Lucas (Saint Luke)

TABLE 1. *Continued*

Date	Religious observances
November 2	Todos Santos (All Souls)
November 25	Santa Catarina (Saint Catherine)
November 30	San Andreas (Saint Andrew)
December 12	Virgen de Guadalupe (Virgin of Guadalupe)
December 21–25	Navidad (Christmas)
January 6	Santa Rey (Epiphany)
March 19	San José (Saint Joseph)
May 3	Santa Cruz (Holy Cross)
May 15	San Isidro (San Isidore)
Movable Feasts	Carnaval (Carnival, including Ash Wednesday)
	Semana Santa (Holy Week, including Palm Sunday and Easter)

Date	Secular and national observances
May 5	Battle of Puebla
May 10	Día de las Madres (Mother's Day)
May 15	Día de los Maestros (Teacher's Day)
May 20	Día de los Padres (Father's Day)
September 16	Independence Day
November 20	Revolution Day
January 31	Año nuevo (New Year)

It is the participation of shamans and the use of paper figures that clearly distinguish the most traditional rituals performed from the more Christianized practices. The paper figures are laid on altars decorated with palm and marigold adornments and ornate, rectangular paper cuttings. Seed spirits are one class of spirits frequently portrayed in paper. The Nahuas, Otomís, and Tepehuas share a belief that each seed has a kind of spirit or life-force that controls the crops in the field. The most elaborate rituals of the year are directed towards these spirits. Seed spirits are usually portrayed as small anthropomorphic figures with hands upraised and with the appropriate vegetable or fruit cut from the body or protruding from the sides. In most rituals the cutouts are destroyed, but all three cultures save examples of the seed figures in sealed wooden cabinets that are kept on special altars. These paper figures are dressed in miniature clothes and have accessories such as tiny hats, earrings, and necklaces. Miniature pieces of furniture and items of daily use accompany the figures. Offerings are made to these seed spirits throughout the year so that their "children"—the crops—will prosper.

Another common class of spirits portrayed in paper images is the *malos aires* ("bad airs"). These airs or winds are the wandering souls of people who died violent or tragic deaths and who, out of revenge, cause disease and misfortune. Shamans control and remove these dangerous spirits in special cleansing ceremonies. These curing rituals are very common in the region, usually performed in conjunction with pragmatic techniques such as herbal medicine, bone setting, and midwifery. The belief that evil winds or airs cause disease is found throughout Latin America in both Indian and non-Indian settings. A similar belief was found historically in Europe and was probably brought over by the Spaniards. The concept survives in the etymology of the word *malaria* ("bad air") and in the belief that drafts cause illness.

Various additional spirit entities are also portrayed in paper cutouts. These images may be the innovation of a single shaman or they may be cut by many shamans throughout the region. Spirits associated with natural phenomena such as thunder, lightning, fire, water, and the sun are cut for use during offerings. Images are commonly made of "witness" and "guardian" spirits, which are believed to watch over people or to act as intermediaries between the human and spirit worlds. Although most paper figures fall within a fairly restricted number of categories reflecting the types of spirits in the pantheon, a great deal of creativity is allowed the shaman who cuts them. Paper images are sometimes cut to depict the spirit of a patient for curing, the life-force of an individual for love magic or sorcery, or man-made objects such as musical instruments and houses for a variety of purposes.

While each culture in the region maintains unique traditions, similarities in their ritual paraphernalia, paper images, shared locations, and spirit pantheons point to a shared body of myths. Only Tepehua myths have been collected systematically (see

Williams García 1972), but both Nahuas and Otomís appear to share elements of Tepehua myth and world view (see also Reyes García 1976 for some Nahua myths). An interesting example of the degree to which traditions are shared in the region can be seen in the role of the shaman. In all three cultures shamans are repositories of esoteric knowledge that gives them power over the spirit world. Their knowledge is recognized regardless of cultural affiliation, and people from one culture do not hesitate to hire a specialist from another (see chapter 2). In a very real sense the shamans occupy a special status that transcends cultural differences in the region.

A key factor in accounting for the similarities among the cultures of the southern Huasteca region is that they partake of common Middle American traditions of great antiquity. Individual cultures are certainly identifiable throughout Middle America, but there is always an underlying stratum of common beliefs and practices. One authority has even suggested that the Huasteca is one of the few areas remaining where pre-Toltec patterns survive (Stresser-Péan 1971, p. 601). Of course no culture is static, and the Nahuas, Otomís, and Tepehuas have changed in response to both internal and external forces. The Otomís of San Pablito, for example, transformed their own economy when they began to sell bark paper to the tourist markets. Additionally, the relative isolation afforded these groups by the topography of the southern Huasteca is breaking down in the face of new roads, transistor radios, and helicopters. It was the absence of mineral wealth that initially caused the Conquistadores to lose interest in the area, but even this factor has changed. In 1901 the first successful oil well was drilled in the region (Williams García 1961, p. 14). The intervening years have brought accelerated change as a host of new invaders, including geologists, surveyors, and drilling crews, have entered the southern Huasteca. Thus the promise of economic development is the latest challenge to the traditional cultures of the paper cult region.

CHAPTER 4

PAPER CULT FIGURES AMONG CONTEMPORARY NAHUA INDIANS

MOST of the information contained in this chapter comes from Amatlán village (not its real name), in Ixhuatlán de Madero, northern Veracruz. Concerning Ixhuatlán, Lenz wrote, ". . . it is dangerous to penetrate the sierra de Ixhuatlán beyond a certain point. This is particularly true if the object of the trip is to gather information on the pagano-Christian customs of the Indians who live there or to collect samples of papers they cut for their offerings and witchcraft" (1973 [1948], p. 139). Years later the ethnographer Roberto Williams García noted Ixhuatlán's reputation as a place of rich cattle ranchers and gunmen (1963, p. 14). In the early 1970s, when we conducted our major fieldwork, Ixhuatlán was still remote and dangerous. We felt, however, that the danger was not so much from the many Indians who inhabit the region as it was from the well-armed soldiers and cowboys we occasionally encountered on the trails.

Ixhuatlán de Madero is a *municipio*—the Mexican political subdivision that corresponds to a county. The majority of the Indians in the *municipio* are Nahuas, although there are also villages of Otomís and Tepehuas. We set up our field headquarters in Amatlán, which is located far off the main road in the northern part of Ixhuatlán. Amatlán has a population of fewer than six hundred people, most of whom are monolingual Nahuatl-speakers and follow a highly traditional lifestyle.

It is appropriate that we begin our examination of the paper images with examples from the Nahuas since they are probably descendants of the Aztecs, the best-known and best-documented Indians of Middle America. We have selected, as a sample, fifty-nine paper images cut by Nahua shamans. We have divided the images into four categories according to the type of spirit represented. The first category contains disease-causing spirits cut for curing rituals. The second contains images of seed spirits used to ensure crop fertility. The third contains witness and guardian spirits that act as intermediaries between the shaman and other more powerful spirits. The final category contains cuttings used as altar adornments to create a proper place for the spirits when they arrive to receive offerings. Following a discussion of the first category—disease-causing spirits —we describe a cleansing ritual in which these same images are employed by a shaman. This description will help to provide the context in which the paper images are used and will be useful in comparing equivalent Otomí and Tepehua rituals. To further set the context of the paper images, an outline of Nahua cosmology is presented which includes a list of the major spirits in their pantheon (see table 2).

As Lenz implied, non-Indian outsiders rarely are allowed to view the paper images or to witness rituals in which they are employed. Local missionaries, government workers, and casual visitors barely are aware that traditional religious practices coexist with Roman Catholic observances. While the Nahuas view Christian and non-Christian observances as part of a single religion, they know that others do not share their view. Hundreds of years of persecution have made them careful to manage the image they present to outsiders. For example, in the village we studied, the schoolmaster had lived among the Nahuas for almost thirty years and yet he had never seen a paper image or attended a traditional ritual. This is all the more remarkable when it is realized that rituals are performed almost continuously during certain times of the year. We lived in the village for many months before people began to reveal aspects of their cosmology and ritual practices to us. They imparted information at such a slow and measured pace that it would take many years of living among them before the complete picture would be revealed.

In an effort to speed the flow of information and our understanding, we questioned people about aspects of cosmology and religious belief. This was difficult in a society that considers direct questions rude. In response to our questions, no matter how gently we posed them, people usually suggested that we speak to a shaman. People often claimed they understood little of such things and that it was the shaman who knew all about them. The shaman, then, not only orchestrates ritual performance, but is the repository of authoritative knowledge on cosmology and religion. In addition, only the shaman can cut the paper images, which are the focus of so many rituals.

A Nahua shaman is called *tlamati quetl,* or "person of knowledge," and also *pachi quetl,* or "curer." In Spanish the shaman is called a *curandero,* meaning "curer," or *adivino,* "diviner," because of his role in diagnosing disease. Any adult man or woman can undergo the training to become a shaman, although most are male. The neophyte becomes an apprentice to an established shaman and slowly learns the complex techniques necessary to control the various spirits. He must learn the sequence of symbolic acts that comprise a ritual, the manufacture and arrangement of altar adornments, the proper chants and prayers, and the techniques for cutting the paper images. In cases where a patient is to be cured the student must learn to diagnose through divination the cause of the ailment as well as to devise the appropriate curing procedure. Probably over 90 percent of a shaman's professional activity involves the diagnosis and curing of disease, a service for which he is paid. To be accepted by the community as successful, a shaman must have a proven record of cures; simple mastery of the ritual techniques is not enough to attract a clientele.

A second type of ritual specialist is the midwife *(tetequetl).* Usually older women become midwives after they have undergone a period of apprenticeship under a master. Along with necessary medical techniques, the neophyte also learns the ritual procedures for cleansing the newborn and mother. Newborn babies are particularly susceptible to spirit attack and must be protected shortly after birth (Williams García 1955, pp. 17ff.; Montoya Briones 1964, pp. 102ff.). Midwives also have a role in larger village rituals, in which they act as censers and dancers *(copalmitoti quetl)*. In the villagewide ritual called Tlacatelilis, a midwife leads the young girls in their procession from house to house.

Shamans occupy a unique status in Nahua villages. They are "people of knowledge," but the knowledge may be used either to benefit or harm other villagers. The word for sorcerer, a person bent on evil, is *tlamati quetl*—the same word used for a legitimate ritual specialist. People of knowledge, then, are viewed with some ambivalence by villagers. In addition, shamans occupy a status that places them outside the usual ethnic boundaries that separate Indians of the Huasteca. Nahua villagers readily engage the services of Otomí or Tepehua ritual specialists believed to be particularly effective. Shamans trade information with each other, even crossing cultural and linguistic boundaries by speaking Spanish. This practice undoubtedly has contributed to the widespread sharing of beliefs and rituals that characterizes the various Indian groups in the Huasteca.

Each Nahua ritual specialist develops a personal style of ritual performance that sets him apart from his colleagues. Paper images may be cut differently, altars may be set up in a unique way, or the chanting may be idiosyncratic. To a large extent, a ritual specialist's reputation depends on charisma and the individualistic way he influences the spirits. Variations in paper cutouts reflect the ritual specialist's attempt to distinguish himself as an effective intermediary between humans and spirits. Underlying all of the variations, however, is a shared set of assumptions about the nature of the spirit world and the strategies effective in dealing with it. In fact, as is argued in the concluding chapter, these assumptions are shared not only among the Nahuas but also among the Otomís and Tepehuas. The effective shaman, then, must develop a definitive personal style, but one within the bounds of the world view of the people who make up his clientele.

The paper images are called *tlatectli* (pl. *tlatecme*) in Nahautl, and they are cut by shamans to represent selected spirits in the Nahua pantheon (Medellín Zenil 1979, p. 118). They provide visual images of spirits as well as beautiful adornments for altars. The paper cutouts are not believed to have ritual potency until they have been sacralized, usually by holding them in copal smoke. After sacralizing, the images have the power to attract spirits, and they pose considerable danger to anyone not initiated as a ritual specialist. When we asked several shamans for samples of cuttings to take with us, each took the precaution of sprinkling the cutouts with cane alcohol to keep wandering spirits away. Although the paper images had not yet been sacralized, the shamans took steps to protect us from accidental encounters with harmful wind spirits.

Once sacralized, the paper images take on an entirely new meaning. While they do not actually become the spirit they are cut to represent, they do acquire the power to attract the life-force or animating principle of that spirit. The Nahuas have two terms for this animating principle, *noyolo* and *notonal.* The word *noyolo* is often translated into Spanish by the Nahuas as *alma* or soul, but it literally means "my heart" or "life-force." *Notonal,* the term less often used, is translated as "my breath," "shadow" *(sombra),* or "life-force"; it contains the root of the Nahuatl word for heat *(tona)* (Hunt 1977, p. 89; see also Montoya Briones 1964, pp. 114, 165). When discussing human beings, the Nahuas say that if heat leaves the body the person sickens and dies. During funerals the *noyolo* or *notonal* of the recently deceased is exhorted to keep away from the surviving kinsmen (see Provost 1981; Williams García 1955, pp. 47ff.). Thus the *noyolo* and *notonal* are nonpersonalized (compare the Otomí concept of *zaki* and the Tepehua *tukuwín* in chapters 5 and 6). Human beings, spirits, plants, animals, and certain objects each have a life-force, and it is this entity that is attracted to the sacralized paper image. The shaman exerts control over the spirits portrayed in cut paper by ritually manipulating their life-forces or animating principles. He can theoretically force a spirit to act against its own will. It is the ability to manipulate the life-force that gives the shaman power to cure, increase crops, produce rain, or engage in sorcery.

The Nahuas conceive the universe to be divided into four

realms, each one a world unto itself. Arching overhead is the sky, called *ilhuicactli* in Nahuatl, which is thought of as a sparkling place or a giant mirror inhabited by the sun and stars (Reyes García 1976, p. 127). The earth is called *tlali*, and it is here that human beings and animals live and that the fields turn green and produce their life-giving crops. Underneath the earth's surface is *mictlan*, a dark, gloomy place where the spirits of people go who die natural and peaceful deaths. In *mictlan* the spirits of the dead marry, build houses, and plant their fields, but their bodies are like air *(como aire)*, with no substance. The sky, earth, and underworld are arranged in layers with the world of human beings located in the middle. The fourth realm is *apan*, "water place," which includes the surfaces and depths of springs, lakes, and rivers, as well as falling water such as rain, and which acts as a kind of connecting passageway among the other three realms. *Apan* is thought of as a pleasant place inhabited by aquatic animals and green grasses and by Apanchane, the Lady of the Water. It is also, however, a home of the angry souls of people who died unpleasant or unnatural deaths.

Each realm is inhabited by large numbers of spirits with different degrees of influence in human affairs. We will discuss only the most important of these. In the sky lives Toteotsi, meaning "Our Honored Deity," who made the universe and the people in it and who now watches over his creation and guards the people on earth. Many Nahuas symbolically equate Toteotsi with the sun and also with Jesus Christ (Reyes García 1960, p. 35; 1976, pp. 127–28; Williams García 1955, p. 55). The sun is a kind of father image, and in fact it is referred to as Tata Sol or "Father Sun" (Lenz 1973 [1948], p. 139). Opposite the sun is the moon *(metstli)*, which is a mother image and which is associated with fertility and the menstrual cycle. Paradoxically, aspects of the moon are associated with dangerous spirits of the dead and also the Devil (Tlauelilo). One ethnographer was told by a Nahua informant that the moon is not a god "because of the evil it does" (Williams García 1955, p. 74). When the sun goes down for the night, stars *(citlali,* pl. *citlame)* come out to take over the sun's duties. At night stones can turn into voracious animals, and the stars shoot arrows (meteors) to kill them. In fact stones with holes in them are thought to have been killed by the star guardians, and they are valued as power objects by Nahua shamans. Catholic saints occupy a special place among the stars called Chicome Iluicactli (Seven-Sky) where they overlook human beings below (Reyes García 1976, p. 127). Another important sky spirit is fire, called Tlixauantsi (Adorned Fire). This spirit comes from the sky, but a part of him resides in the three fireplace stones of each household where he guards over family members (Reyes García 1976, p. 128).

The most important spirit in Nahua religious thought originates from the sky, is associated with positive aspects of the moon, and now lives in a sacred cave on the earth. She is called Tonantsi (Tonantsin in other dialects), meaning "Our Sacred Mother." The Nahuas believe that she controls the fertility of both human beings and the earth. The concept of Tonantsi dates to pre-Columbian times when a deity of the same name was also believed to have the power of fertility. The Nahuas, along with most other Indians in Mexico, have syncretized the pre-Columbian Tonantsi with the Virgin Mary in the person of the Virgin of Guadalupe (see Wolf 1958). Statues of the Virgin of Guadalupe are called Tonantsi by the Nahuas, and she is invoked to increase harvests and to help women who are having difficulty conceiving. Tonantsi is the subject of an elaborate ritual called Tlacatelilis (Causing Birth), which is held each year at the time of the winter solstice. In this ritual, her statue is taken to each house in the village by a procession made up of ritual specialists and young girls. The members of each household make offerings to Tonantsi so that she will confer the blessing of fertility on them (see Sandstrom 1982).

Although Tonantsi originates from the sky, she has become part of the earth realm. She controls general fertility, while her children, the seed spirits, control the productivity of specific crops in the field. These seed spirits, called by the collective noun *xinaxtli,* which simply means "seed" in Nahuatl, are thought to live either in sacred caves located some distance from the village or in the sea with a water spirit. Chief among the seeds is Chicomexochitl (Seven-Flower), the spirit of maize (see Reyes García 1976, p. 128; and chapter 2). Both the seed spirits and the rituals in which they are invoked are discussed below. Additional spirits inhabiting the earth realm include ancestors called Itecu (Señores or Lords) who live inside of sacred hills or in the underworld (Reyes García 1976, pp. 127–28). Through intermediary spirits called "witnesses" or "guardians" *(onipixtoc aquiqui'ixtoc)*, the ancestors guard over the daily lives of villagers. House spirits called *mu'axcatl*, which guard over the people and their belongings, are portrayed in the small saints' pictures that villagers display on their house altars. Among the lesser spirits in the earth realm are the Viejos or Huehuetsitsi (Old Ones), which include Thunder (Tlatomoni) and Lightning (Tlapetlani), all of whom live in caves on special hills. These spirits transport water from the sea to the sacred hills before releasing it to germinate and nourish the seeds (Reyes García 1976, p. 127). The twelve sacred hills (Santo Tepeme) are conceived of as spiritual beings in their own right that house other spirits and reach towards the sky realm.

One key spirit in the earth realm is the earth itself. The Nahua view of the earth is complex and will require further research before it is clearly understood. We know, however, that the Nahuas see one manifestation of the earth as a kind of unified duality called Tlaltepactli or Tlalticpac (Earth's Surface). Within the unity are two aspects: Tlaltetata, "Father Earth," and Tlaltenana, "Mother Earth" (Reyes García 1976, p. 127). These aspects of the earth are positive and beneficial. They are responsible for the crops and, ultimately, for life itself. The positive aspects of the earth are balanced by a negative aspect called Moctezuma. The name Moctezuma recalls one of the last Aztec emperors (Moctezuma Xocoyotzin) at the time of the Spanish Conquest, but the villagers were unable to connect the spirit to the historical figure. Moctezuma, for contemporary Nahuas, is a kind of magician who builds churches in the cities and pre-Columbian ruins in local villages (Reyes

García 1960, p. 36; Williams García 1955, pp. 76ff.). The spirit is thought to consume dead bodies and is associated with frightening underworld figures (see below). The earth as a whole is a living creature whose flesh is the soil and whose bones and blood are the rocks and water. The activities of humans, such as defecating, giving birth on the house floor (Williams García 1955, p. 18), and planting crops, annoy the earth; thus, humans are obliged to make recompense in the form of offerings. When the earth must be placated for particularly large offenses, Nahua shamans bury sacrificial fowl alive (see Reyes García 1960, pp. 35–37; Lenz 1973 [1948], pp. 137–38).

Two additional types of spirits complete the earth pantheon. The first type includes extremely dangerous creatures, often taking the form of nocturnal birds that suck the blood out of their victims. Three manifestations of these spirits have been reported: the *nagual*, which we were told about in Amatlán and which is believed to be a transformed sorcerer; the *teyolcuahetl*, a buzzard that sucks blood and devours human hearts (Williams García 1955, p. 48); and the *tlahuepoche*, a spirit similar to a *nagual* that attacks newborns (Montoya Briones 1964, pp. 102–103, 173). These last two are probably variants of the *nagual* concept widespread throughout Middle America.

The second class of earth spirits are the Antiguas (Ancient Ones), called Teteyome in Nahuatl (Medellin Zenil 1979, p. 119). These spirits were once ancient humans who lived in darkness. When the sun was born they went to live in caves and pre-Hispanic ruins (called *cubes* in regional Spanish) to avoid the light. Now they send the clouds so that it will rain. They are represented by small prehistoric figurines and heads that are occasionally found in the jungle and are kept on shamans' altars as power objects.

Mictlan, the underworld, contains the *noyolo* (hearts or life-forces) of people who died natural deaths. These spirits have a strong desire to rejoin their kinsmen on earth, but they must be prevented from doing so. Spirits of the dead are unaware of their power and can inadvertently cause serious illness and even death among the living. When not in Mictlan they lurk around graveyards and may search for their relatives. Spirits of the dead are placated during a ritual observance called Xantolo, which has been syncretized with All Souls' Day. During the observance the spirits are ritually fed and their grave plots are cleaned up and put in order (Reyes García 1976, p. 127; Williams García 1955, pp. 52ff.; Montoya Briones 1964, pp. 151–52).

Spirits of the dead are led by a fearsome creature called Tlacatecolotl (Owl Man). Owls are considered to be messengers of Tlacatecolotl by the Nahuas and are feared as harbingers of death. The ruler of the underworld is served by ambivalent spirits called *mecos* and by the dreaded Miquilistli (in Spanish La Muerta, or Death), who is depicted by the Nahuas in paper as a skeleton (Reyes García 1960, p. 36; see figure 12). The *mecos* are impersonated by young men wearing costumes and masks during an annual observance called Nanahuatili, which has been syncretized with the Christian celebration of Carnaval (Williams García 1955, pp. 71ff.; Montoya Briones 1964, pp. 132ff.; see Reyes García 1960; Provost 1975; and Sandstrom and Provost 1979). The final major figure associated with Mictlan is Tlauelilo (literally, Wrathful One) translated into Spanish as el Demonio (the Demon) or el Diablo (the Devil). This spirit, which is sometimes called Señor de la Noche (Lord of the Night), lives in the pre-Columbian stone ruins found throughout this region of Mexico. The ancient ruins are thought by the Nahuas to be doorways between Mictlan and the earth's surface. The Devil leads other harmful spirits from the underworld, collectively called "devils," *judíos,* or *ejecatl* (the *malos aires,* "bad airs" or "bad winds") to the villages where they can cause disease and death (Montoya Briones 1964, pp. 158ff.; 1981; the Indians' use of the term *judío* is explained in chapter 5). The Devil is also thought to lead animals, and some Nahuas believe that people turn into animals when they die (Williams García 1955, pp. 52, 74). Tlacatecolotl and the Devil are two separate spirits according to Nahua religious belief, but in some cases neighboring Indian groups have borrowed the Nahua spirits and combined them into a single spirit, which resembles the Christian Devil (see chapter 6).

The water realm contains the spirits of people who were murdered, drowned, struck by lightning, or killed by certain diseases. These spirits are also called *ejecatl,* and they possess characteristics like those of the spirits led by the Devil. Angered over their untimely deaths, they seek revenge on all living people. They are the servants of Apanchane, the Lady of the Water, who may send them into the village if she feels neglected or if people fail to repay her for using water. By rendering a continual flow of gifts, often consisting of eggs cracked into a stream or spring, people hope to avoid her reprisals. In addition, she releases the rain that has been brought to the hills from the sea by thunder and lightning spirits (Reyes García 1976, p. 127; Montoya Briones 1964, p. 162; Lenz 1973 [1948], p. 139; Williams García 1955, p. 67). Because Apanchane's realm communicates with the sky, earth, and water, all rituals held by the Nahuas are partially dedicated to the water spirit. She has been syncretized with Saint John the Baptist (San Juan) in Nahua thought, and some Nahuas conceive of Saint John as the male aspect of water and Apanchane as the female aspect (Reyes García 1960, p.38; 1976, p. 128). Finally, Santa Rosa ("Sacred Rose," or perhaps Saint Rose of Lima), which is the Nahua name for marijuana, is considered a female spirit associated with the water. Santa Rosa is invoked during ceremonies in which marijuana is ingested. Most Nahuas agreed that although their shamans occasionally eat marijuana in order to establish contact with spirits, this practice is more commonly found among the Otomís (Williams García 1955, p. 67; see chapter 5).

The four realms of the universe, along with their spirit leaders, are neatly tied together in a Nahua myth about the children of Tonantsi. They say that Tonantsi has four sons. The first is Tlauelilo (El Demonio or the Demon), who is viewed in some cases as an ambivalent figure but more often as a dangerous troublemaker. As previously mentioned, he is associated with Tlacatecolotl and the realm of the underworld.

The second child is San Juan (Saint John the Baptist, probably Apanchane in male aspect), who controls all fresh waters. San Juan is also viewed with some ambivalence since he threatens to flood the entire earth, thus rendering it uninhabitable. The third son is Moctezuma, the magician, who wanders around at night. He is closely associated with the earth and is believed miraculously to have built the pre-Columbian ruins in the region where Tlauelilo emerges from the underworld. The last child is Jesus, who is symbolically connected to Toteotsi and the sun and who, as the youngest child, has less power than his older brothers. Thus Tonantsi, who symbolizes fertility, gives birth to four sons, each of whom is associated with one of the basic realms: Tlauelilo with the underworld; San Juan with the water; Moctezuma with the earth; and Jesus with the sky. The myth is historical in two senses: it recounts the four ages of the past when the universe was ruled, in progressive order, by the underworld, the water realm, the earth realm, and the heavenly realm; and it recounts the coming of Christianity as Tonantsi gives birth to her last child (Provost 1981, p. 81). See table 2 for a summary of Nahua spirits.

NAHUA DISEASE-CAUSING SPIRITS

Nahua shamans are selective about which spirits they portray with their paper images. The ones most often depicted are a class of dangerous, disease-causing spirits that infest all four realms of the cosmos. They are the *ejecatl* (pl. *ejecame*, used hereafter in singular form as a collective noun), which literally means a "gust of wind" (Williams García 1955, pp. 42ff.; Montoya Briones 1964, pp. 158ff.; Reyes García 1976, p. 127; Knab 1979a, p. 134). As mentioned in the previous chapter, the idea that winds or *malos aires* (bad airs) cause disease is widespread throughout Latin America (Montoya Briones 1981, pp. 11ff.). For the Nahuas, the *ejecatl* are responsible not only for disease, but also for any misfortune, including drought, barrenness, and death. They lurk about trails, houses, bathing areas, or any place that people might frequent. At the most unsuspecting moment they enter a victim's body and cause it to fester until the person is too sick to move. They are particularly fond of attacking children, the aged, and anyone who has been weakened in any way.

TABLE 2. The Nahua Pantheon

Realms of the Universe and Associated Spirits

Ilhuicactli (Sky)
    Toteotsi (Our Honored Deity, Sun, Jesus)
    Metstli (Moon, also associated with Tlauelilo)
    Citlame (Stars)
    Catholic saints
    Tlixauantsi (Adorned Fire)
    Ejecatl (Wind)

Tlali (Earth)
    Tonantsi (Our Sacred Mother, Virgin of Guadalupe, also associated
      with the moon)
    Tlaltepactli (Earth's Surface); also
      Axcatlaltipatli (Earth as a Whole)
      Tlaltetata (Father Earth)
      Tlaltenana (Mother Earth)
      Moctezuma (devouring Earth) etc.
    Xinaxtli (Seeds)
      Chicomexochitl (Maize)
    Santo Tepeme (12 sacred hills)
    Huehuetsitsi (Old Ones); also Itecu (Ancestors)
      Tlatomoni (Thunder)
      Tlapetlani (Lightning)
    Onipixtoc Aquiqui'ixtoc (Witnesses)
    Mu'axcatl (House Guardians)
    Nagual (transforming sorcerer)
    Teteyome (Ancient Ones)
    Ejecatl (Wind)

Mictlan (Underworld)
    Tlacatecolotl (Owl Man)
    Tlauelilo (Devil, Demon); also
      Señor de la Noche (Lord of the Night)
    Miquilistli (Death)
    Mecos (servants of Tlacatecolotl)

TABLE 2. *Continued*

Realms of the Universe and Associated Spirits
Noyolo (Heart, Spirits of the dead) Ejecatl (Wind)

Apan (Water)
  Apanchane (Lady of the Water); also
    San Juan
  Noyolo (Heart, Spirits of the dead)
  Santa Rosa (Marijuana)
  Ejecatl (Wind)

Because they are ubiquitous, the *ejecatl* are constantly on people's minds. An incident that occurred while we were living in the village illustrates the point. Near the end of our stay, we visited the village headman, who was outside playing with his fourteen-month-old daughter. He continued to play with the child as we sat watching from under the eave of his house. Suddenly a gust of wind swept through the clearing in front of us. Immediately the headman clutched the child to protect her from the wind. His wife rushed from the house carrying a shawl, fearfully shouting *"Ejecatl!"* She wrapped the child and carried her inside out of the wind. We had seen similar events take place but never with such evident panic. We later found out that the couple had lost a child the previous year to *ejecatl* attacks. Given the danger posed by the *ejecatl*, it is not surprising that the major portion of a shaman's activity is directed towards controlling these malevolent spirits.

Ejecatl spirits as a class are sometimes called different names by different shamans. One shaman calls them by the term Xochiejecatl, which means "Flowery Wind." Another calls them Chicome Ejecatl, or "Seven-Wind," to stress that there are seven basic types of *ejecatl* spirits. A third name recorded by Reyes García (1976, p. 127) is Tlatokxochiehakameh or "Polychrome Winds of Cultivation." This last name is used to emphasize the danger posed to crops by *ejecatl* spirits. The *ejecatl* are categorized by the Nahuas into seven color classes, each associated with a realm of the universe. The color of a particular *ejecatl* reveals not only its type but also its place of origin. Blue or green paper is used to portray spirits that come from the water. Red or yellow paper indicates that the spirits come from the sky realm. White *ejecatl* come from the underworld, and black or purple/rose *ejecatl* come from the earth realm. When conducting curings, shamans may sometimes leave out one or more types of *ejecatl* spirits, but they usually include representatives from each of the realms (cf. Montoya Briones 1981, pp. 12ff.; see table 3).

TABLE 3. Nahua Ejecatl Spirits

Figure Number and Spirit Name	*Color*	*Realm*
First shaman:		
1. Atl, Water	Yellow	Celestial
2. Tlasole Ejecatl, Filth Wind	Red	Celestial
3. Mictlan Tlasole Ejecatl, Underworld Filth Wind	White	Underworld
4. Mictlan Tlasole Ejecatl, Underworld Filth Wind	White	Underworld
5. Tlali Ejecatl, Earth Wind	Black	Earth
6. Atl, Water	Green	Water
7. Apan Ejecatl Siuatl, Water-Wind Woman	Green	Water
Second shaman:		
8. Mictlan Tropa Ejecatl, Underworld Horde Wind	Red	Celestial
9. Tonal Ejecatl, Sun Wind	Yellow	Celestial
10. Tonal Ejecatl, Sun Wind	Red	Celestial
11. Tonal Ejecatl, Sun Wind	Yellow	Celestial
12. Miquilistli, Death	White	Underworld
13. Tlecate Ejecatl, probably Owl Man Wind	Rose	Earth
14. Tlali Ejecatl, Earth Wind	Black	Earth
15. Tlachichi Ejecatl, Suckling Wind	Purple	Earth
16. Tlali Ejecatl, Earth Wind, or Tecacual Ejecatl, Wind from the Ruins	Black	Earth

TABLE 3. *Continued*

Figure Number and Spirit Name	Color	Realm
17. Apantlasole Ejecatl, Water Filth Wind	Blue	Water
18. Apantlasole Ejecatl, Water Filth Wind	Green	Water
19. Aixcutla Ejecatl, Wind of the Water- Face Plant (Water Hyacinth?)	Green	Water
Third shaman:		
20. Xochiejecatl, Flowery Wind	Red	Celestial
21. Xochiejecatl, Flowery Wind	Red	Celestial
22. Xochiejecatl, Flowery Wind	Black	Earth
23. Xochiejecatl, Flowery Wind	Purple	Earth
24. Xochiejecatl, Flowery Wind	Purple	Earth
25. Xochiejecatl, Flowery Wind	Green	Water
26. Xochiejecatl, Flowery Wind	Blue	Water

Each shaman has his own particular way of portraying *ejecatl* spirits, and each may direct his ritual procedures to a slightly different inventory of spirits. Paper cuttings of the *ejecatl* often symbolically reflect aspects of the spirit's character or habits. Some have animal horns to reveal their animallike temperaments. Also, the Devil is considered master of all animals and thus, by association, master of the *ejecatl*. Others are cut with crowns or clothing symbolizing their place of origin or where they are most likely encountered. Many of these spirits have a spiky appearance, which, according to one shaman, helps explain how the *ejecatl* cause pain when they lodge in their victim's bodies.

Following are twenty-six paper images of *ejecatl* spirits cut by three different shamans. Figures 1–7 are a complete series cut for a curing ritual. A second complete curing set is included in figures 8–19, and a third set is included in figures 20–26. Usually seven to ten duplicates of each cutting are made for a single cure.

Figures 1–7 were cut by a female shaman who practices in the village of Amatlán. She cuts multiple identical images of spirits to emphasize their power and danger.

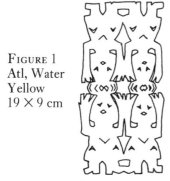

FIGURE 1
Atl, Water
Yellow
19 × 9 cm

The *ejecatl* spirit portrayed in figure 1 originates from the sun but now lives in the water. It attacks mothers and children when they go to the stream to wash clothes and makes them sick. Central V cuts represent the spirit's heart, while other cuts signify clothing. It is portrayed wearing a crown *(corona)*, which the shaman said helps people to identify which *ejecatl* it is.

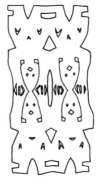

FIGURE 2
Tlasole Ejecatl, Filth Wind
Red
18 × 8.5 cm

Figure 2 portrays an *ejecatl* that originates from the sky realm but now travels on the wind in search of victims. *Tlasole ejecatl* is found in "filthy" places or in the tangled refuse on the jungle floor. The central V cuts represent the spirit's heart; the other cuts signify pockets and decorations on its clothing. As is often the case with dangerous spirits of this sort, the spirit is portrayed wearing shoes or boots. These may serve to identify the spirit with outsiders, since most Indians wear sandals or go barefooted.

FIGURE 3
Mictlan Tlasole Ejecatl,
    Underworld Filth Wind
White
18 × 10 cm

Also associated with filth and trash, this disease-causing spirit comes from Mictlan, the realm of the dead souls. The shaman said that it rides on the wind, constantly searching for unsuspecting victims. The spirit's power is emphasized by the eight-fold duplication of the figure.

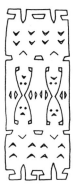

FIGURE 4
Mictlan Tlasole Ejecatl,
    Underworld Filth Wind
White
34 × 10.5 cm

The *ejecatl* depicted in figure 4 comes from the underworld and rides on winds blowing from hills or the sea. The paper image is used to cleanse the patient and is then left on a sacred hill or nearby crossroads. In this way the shaman hopes to attract the *ejecatl* away from the patient's surroundings. This spirit is found where there is filth, or piles of tangled vines and branches in the jungle. Central V cuts represent the heart, while other cuts indicate clothing.

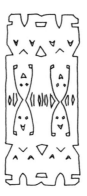

FIGURE 5
Tlali Ejecatl, Earth Wind
Black
24 × 8.5 cm

Originating from the soil, this spirit strikes children at midday, making them sick. The black color indicates that the spirit comes from the earth, although like other *ejecatl* it rides on gusts of wind. As in previous cuttings, V cuts represent the heart and other cuts signify clothing.

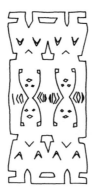

FIGURE 6
Atl, Water
Green
23.5 × 11.5 cm

The *ejecatl* portrayed in figure 6 originates from the stream that flows by the village, hence its green color. Nahua Indians make frequent use of the stream for bathing, fishing, and washing clothes. This spirit is associated with trash or filth in the water and is believed to cause many diseases.

FIGURE 7
Apan Ejecatl Siuatl,
   Water-Wind Woman
Green
24 × 11 cm

This *ejecatl* specializes in attacking women. The shaman said that it comes from the water, which is why she uses green paper, and that it is the wife of figure 1, Atl. She gives it a crown, a heart, and a set of clothes.

Figures 8–19 were cut by a male shaman from Amatlán. In contrast to the previous shaman, he portrays spirits as single anthropomorphic figures (see color plate 7).

FIGURE 8
Mictlan Tropa Ejecatl,
   Underworld Horde Wind
Red
16.5 × 5 cm

The name of the spirit shown in figure 8 implies that it originates from the underworld, although it is cut out of red paper, which associates it with the celestial realm. The shaman said that the spirit comes from the sun but now lives in Mictlan, adding that "it rides the wind making people sick." It is cut wearing a hat, poncholike *jorongo,* and boots.

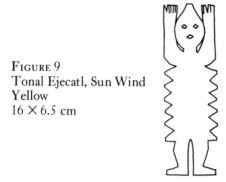

FIGURE 9
Tonal Ejecatl, Sun Wind
Yellow
16 × 6.5 cm

This *ejecatl* comes from the sun but lives in rocks. It is released into the air to cause disease and misery when "someone says something bad." The spiny clothing causes pain when the spirit enters a victim's body.

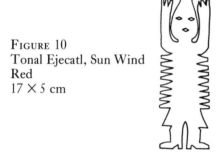

FIGURE 10
Tonal Ejecatl, Sun Wind
Red
17 × 5 cm

Originating from the sun, this spirit is portrayed with animal horns to symbolically link it to the Devil (Tlauelilo), and a crown and a suit of spines. As in other examples, it is wearing boots or shoes. When cutting this figure, the shaman commented that "the Devil also has spines."

FIGURE 11
Tonal Ejecatl, Sun Wind
Yellow
17.5 × 5 cm

The spirit shown in figure 11 also comes from the sun. It is released into the air when a person loses his temper. It has animal horns, a spiky crown, spiny clothes, and boots.

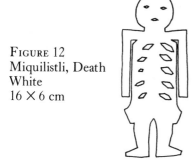

FIGURE 12
Miquilistli, Death
White
16 × 6 cm

The skeleton has been used to represent death in Middle America since pre-Columbian times. Modern Nahuas say that this spirit comes from the underworld but can usually be found lurking around graveyards. The only paper figure cut with downturned arms, this image is used by shamans when it is feared the patient is dying (see color plate 8). By making offerings to Miquilistli, the the shaman tries to remove it from the patient's surroundings, thus eliminating any threats to life. Miquilistli is an underling of Tlacatecolotl (Owl Man), chief of the underworld.

Figure 13
Tlecate Ejecatl, (probably
    Tlacatecolotl Ejecatl,
    meaning Owl Man Wind)
Rose
17.5 × 5 cm

The shaman remarked that the spirit Tlecate Ejecatl is attracted to the village "when women gossip." It comes from the earthly realm and lives inside solid rock. It has animal horns and a crown, and it wears a woman's dress.

Figure 14
Tlali Ejecatl, Earth Wind
Black
17 × 6 cm

The horns on the head symbolize that this *ejecatl* has the temperament of a bull. The shaman explained that it is a "worker for the Devil." It comes from the earth and wears clothes, boots, and a hat.

FIGURE 15
Tlachichi Ejecatl, Suckling
    Wind
Purple (called rose by the
    shaman)
17 × 5 cm

Gossip or "bad talk" attracts the Tlachichi Ejecatl spirit to the village. It specializes in attacking nursing babies, hence its name. The shaman said that it comes from the earth and that it is a female, which is why he cuts it with a dress.

FIGURE 16
Tlali Ejecatl, Earth Wind, or
    Tecacual Ejecatl, Wind
    from the Ruins
Black
17 × 6.5 cm

The *ejecatl* portrayed in figure 16 originates from the earth and lives in the pre-Columbian ruins *(cubes)* that dot the Nahua area of northern Veracruz. The Nahuas view these ancient ruins as doorways between the underworld and the earth's surface and as the residence of the Devil. This *ejecatl* spirit is a servant of the Devil. It follows its master in search of victims. Besides its crown and animal horns, the spirit is cut wearing a suit of freshwater mollusk shells. It can be released into the air when a person loses his temper.

FIGURE 17
Apantlasole Ejecatl, Water
   Filth Wind
Blue
17.5 × 5 cm

Also a servant of the Devil, this spirit attacks its victims at midday. It is cut with animal horns, a crown, and clothes. The shaman said that it is found in the filthy scum that forms on the surface of water.

FIGURE 18
Apantlasole Ejecatl, Water
   Filth Wind
Green
16 × 6.5 cm

Originating from the water, the disease-causing agent shown in figure 18 is covered with matted, dirty hair. It is dangerous to everyone who goes near rivers, springs, or lakes.

FIGURE 19
Aixcutla Ejecatl, Wind of the
    Water-Face Plant (Water
    Hyacinth?)
Green
16.5 × 6.4 cm

This *ejecatl* originates from the surface of the water and is portrayed with animal horns, a crown, and a suit made of waves. The spirit causes disease by entering the bodies of unsuspecting victims when they go near water. While cutting this figure, the curer said that the spirit is a male, but dresses like a woman.

Figures 20–26 were cut by a male shaman from a neighboring village who specializes in disease-prevention rituals. Like the first shaman, he cuts multiple images of each figure to emphasize its power. This curer is unusual in that he does not distinguish the various *ejecatl* spirits by name. Instead he classes them all under the name Xochiejecatl, meaning "Flowery Wind." The next section describes a ritual in which these particular paper images are used by the shaman to effect a cleansing.

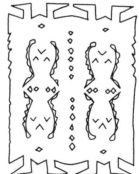

FIGURE 20
Xochiejecatl, Flowery Wind
Red
19 × 11.5 cm

The *ejecatl* portrayed in figure 20 is from the sky realm but is encountered in the mountains and forest. The spirit is cut wearing a crown and clothes; the central diamond cuts represent the heart.

FIGURE 21
Xochiejecatl, Flowery Wind
Red
16.5 × 11.5 cm

Eight heads characterize this *ejecatl,* which also comes from the sky realm. It somewhat resembles the underworld spirit Mictlan Tlasole Ejecatl in figure 3, which was cut by the first shaman.

FIGURE 22
Xochiejecatl, Flowery Wind
Black
18 × 11.5 cm

Identical to figure 20 except for color, this spirit originates from the earthly realm. According to the shaman, it is prone to attack people who are in a susceptible, weakened state, such as children or anyone who has been frightened.

FIGURE 23
Xochiejecatl, Flowery Wind
Purple (called rose by the
    shaman)
16.5 × 9 cm

The *ejecatl* in figure 23 is cut with animal horns, which indicates its bull-like temperament and symbolic association with the Devil. It comes from the earth, rides on the wind, and makes people sick.

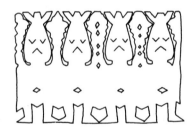

FIGURE 24
Xochiejecatl, Flowery Wind
Purple (called rose by the
    shaman)
15 × 12 cm

This earth *ejecatl* is portrayed as a series of identical figures standing side by side. Animal horns emphasize the spirit's dangerous temperament, and the central diamond cuts signify the creature's heart.

FIGURE 25
Xochiejecatl, Flowery Wind
Green
18 × 13 cm

This eight-headed spirit comes from the water and is believed to attack at midday. In some cases the time of day, or perhaps the position of the sun, can stimulate disease-causing spirits to attack unwary people.

FIGURE 26
Xochiejecatl, Flowery Wind
Blue
18 × 15.5 cm

The blue color means that this *ejecatl* also comes from the water realm. It specializes in attacking people who are bathing.

The significance of these *ejecatl* spirits can be clarified if they are placed in the context of Nahua world view. The Nahuas attribute the good things in life—children, crops, and health —to spirits such as the Earth, Tonantsi, Toteotsi, and Apanchane. As long as offerings are made to compensate the spirits, they will continue to send benefits from the sky, earth, and water. Dealing with the underworld is a different matter, but here too, if the spirits of the dead can be enticed to keep away, the ensuing state of health is beneficial. If the offerings are forthcoming, human beings can remain in a balance or harmony with the forces of the cosmos. This is not to say the Nahuas are fatalists; far from it. They work hard to manipulate and exploit their natural and social environment, but they believe that labor and planning are not enough to assure that their desires will be met.

Three points help clarify how the *ejecatl* spirits fit into the Nahua cosmos. First, they are often associated with filth and disorder. Many of them have names containing the word *tlasole*, which means "trash" or "filth." The second aspect of *ejecatl* spirits is that many of them are brought in or attracted by people's misbehavior. Gossip, anger, saying bad things, or acts of sorcery draw *ejecatl* spirits into the village. Once in the village, they may attack anyone, including innocent bystanders or children. The third aspect is that many *ejecatl* spirits are portrayed with animal horns, indicating that they are servants of Tlauelilo, the Devil. In other words, they are the spirits of dead people.

Anthropologists have found that in cultures all over the world elements of disorder are thought of as being "dirty" or "filthy"; in short, "polluted" (see Douglas 1968). For example, incest is polluting because it disrupts the kinship system. Or a tennis shoe on the dining room table pollutes because it disrupts the order of the household. The *ejecatl* spirits seem to be part of this universal association of disorder with dirt and can best be looked at as agents of pollution. As such they represent viola-tions or disruptions of social norms and the culturally accepted arrangement of things. The *ejecatl* interfere with the benefits that would naturally flow from a harmonious universe. But they are pollutants put there by actions of the very human beings upon whom they prey; it is people in general who are ultimately responsible for their own misfortunes. The spirits of the dead have become associated with antisocial behavior and are taking revenge on the living. The whole cosmos is infested with them, such that they now permanently live in all four realms. Interestingly, the curing ritual is called *ochpantli* or *tleuchpantle*, which means a "cleansing," "sweeping clean," or "reordering," and its purpose is to rid the patient and his surroundings of *ejecatl* spirits. Ultimately the purpose of a cure is to restore the balance between the patient and the natural order (see Sandstrom 1978a).

Examination of figures 1–26 also reveals the distinctive style of each shaman's cuttings. Even the images of the two specialists who cut multiple images are easily distinguished from one another. As different as they are, however, they are distinctively Nahua, as is seen in succeeding chapters. Some of the common features among the paper images reveal a striking uniformity of overall style and symbolic convention. All images are front-facing, anthropomorphic, and, except Miquilistli (Death, figure 12), have hands which are upraised by the side of the head. Many of the images are cut wearing crowns, which serve to identify them. In addition the heads have a characteristic pointed appearance, with the features of the face always completed. The shamans who cut the multiple images are much more concerned with representing the heart and clothing features than is the shaman who cuts single images. All of the images are cut wearing shoes, supporting an observation by Christensen with regard to the Otomís that dangerous spirits are often identified with shoe-wearing mestizos, while salutary spirits are often cut with bare feet, like Indians (Christensen 1971, p. 21). Finally, it is remarkable, considering the dangerous nature of the *ejecatl* spirits, that their images are so benign. They do not look dangerous, and their suits of hair, shells, and waves do not appear threatening. All of these features are discussed in greater detail in the concluding chapter.

A NAHUA RITUAL

The simplest way to illustrate how these paper figures are used is to describe a Nahua ritual. We have selected, among the many we witnessed, a cleansing ritual—used in this case to prevent disease—that is held annually to protect village political authorities. It is sponsored and paid for by an important man in the village as a kind of gift to the community. Only political authorities participate directly in the ritual, but everyone agreed that it ultimately benefits the entire village.

THE SETTING

The ritual is called *ochpantli*, or *limpia* in Spanish, which means "to cleanse"or "straighten out." It was conducted at the sponsor's house by a shaman from a neighboring village. The shaman has a large clientele from many surrounding villages and is considered extremely able and powerful. He arrived in the morning for what turned out to be a twelve-hour ritual. After being seated in a special guest's chair, which is part of the Nahua welcoming custom, he was greeted respectfully by everyone in attendance. He is an affable man with a voice made permanently hoarse from chanting. He was paid two hundred pesos for the ritual, an indication of his stature, since 12.50 pesos was considered fair pay for a day's work. A description of the ritual as we witnessed it follows.

PREPARATIONS

Almost immediately upon arriving, the shaman begins to cut dozens of paper images using scissors and paper he has brought with him (see color plate 2). He uses plain white paper sheets to cut the witness spirits and colored sheets for the *ejecatl*. He carefully stacks the finished products in separate piles. The paper is folded before being cut, which accounts for the symmetry of the figures. Near him, aromatic copal smoke pours from a clay incense brazier, sacralizing the area. At the other end of the small house six men are busy making floral adornments on a sheet of plastic spread on the earthen floor. After a short while several men enter the house carrying chickens and a turkey. The shaman receives the birds and holds each one over the smoking brazier while he chants. His chant dedicates the birds to the house guardian spirits *(mu'axcatl)* and asks them to watch over the village political authorities. Then, one by one he breaks each bird's neck and lays it before the narrow table that serves as the house altar. As he resumes cutting paper images, an old woman enters and removes the birds to a neighboring house where she cooks them for use later in the ritual.

THE PRELIMINARY CLEANSING

When everything is ready, the shaman digs a small hole in the earth floor, symbolizing Tlaltetata, Father Earth. He places a white tallow candle nearby, symbolizing the earth and underworld, and then lays out bunches of sacred plants. On top of and between these plants he lays out the *ejecatl* images in a circle around the hole. The images he lays out are reproduced in figures 20-26. As he chants, he sprinkles white rum *(aguardiente)*, raw egg, tobacco, and cornmeal on the paper images (see color plate 3). After dropping offerings in the hole, he picks up one group of paper images and violently tears it apart. Next he forms a bundle of the paper images and herbs and, after sacralizing it in incense, he vigorously rubs it over each of the political officeholders. Then, standing before each man in turn, he violently and with great energy tears the bundle to shreds. During his chant the shaman repeats the phrases *"Axcana Xochiejecatl"* ("No Flowery Wind!"), and *"Xiahque Ejecatl"* ("Begone Wind!").

The shaman then goes to the neighboring house where the birds are being cooked and lays out paper images on the floor near the fireplace. After lighting a beeswax candle symbolizing the sky realm, he sprinkles offerings on the images and destroys them. During this act he chants repeatedly, *"Xiahque, Xiahque"* ("Get out! Get out!"). Next, he proceeds to a point outside the original house and assembles an array of *ejecatl* images along with a burning candle. While chanting, he sprinkles them with offerings and then violently rips them to pieces. The procedure of laying out paper images, sprinkling them with offerings, and destroying them is repeated at four additional places: along the trail, at the base of a stone ruin, at a nearby spring where people get water, and where trails cross. In all, seven locations are visited, including the house floor.

Similar locations are visited during any cleansing or curing ritual. They represent places where *ejecatl* attack is likely to occur. Equally important, the sequence of locations symbolically reproduces the average daily activities of the men. People sleep on the floor and, upon rising, eat food cooked over the fire. Then they leave the house to cross and travel over trails to the fields. In the evening they bathe before returning home. The ruins are visited because they represent doorways between the underworld and the earth, and, thus, most *ejecatl* spirits come from them. This first section of the ritual is a preliminary cleansing which also protects the village authorities during their daily rounds (see Sandstrom 1982).

THE OFFERING

In the second part of the ritual the shaman continues to rid the village political authorities of the *ejecatl* while enlisting the help of various protector spirits to watch over them. He has the men stand inside a large marigold-covered loop while he rubs them vigorously with a bundle containing witness spirits (see color plate 4). Should the men encounter harm anytime during the year, the witnesses will report this to the house-guardian spirits. Among other things, house guardians have the power to intervene and dispel attacking *ejecatl* spirits. The loop is then passed over the men to remove any stubborn *ejecatl* spirits that remain. After the loop cleansing, some of the men proceed to decorate the house altar and the hole in the earthen floor with the prepared floral adornments. The shaman lays paper images of witness spirits on the altar, while women and girls bring in plates of food and place them on the altar and by the hole. The shaman dedicates the offerings in a long chant, and the spirits are finally fed when the men pour all of the food offerings over the altar and into the hole. Tlixauantsi, the hearth spirit, is included in the offerings by casting food on the three stones surrounding the fireplace.

After several more episodes of cleansing with bundles of witness spirits and the marigold loop, the shaman instructs the men to pack ritual paraphernalia and offerings into carrying baskets so that the ritual can be continued at the top of one of the twelve sacred hills *(santo tepeme)* that surround the village. He directs everyone to Tepetl Ahuimutl, a sacred hill where the first humans are said to have been placed on earth after being created by Toteotsi. The ancestor spirits (Itecu) now live inside of this hill, and they stand guard over the village below. At the top of the hill the village political authorities set up an ornate altar dedicated to these ancestor protectors (see color plate 5). At the center of the altar is a paper cutout of the sun as well as a dozen paper images of witness spirits, some of which are laid on a paper "bed." (The witnesses, bed, and sun used in this ritual are reproduced in figures 27–30, 55, and 59). Bread, tamales made from the sacrificial birds, cups of coffee and chocolate, bottled beer and soft drinks, tobacco, *aguardiente*, and many other offerings are placed on the altar (see plate 6). After chanting and censing the altar, the shaman puts bits of a chicken-heart tamale into the mouths of the paper images. Following this the men spread the food over the entire altar. The remaining food is consumed by the men before they return to the village.

Back in the house where the ritual began, the shaman conducts yet another cleansing, this time using beeswax candles. While breathlessly chanting, he rubs each man wildly with the candles. At the end he gives each man one of the candles to be burned at home sometime during the next several days.

PAPER IMAGES AND THE RITUAL

The description illustrates several of the basic elements found in nearly all Nahua rituals and first described in chapter 2. First is the manufacture and use of paper images to portray selected spirits. The images become powerful magnets capable of attracting spirits, and thus only the shaman cuts and handles them in a ritual. A second element is the construction of altars to hold the paper images. Altars *(tlaixpamitl)* are designed to be beautiful places that are attractive to spirits. Third is the dedication of offerings to the spirits. These offerings include *aguardiente*, tobacco, cornmeal, raw egg, and the meat or blood of sacrificed animals. The offerings are symbolically fed to the spirits by pouring them on the paper images or by putting them in the images' mouths (see color plate 10). Ultimately most of the food offerings are consumed by ritual participants. The fourth element is the chanting addressed to paper images by shamans. Usually the chants are a listing of the offerings that have been made as well as a specific statement detailing what is requested of the spirits (see color plate 11). Fifth is the over-all strategy of Nahua rituals, which is to make offerings and sacrifices to spirits as a way of inducing them to cooperate. In the case of lesser spirits, the rituals are, more accurately, a way of controlling the spirits by manipulating their life-forces.

The cleansing of the political authorities is really a combination of two separate rituals, each of which contains the basic elements described above. The first sequence (labeled the preliminary cleansing) is simply a standard curing ritual usually performed by itself to remove disease-causing *ejecatl* from a patient's body and surroundings. The second sequence is the actual offering to the house guardians and ancestor spirits. The repeated cleansing episodes come before the two offerings, just as in the ritual described in chapter 2, so that dangerous spirits lurking in the environment will be lured away from the proceedings. The altars and offerings are as attractive to harmful spirits as to their intended recipients, and care is taken to address this potential danger to the participants. The techique for removing *ejecatl* spirits can be reduced to three steps: first, the herbs and paper images are carefully arranged in a kind of abbreviated altar; second, offerings are spread on the images; and third, the images are suddenly destroyed. The techniques are similar when making offerings to beneficial spirits, except that the paper images are not destroyed.

The offering sequence is also directed to the paper images. It may seem curious, however, that the images that are placed on the altars and that receive the offerings do not represent the spirits whose protection is being sought. Instead, witnesses acting as intermediaries are the focus of attention. The indirectness of the offering sequences differs from the almost brutal confrontation between the specialist and *ejecatl* spirits in the cleansing sequence. A clue to these differing approaches can be found by examining general interactional patterns in the village. In-

directness of behavior characterizes many types of social inter-
action among the Nahuas, particularly between people of differing statuses (see Provost 1975). Marriage proposals, gift
giving, and requests made to social superiors are always conducted through intermediaries. Thus the use of witness spirits
is a reflection of the general pattern and is indicative of the
extremely respectful relationship between the Nahuas and their
salutary spirits.

Additional Nahua rituals are listed in table 4.

TABLE 4. Major Nahua Rituals

Ochpantli: Curing-cleansing ritual varying from two to twenty-four
hours in length. Paper images: *ejecatl* figures, tortilla napkins, witnesses and guardians, the sun (Lenz 1973 [1948], pp.137ff., 144;
Sandstrom 1975, pp. 147ff.; 1978a; 1982; Williams García 1955,
pp. 40ff.).

Xochitlalia or Chicomexochitl: Prerainy season crop-fertility ritual.
Paper images: *ejecatl* figures, tortilla napkins, seed images, additional spirits connected to rain (see chapter 2; Medellín Zenil 1979,
pp. 115–16; Sandstrom 1975, pp. 232ff.; Williams García 1955, pp.
56ff.).

Quitlacuahti Xinaxtli Pilsintsi: Offering to young maize plant held
after planting. Paper images: figure of young maize (Sandstrom
1975, pp. 221ff.).

Sintlacua: Offering to mature maize plant; held at harvest time. Paper
images: figure of mature maize (Sandstrom 1975, pp. 221ff.).

Tlamanas: Ritual held at harvest of first young ears of corn. Paper
images: no information (Medellín Zenil 1979, pp. 116; Williams
García 1955, pp. 14, 65ff.; 1966, pp. 345ff.).

Xantolo: Ceremony to feed the souls of ancestors; syncretized with
All Souls. Paper images: shawls for female ancestors (see color
plate 9) (Medellín Zenil 1979, pp. 116–17; Montoya Briones 1964,
pp. 151ff.; Reyes García 1960, pp. 39–40; Sandstrom 1975, pp.
247ff.; Williams García 1955, pp. 53ff.).

Tlacatelilis: Fertility rite connected to the winter solstice. Paper

TABLE 4. *Continued*

images: *ejecatl* figures and tortilla napkins used in preliminary cleansing (Sandstrom 1975, pp. 188ff.; 1982).

Yancuic Xiuitl: Feast given for old and new year spirits; syncretized with New Year's Day. Paper images: *ejecatl* figures and tortilla napkins used in preliminary cleansing (Montoya Briones 1964, p. 148; Reyes García 1960, p. 39; Sandstrom 1975, pp. 215ff.).

Nanahuatili: The Devil and his servants, impersonated by young men, dance and demand "payment" from each household; syncretized with the Christian celebration of Carnival. No paper images used (Montoya Briones 1964, pp. 132ff.; Provost 1975; Reyes García 1960, pp. 39, 54ff.; Sandstrom 1975, pp. 254ff.; Williams García 1955, pp. 71ff.).

Xantucarus: Ritual feeding of the spirits of those who died violently; syncretized with Holy Cross. No paper images used (Sandstrom 1975, pp. 259ff.).

House Blessing: Held after a house is built to insure protection of the family. Paper images: no information (Lenz 1973 [1948], pp. 139ff.; William García 1955, pp. 70–71).

Maltiscone: Naming ceremony and cleansing ritual for newborn infant. Paper images: no information (Williams García 1955, pp. 17ff.; 1957, pp. 52ff.).

Momapacas or Tlapahpacayotl: Handwashing ceremony held among ritual kinsmen of newborn infant. Paper images: no information (Medellín Zenil 1979, pp. 117–18; Reyes García 1960, p. 41; Williams García 1955, pp. 30ff.; 1957, pp. 55ff.).

Titeixpia: Funeral ritual to keep away spirit of the dead. Paper images: no information (Montoya Briones 1964, pp. 109ff.; Provost 1981; Sandstrom 1975, p. 260; Williams García 1955, pp. 48ff.; 1957, pp. 62–63).

Tliquixtis: New flame ceremony held approximately nine days after death; signals final departure of spirit of the dead. Paper images: no information (Sandstrom 1975, p. 262; Williams García 1955, pp. 51ff.; 1957, p. 63).

Cabo de Año: Rite marking first-year anniversary of death. Paper images: no information (Williams García 1955, pp. 51–52).

It is impossible to make a complete list since shamans are continually creating rituals or adding innovations to the ones that have become somewhat standardized. The table indicates the range of rituals performed and the types of paper images associated with each one.

NAHUA WITNESS AND GUARDIAN SPIRITS

The importance of spirits that act as intermediaries between humans and more powerful spirits is clearly illustrated in the ritual just described. As mentioned, the witnesses cut for the ritual appear in figures 17–30. Figures 27 and 29 are female witnesses, while figures 28 and 30 are their male companions. All are portrayed wearing shoes and poncholike clothing called *jorongos*. The shoes in this case symbolize the traveling these witnesses do between the human and spirit realms. Designs cut into the clothing represent decorations in figures 27 and 29 and doorways *(puertas)* in figures 28 and 30. The doorways act as conduits to the ancestor spirits.

Figure 27
Onipixtoc Aquiqui'ixtoc,
    Senior Witness
White
24.5 × 8 cm

Figure 28
Onipixtoc Aquiqui'ixtoc,
    Senior Witness
White
24.5 × 7.5 cm

Figure 29
Onipixtoc Aquiqui'ixtoc,
   Senior Witness
White
24.5 × 8 cm

Figure 30
Onipixtoc Aquiqui'ixtoc,
   Senior Witness
White
23 × 7.5 cm

Note that the shaman calls them "senior" witnesses to indicate that they have greater power than ordinary witnesses. The
headdresses of these spirits are difficult to interpret. When
asked about them, the shaman simply said that they are crowns
(coronas) that serve to identify each image. The comblike crown
in figure 30 is sometimes identified as a symbolic representation
of the devouring jaws of the earth. Finally, the head shape is
reminiscent of the form exhibited in *ejecatl* spirits.

The following seven images are witness and guardian spirits
cut by other shamans. Both witness and guardian spirits can act
as intermediaries. As previously seen, witnesses generally watch
over people and report to the ancestors if someone is sick,

that is, if they are attacked by *ejecatl* spirits. Occasionally the shaman enlists the aid of witness spirits to cure a patient or watch over people recovering from an *ejecatl* attack. Guardian spirits, on the other hand, generally take a more active role and are able to ward off attacks from the *ejecatl* or from a sorcerer. They have the power to intercept misfortune themselves without the aid of more powerful deities. The distinction between witness and guardian spirits is not completely clear, however, since sometimes guardians act like witnesses. In this case they are called guardian-witnesses (see figures 36 and 37).

Figures 31 and 32 were cut by a female shaman, and they are some of the very few examples we have seen in which the images are cut side by side (see figure 24).

Figure 31
Onipixtoc Aquiqui'ixtoc,
   Senior Witnesses
White
34 × 10.5 cm

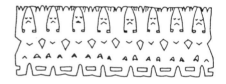

The shaman said that these eight figures represent witnesses who take offerings to the ancestors inside the sacred hill. Each figure has a V-shaped heart and additional cuts represent clothing. She added that these spirits are good *(cuali)* because they ask the ancestors to watch over people. During rituals, this paper image is laid on a paper bed (figure 57) and sprinkled with offerings.

Figure 32
Tlali, Earth (Guardian)
White
34 × 11.5 cm

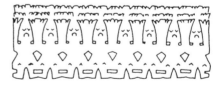

The cutout in figure 32 represents a specialized category of guardian spirits associated with the earth. The shaman cut them with clothing decorations and multitiered crowns. The guard-ians intercept disease-causing spirits before they can harm pa-tients. During rituals they are laid out on a paper bed (figure 58), and offerings are sprinkled on them. As with other guardian and witness spirits, they are not destroyed after the offering.

Figures 33, 34, 35, and 53 were cut as a complete set of witness spirits with accompanying bed. The shaman makes offerings to the images and then leaves them on the patient's home altar.

Figure 33
Onipixtoc Aquiqui'ixtoc (Tepetl),
    Hill Witness
White
18.5 × 6.5 cm

This cutting is a companion of figure 35. It represents a male witness spirit propitiated during elaborate curing rites. It is portrayed with a crown and four pockets in its clothes. The spirit lives on the tops of hills and says good things to powerful ancestor spirits on a person's behalf. The shaman added that this hill witness can also guard over people and report to the ancestors if someone is sick.

Figure 34
Onipixtoc Aquiqui'ixtoc (Tlali),
    Earth Witness
White
13.5 × 5.5 cm

Like figure 32, this spirit is associated with the earth, although in this portrayal it wears no crown. The four cuts represent pockets. This image, like figure 33, is also a male companion of figure 35 and is used in rituals held to cure and protect people.

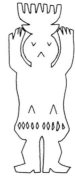

Figure 35
Onipixtoc Aquiqui'ixtoc (Tepetl),
    Hill Witness
White
17 × 7 cm

The female hill witness portrayed here is the companion of both figures 33 and 34. It is portrayed with a crown, two pockets, and a row of cuts representing a woman's dress. Like the others, this spirit is cut by shamans to cure disease, watch over patients, and intercede with more powerful entities on people's behalf.

The last two figures in this series are guardian witnesses. Note that they are cut with the bare feet, which symbolically place them in the Indian world. The absence of shoes further indicates that they, unlike the witnesses, are something more than simple go-betweens.

Figure 36
Onipixtoc Aquiqui'ixtoc (Guardián),
  Guardian Witness
White
18.5 × 6 cm

This unusual guardian witness of unknown sex has a hornlike headdress and winglike cuts on each side. Since the spirit has the power to protect people from harm, offerings are specifically dedicated to it by name in curing rituals. The cutout image is part of a sacred bundle that includes a companion spirit (figure 37), palm and marigold adornments, a mirror used in divinations, and a paper "bed" (see figure 52). The bundle is rubbed over a patient to remove harmful spirits that may have entered his body. This spirit, like figures 32 and 34, originates from the earth.

Figure 37
Onipixtoc Aquiqui'ixtoc (Guardián),
  Guardian Witness
White
17.5 × 5.5 cm

A female companion of figure 36, this spirit is also a guardian witness that protects people from harm and is included as part of the sacred bundle used to cleanse and cure patients. If the bundle also contains cutouts of disease-causing spirits, it is destroyed and discarded outside of the village. If the bundle contains only guardian-witness spirits such as the ones portrayed here, it can be kept on the house altar indefinitely.

NAHUA SEED SPIRITS

Nahua shamans also conduct private and public rituals to insure success in the villagers' fields. A central feature of these rituals is the propitiation of seed spirits called Xinaxtli, which are believed to have direct control over crop productivity. Each cultigen has its own spirit, although paramount among them is maize, called Chicomexochitl, "Seven-Flower" (see annotation under figure 40). The seeds are controlled by Tonantsi, who is viewed as their mother. Seed spirits are not seen as awesome and powerful like the ancestors who have to be dealt with through the aid of intermediaries. Rather they are viewed almost as obstreperous children who must be controlled. They are necessary for the crops to succeed, but the earth, water, and sun are considered more important. Thus at planting and harvesting rituals offerings are made to a number of spirits involved with crop growth.

During crop increase rituals, the typical offerings of food, drink, and tobacco are made before the paper images of the seed spirits. In most rituals the paper images are left on the altar following the offering or after several days are wrapped into a bundle and placed outside. In other cases the images are carefully preserved in a special wooden cabinet throughout the year. While neighboring San Pablito Otomí Indians cut a paper image of each of the scores of crops grown, the Nahuas and Tepehuas cut very few seed images. The Nahuas most commonly cut the maize seed figure. However, certain crops, such as squash (figure 49), chile (figure 50), or palm nut (figure 51), may be cut on special occasions.

An important planting ritual held that acknowledges the stages of crop growth is called Quitlacuati Xinaxtli Pilsintsi, meaning "To Feed the Infant Maize Spirit." For this offering the shaman cuts paper images of immature maize (figures 38 and 39). Just prior to harvest the Nahuas hold a ritual called Sintlacua, which means "to Feed the Maize Spirit." At this time the shaman cuts an image depicting maize as an "old man" (figure 40). In both of these rituals the people give the seed spirit a big welcome so that maize will flow freely into the village.

Figure 38
Pilsintsi, Young Maize Spirit
White
20.5 × 6.5 cm

Figure 38 represents the spirit of immature maize. The ripening tassel serves as a crown, and undeveloped ears of corn are cut in the spirit's body. Cuts in the heels of the shoes represent roots. Seed spirits live in caves and are ruled by their mother, Tonantsi.

Figure 39
Pilsintsi, Young Maize Spirit
White
20.5 × 6 cm

Another representation of immature maize, this spirit is portrayed with a heart and four developing ears of corn. It wears a tassel crown on its head. The cuts on the back of each leg signify roots.

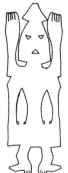

Figure 40
Sintle, Maize Spirit
White
20.5 × 6.5 cm

Figure 40 portrays the spirit of mature maize, sometimes called Chicomexochitl (Seven-Flower). The origin of the name is not certain, but Seven-Flower was an Aztec day name whose symbol was corn. Seven-Flower was also a deity who protected seamstresses and painters (Berdan 1982, p. 135) and who is related to the Aztec deities Xochipilli and Pilzintecutli (Lord of the Young Maize) (Monnich 1976, p. 143). The Nahuas state that the name derives from a miraculous corn plant that was discovered with seven ears of maize (Reyes García 1976, p. 128; Williams García 1955, p. 61; 1966a, p. 343). Ripened ears of corn are cut into the body, and the tassel crown is replaced by a hat. The heels of the shoes are cut to represent roots.

Note that these and some other seed spirits are cut wearing shoes. It is difficult to explain why this is so, since shoes among the *ejecatl* spirits symbolize outsider *(mestizo)* status. When asked, the shamans who cut these said simply that "this is the way we do it, it is our custom *(costumbre)*."

Nahua shamans also cut images of seed spirits that are placed in a special wooden cabinet. The cabinet is kept on an altar and is the focus of offerings at various times. The images stored inside it are prepared from a type of plasticized paper that lasts longer in the tropical climate than regular paper. With few exceptions the images represent the seed spirits of maize. These cutouts are dressed in tiny clothes, including hats, necklaces, and earrings. In addition the cabinet contains miniature chairs, tables, *manos* and *metates* for grinding corn, and other furnishings. The cabinet is a microcosm of the Nahua world for the seed spirits who live inside.

The idea behind the cabinet is complex and paradoxical. Shamans state that the seeds must be kept in the box so that they do not run away. Should they do so, the people would starve. At the same time, however, people insist that seed spirits live in caves at the tops of sacred hills. It is unclear whether the seeds have multiple spirits or whether the cabinet symbolizes the caves. In any event, in the early spring during an elaborate ritual called Xochitlalia or "Flowery Earth," the cabinet is opened and the paper images are removed. All of the clothes are washed and an extensive offering is made to the seed spirits. For a description of this ritual see chapter 2. Figures 41-51 are a sample of the paper images kept in the cabinet (see also color plate 1). To our knowledge this is the first time that the contents of a cabinet have been revealed to outsiders since Frederick Starr was permitted to view the statues in the Otomí cabinet at the turn of the century (see chapter 1). Except in figures 45 and 50, the clothes have been removed so that the paper image itself is revealed.

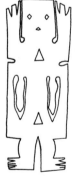

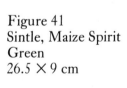

Figure 41
Sintle, Maize Spirit
Green
26.5 × 9 cm

In this maize spirit, triangular cuts represent the heart and genitals. Oblong cuts in the body signify ripened ears of corn ready for harvest. The square head on the figure is unusual.

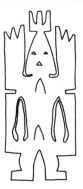

Figure 42
Sintle, Maize Spirit
White
23 × 10 cm

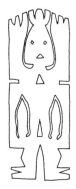

Figure 43
Sintle, Maize Spirit
White
25 × 9 cm

A three-pronged crown identifies these portrayals of the spirit
of the maize plant. They are the most common styles of maize
spirit found in the cabinet. The three-pronged crown may indicate that these represent the generalized maize plant. Head
and crown shape in the other maize spirits reproduced here may
indicate specific varieties of maize. Cuts representing the spirit's
heart and genitals separate upright ears of corn.

Figure 44
Sintle, Maize Spirit
Green
33 × 12 cm

Because of its unusual design the paper image in figure 44 most likely represents one specific type of the several varieties of maize grown by the Nahuas. Lines of diamond and oblong cuts are clothing decorations. The cut beneath the diamond-shaped heart may signify the spirit's stomach. Four spikes of the maize plant are cut from the spirit's body.

Figure 45
Sintle, Maize Spirit
White with pink, blue, and
    white cloth dress
29 × 7.5 cm

This seed spirit represents white corn. It is clothed in a single-piece dress much like that worn by unmarried Nahua girls. The crown is a maturing ear of corn.

Figure 46
Sintle, Maize Spirit
White with white cloth outfit
29 × 7.5 cm

This companion to figure 45 is dressed in white shirt and pants, the usual dress for Nahua men and boys who are old enough to work the fields. The bunlike headdress represents a newly forming ear of corn.

Figure 47
Sintle, Maize Spirit
White
23.5 × 8.5 cm

Illustrated here is another image of the maize spirit. Ears of corn are cut in the figure's body along with triangular cuts representing the heart and genitals.

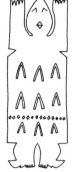

Figure 48
Sintle, Maize Spirit
Yellow
35.5 × 12 cm

This paper image represents the spirit of yellow corn, the staple of the Nahua diet. Pointed cuts symbolize the growing ears of corn, and the diamond cutouts are clothing decorations. Cuts in the boot heels represent roots.

Figure 49
Ayotli, Squash Spirit
White
34.5 × 12 cm

The seed spirit portrayed here is that of the squash plant. Squash is an important component of the Nahua diet and is grown in each field along with maize. The round cuts are the developing squash, while diamond cuts are clothing decorations. The boot heels are cut to represent roots.

Figure 50
Chile, Chile Spirit
Red
size of original unknown

The seed spirit of the chile plant is illustrated here. Six oblong cuts symbolize growing chile peppers, while diamond cutouts are decorations on the spirit's clothing. Chile is commonly used as a condiment in Nahua cuisine.

Figure 51
Coyoli, Palm Nut Spirit (?)
Green
35 × 12 cm

The identification of this unusual seed spirit is uncertain. It is likely that the spirit symbolizes the palm nut, which is a food crop with important ritual connotations. The flower of the palm nut is used as an altar adornment and ritual object during crop increase rites. Besides the identifying crown, the figure is cut with winglike projections beneath the upraised arms. The four jagged cuts in the body may represent the palm flower, while the smooth cuts that come to a point are the palm nut itself. Diamond cuts are clothing decorations, while the triangular cutouts beneath these are genitals. The boot heels are cut to represent roots.

Compared to those of the Otomís of San Pablito, the varieties of seed images cut by the Nahuas are restricted. Although we have presented only fourteen specimens, these represent all of the major styles of seed spirits we were able to collect. The distinctive feature of Nahua seed images is the silhouette of the crop that is cut out of the body of the figure. The shapes are readily identifiable by everyone in the village, including children. Seed spirits are also distinguished by the roots that are cut out from the feet or legs of several specimens. Once again, similar to the witness and *ejecatl* spirits, the structure of the headdress or the lack of a headdress are important identifying features of the images. We are not certain of the precise meaning of the headdresses at this time. Finally, we are not completely certain of the connection between paper color and seed spirit portrayed. Young corn is cut from white paper, figures 41 and 44 are green and figure 48 is yellow. These are all colors one would associate with the corn plant, and perhaps that is the extent of the meaning. The palm nut spirit is cut from green paper and the chile spirit from red, which seems straightforward; but we are uncertain why the squash spirit is white.

NAHUA MISCELLANEOUS PAPER CUTTINGS

Not all paper images cut by Nahua shamans are meant to represent spirits. Some are decorative in nature; they are called *amatl tlapopostectle*, which means "paper adornments." Figures 52–58 are examples of large sheets of paper called *tlaxcali yuyumitl* (tortilla napkin) also, *cama* (bed) or *petal* (sleeping mat), which are cut so that the images of spirits can be placed on them during rituals. They are usually highly decorated so that the altar will be a beautiful place for the spirits in attendance. The unusual name given to these altar mats probably is taken from the embroidered cloth tortilla holders sold at the market. Each mat is covered with designs representing stars, flowers, or, in some cases, small images of the cutout paper images they are to hold during the ritual (see figure 53). During a ritual, paper images of spirits are carefully arranged on the altar mats. Special flower and palm decorations are then laid on top of each image. After offerings have been sprinkled over the cutouts, the mat is often folded up with the contents inside and then rubbed over the patient or people in attendance. This bundle is believed to have the power to cleanse people by getting rid of disease-causing spirits.

Figure 52
tlaxcali yuyumitl, tortilla napkin
   (altar mat)
White
43 × 36 cm

This altar mat is used to form the bundle which holds figures 36 and 37 (guardian witnesses). The geometric designs are identified as flowers or guardian stars.

Figure 53
tlaxcali yuyumitl, tortilla napkin, also
   yuyumitl para tlaltepactli, napkin to
   guard the earth (altar mat)
White
35 × 24 cm

This altar mat is used to hold witness spirits, figures 33, 34, and 35, during rituals. Four earth guardian witnesses along with various geometric designs are cut into the mat. In the center of the cutout is a flower. The fringed ends are very common in Nahua altar mats.

Figure 54
tlaxcali yuyumitl, tortilla napkin
   (altar mat)
White
36 × 25 cm

The geometric designs on this altar mat are all guardian stars, with the exception of the central feature, which is a flower. This mat is used to hold palm and marigold altar adornments and paper images of hill witnesses.

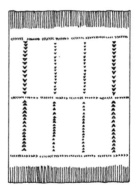

Figure 55
tlaxcali yuyumitl, tortilla napkin
   (altar mat)
White
48 × 34.5 cm

The mat in figure 55 is used to hold the witness spirits (figures 27–30) that were cut for the major cleansing ritual described earlier. The designs are decorations to make the bed beautiful.

Figure 56
tlaxcali yuyumitl, tortilla napkin
    (altar mat)
White
38 × 28 cm

This variation of figure 55 is also used to hold witness spirits. When asked about the type of cuts, the shaman said they are simply decorations.

Figure 57
tlaxcali yuyumitl, tortilla napkin
    (altar mat)
White
34 × 25 cm

The designs cut into this altar mat make a beautiful place for the spirits laid on it. The central design is a flower. During more elaborate curing rituals, figure 31, a senior witness, is placed on the mat along with altar adornments and offerings.

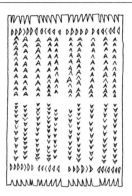

Figure 58
tlaxcali yuyumitl, tortilla napkin
   (altar mat)
White
34 × 23.5 cm

This mat is cut to represent the earth. During major curing rituals the earth guardian spirits in figure 32 are placed on it along with altar adornments and offerings. The significance of the cuts is unknown.

The primary function of the altar mats appears to be the beauty they create for the spirits that are invited in during rituals. In addition they serve as beds for paper images and are handy for forming bundles of images for use during cleansings. The shamans who cut these did not seem concerned about any particular meanings attached to the designs. The Otomís of San Pablito also cut elaborate sheets like these, but they attribute more specific meanings to them (see chapter 5).

The final Nahua figure is the sun. While this figure is not an altar mat or a bed, it is an adornment that decorates altars. It stands for the physical sun and not its spiritual manifestation, Toteotsi.

Figure 59
tonati (sometimes
tona or
tonatl), sun
White
22 cm diameter

Most Nahua altars are composed of an arch beneath which are placed paper figures and offerings. On some ritual occasions, such as the one to protect the village political authorities described earlier, this cutout is attached to a stick and either leaned against the arch or stuck into the ground just beneath it. The arch, which is usually covered with sacred leaves, symbolizes the arc of the sky. The sun cutout completes the symbolic representation of the sky realm.

The front-faced stance of the figures is a common stylistic feature of the majority of paper images among the Nahuas as well as among the Otomís and Tepehuas. In pre-Hispanic times artists rarely portrayed figures *en face*, preferring instead depictions in profile. Cecelia Klein found that *en face* images in pre-Hispanic art are symbolically linked to the earth, fertility, and end points in the space-time continuum (Klein 1976). The Nahua spirits fit the pre-Hispanic pattern in that they are front-faced and the majority are linked to the earth or to crop fertility. The *ejecatl* spirits are found in all realms, but they are linked to death and by implication to the earth and the underworld. Witness guardian spirits are frequently linked to the earth or hills, and the seed images are associated with crop fertility. As is noted in the following chapters, this pattern is also found among the other two cultures. The issue of frontality is discussed in chapter 7.

The large variety of paper cuttings in this chapter reflects not only the number of uses to which they are put, but also the scores of spirits in the Nahua pantheon. This array of spirits is bewildering for two reasons. First, there appears to be no end to the number of spirits found in a village. For example, the Earth is known as Tlali (Earth); Tlaltepactli, Tlalticpac, Tlaticpa (all aspects of Earth's Surface); Axcatlaltipatli (Belongings of the Earth or Earth as a Whole); Tlalimematsi (the Wife of the Lord of the Earth); Tlaxueuentsi (Lord of the Earth); Tlaltetata (Father Earth); or Tlaltenana (Mother Earth). Other manifestations of the Earth spirit that play a role in religious rituals include Tlalsisme (Aunt of the Earth), Tlaltepa (Earth Place), and Semanawak Tlaltentle (Edge of the Earth) (Reyes García 1960, p. 35; 1976, p. 127). In another example, the spirit of corn has nine different names in addition to Chicomexochitl (Seven-Flower). These names, like those for the earth, are not synonymous but rather stand for special aspects, or perhaps alter egos, of each spirit. The second source of confusion is that spirits can have contradictory characteristics or roles. The moon, for example, is associated with Tonantsi; in fact, in some villages the moon is called by the name Tonantsi (Reyes García 1976, p. 127). Yet Tonantsi (Our Sacred Mother) is the most salutary spirit among the Nahuas, while the moon receives no offerings because of the evil it causes.

An additional problem in trying to understand Nahua spirits is that they defy outside attempts to order them. Although most spirits more or less fit into one of the four cosmological realms—sky, earth, underworld, and water—several do not. Tlauelilo (the Devil), for example, lives in the ruins *(cubes)* that lie between the underworld and the earth. Tlauelilo also is associated with the moon and the celestial realm. The *ejecatl* come from the underworld and now inhabit all four realms, but they threaten people on earth. Tonantsi comes from the sky but lives in a cave. And Tlixauantsi (Fire) comes from the sky but lives in the stones surrounding the fireplace. In sum, we find that spirits have shifting identities and that they move between the realms. These puzzles are also found among the spirit worlds of the Otomís and Tepehuas, the subjects of chapters 5 and 6. The reasons for the apparent lack of organization in the pantheons of these cultures are discussed in chapter 7.

CHAPTER 5

PAPER CULT FIGURES AMONG CONTEMPORARY OTOMÍ INDIANS

THE Otomí Indians have long had a reputation for ferocity and power. They were viewed as uncivilized and brutish by the ancient Aztecs, who used the term Otomí as an epithet. Witness the scolding given a misbehaving Aztec child as recorded by Sahagún: "Now thou art an Otomí. Now thou art a miserable Otomí. O, Otomí, how is it that thou understandest not? . . . Not only art thou like an Otomí, thou art a real Otomí, a miserable Otomí, a green-head, a thick-head, a big tuft of hair over the back of the head, an Otomí blockhead" (quoted in Berdan 1982, p. 87). On the other hand, the Aztecs admired the Otomís as great warriors. One of their most prestigious military societies was called the Order of the Otomí. By becoming a member of this society, a man gained in social status and had the opportunity to receive economic advantages (Berdan 1982, p. 65). The Otomís of today have the same ambiguous reputation among neighboring Indian groups. The Nahuas, for example, view them as an unruly people who like to fight. At the same time, they claim that Otomí shamans are among the most powerful in the region.

In this chapter we examine the paper images cut by Otomí shamans. For ease of presentation and to facilitate comparison we have divided the ninety-seven images into five categories. The first contains those spirits that cause disease and misfortune and that are the focus of curing and cleansing rituals. The second includes the seed spirits used by shamans to ensure crop fertility. Third are the mountain spirits, which act as protectors and intermediaries. The fourth category contains adornments that in some cases serve to protect the people from wandering, dangerous spirits. Last we present miscellaneous images of spirits cut by shamans for special-purpose rituals. Following a discussion of the first category of disease-causing spirits, we include a description of a curing ritual, recounted, for the most part, by an Otomí shaman. The purpose of this description is to show how the paper images are employed by the shaman.

All but six of the figures were cut in the village of San Pablito, the same village in which Frederick Starr first witnessed papermaking and first saw paper images laid on an altar. Beginning in the 1930s or 1940s, a San Pablito shaman named Santos García developed a distinctive style of portraying the spirits that led to his renown as a master ritual specialist. Later when the bark-paper market began to grow, he offered examples of his cut images to Mexican folk-art dealers. Within a few years the paper images became popular tourist items, and a huge demand soon developed. By the 1970s virtually every tourist-oriented market in Mexico had stacks of the paper images for sale. Before long, import shops in the United States and Europe were also selling the images. After Santos García's death, his son, Alfonso García, continued the tradition. Today he is a leader in the enormous production of paper images in San Pablito. The son has carried on the style of the father, and most of the images presented here were cut by one or the other of these two shamans (Fitl 1975, p. 105; Dow 1982, p. 630).

The tourist trade has revolutionized the economy of San Pablito and undoubtedly has caused changes in traditional practices. In fact, an important shaman in San Pablito now holds curing ceremonies for paying tourists. One researcher has suggested that San Pablito is atypical of Otomí villages because it has been invaded by tourists, ethnographers, and travelers and because it has been influenced by neighboring Nahua villages (Fitl 1975, p. 162). These assertions are difficult to prove, however, since no one has published a thorough ethnographic study of the village. In spite of changes, Manrique concluded as late as 1969 that "pagan ritual has more manifestations in San Pablito, Puebla, than in any other place" (1969, p. 715).

One researcher has even noted the active support given to the native religion by Otomís in and around San Pablito (Dow 1982, p. 630). The question of the degree of influence that one Indian group exerts upon another is difficult to resolve given the region's ethnic diversity. In the concluding chapter we will argue that similarities among Nahua, Otomí, and Tepehua religious systems go beyond simple borrowing. Meanwhile, we have selected San Pablito as the focus of this chapter because of the numbers and varieties of paper images produced there and because we believe that these paper cuttings still reflect Otomí religious beliefs.

The information we have on Otomí religion as presented below is a composite derived from published reports of ethnographers who visited San Pablito and from data published on neighboring Otomí villages. Some of the rituals and beliefs recorded in the 1940s have undoubtedly undergone change. Some of the paper images collected by Lenz and Christensen are probably no longer cut. But the patterns of beliefs and the underlying world view of the Otomís remain. Otomí religion, like that of the Nahuas and the Tepehuas, is a blend of the Indian and the Christian, and it has proven its durability over the last 450 years (see Galinier 1980a).

Unfortunately, certain classes of ethnographic data on the Nahuas are not matched by data on the Otomís of San Pablito. For example, Galinier has written that some Otomís in the region conceive of the universe as consisting of seven layers *(mondes):* three in the celestial realm; three in the subterranean realm; and finally, the earth's surface. However, he provides no information on the functions or nature of these layers. He makes assertions about Otomí concepts of space, time, and directionality that are difficult to assess with the data he provides (see Galinier 1979a). Furthermore, the degree to which his assertions apply specifically to the people of San Pablito is not known. Because of these shortcomings in the ethnographic record, we have organized the Otomí data in much the same way that the Nahua information was presented. The Otomís may or may not have a formal cosmology identical to that of the Nahuas, but they do associate spirits with the sky, earth, underworld, and water. We do not intend to force ethnographic information into preconceived categories, but similar organization of the data will greatly aid in cultural comparison.

Like the Nahuas, the Otomís have many more spirits in their pantheon than they depict with paper images. Usually images of benevolent deities such as the Madre de la Tierra (Mother Earth) or the Sirena de la Laguna (Siren of the Lake) are not cut from paper. Lopez, in his handwritten books (see chapter 1; see also Sandstrom 1981), illustrates benevolent spirits with an undifferentiated, unidentifiable paper cutout. For example, the "Earth Mother" looks the same as the "Lord Siren" (Sandstrom 1981, pp. 66, 68), and Dios de Antigua (Ancient God) looks like Hombre Bueno (Good Man) (Sandstrom 1981, pp. 51, 30). This indicates that these important spirits do not have conventionalized images with distinguishing symbolic features. Apparently Lopez included the generalized images simply to fill blank pages in his book. Finally, the numerous Catholic saints that have been incorporated into the Otomí pantheon are never cut from paper (Dow 1982, p. 646).

Religion among the Otomís like that among the Nahuas, can best be characterized as flexible and variable. Religious practices and beliefs in any particular village depend on important factors such as economic development, the history of missionary activities in the area, the influence of neighboring villages, and the capabilities and interests of specific shamans operating at a given time. In some areas of the Sierra Norte de Puebla, the Otomís have adopted much of the official doctrine of the church, and they refuse to go to the shamans. In other areas, however, they support the traditional religion (Dow 1974, pp. 105–106). Even within a single village variation exists both in adherence to traditional beliefs and in how these traditional beliefs are understood. However, the cutting of paper images is one practice shared by all traditionally oriented Otomí villages in the region. Use of paper images implies a shared set of assumptions about the nature of the world and about the best strategies for dealing with spirits.

Otomí shamans occupy the same ambivalent status as their Nahua counterparts. They are possessors of secret knowledge that can be used to cure or kill. They are called *páti* in Otomí, which means "person of knowledge" (Dow, personal communication; Galinier 1976c, p. 166). Shamans who use their powers to destroy enemies or harm people are seen as sorcerers, and sorcerers are an intolerable presence in a village. It has been reported that as late as the mid-1960s an Otomí shaman in San Pablito was killed by fellow villagers on suspicion of practicing sorcery (Lannik, Palm, and Tatkon 1969, pp. 7–8).

The occupation of shaman is open to men or women equally, although apparently the majority are men (Dow 1975, p. 68). A person who wishes to become a shaman apprentices himself to an established person of knowledge. Signs that one should become a shaman include miraculous recovery from a disease and recurring strange dreams. The apprentice who is effective, that is, one who convinces people that the rituals work, will earn a reputation and begin to establish a clientele. The shaman must be able to carry out many different complex rituals and master the cutting of the numerous paper images that the rituals require. A renowned shaman may even create whole new rituals.

Dow (1975, p. 68) reports that shamans from neighboring Otomí villages sometimes employ the services of female vision specialists called *zidöni* or *t'ädi* in their rituals. These women are called upon because of their special ability to make contact with the spirit world. Vision specialists often ingest marijuana (Santa Rosa) to help them speak to the spirits, and during rituals they are frequently off to one side weeping hysterically. Whether shamans in the village of San Pablito also use vision specialists is not clear from the published reports. It is the shaman, in any case, who is the authority on ritual performance and the system of myths associated with rituals. The shaman's most important attributes are his ability to make contact with spirits and to control or deflect them for the benefit of other villagers.

Paper cutouts are called *dāhi* in Otomí and *muñecos* in Spanish

PLATE 1. Nahua images of seeds that have just been removed from the sacred cabinet for the observance of Xochitlalia. The figures are dressed as unmarried village girls.

PLATE 2. The shaman cuts dozens of paper images in preparation for the cleansing ritual (Figs. 20-26). Photo courtesy of Paul Jean Provost.

PLATE 3. The shaman lays out sacred plants, offerings, and paper images of *ejecatl* spirits (Figs. 20–26) around a hole symbolizing Tlaltetata, Father Earth. In his chant he lists the offerings and exhorts the disease-causing spirits to return to the underworld.

PLATE 4. The shaman has the village authorities stand inside a marigold loop as he cleanses them with a bundle containing paper figures of witness spirits (Figs. 27–30).

PLATE 5. The shaman and the village authorities set up an altar dedicated to the ancestor spirits at the top of a sacred hill. A paper sun is attached to an arch of marigolds symbolizing the sky realm. Beneath the arch are paper images of witness spirits (Figs. 27–30, 55, 59).

PLATE 6. The shaman chants before the completed altar dedicated to the ancestor spirits. Beeswax candles surround the altar, which holds food offerings and a smoking incense brazier.

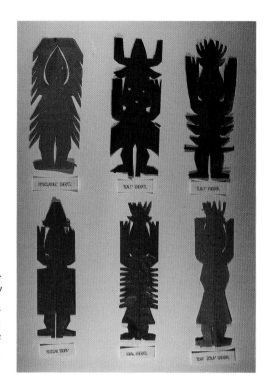

PLATE 7. Paper images of *ejecatl* spirits cut by a male shaman from the Nahua village Puyecaco (Figs. 18, 14, 16, 8, 10, 13).

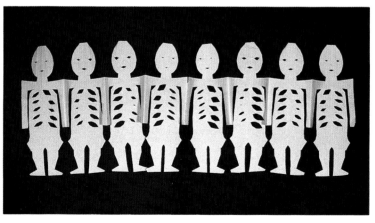

PLATE 8. A paper image of Death cut by a Nahua shaman, unfolded to show the eightfold duplication of figures (Fig. 12). Death is the only figure cut with downturned arms.

PLATE 9. A Nahua family places paper shawls on the graves of female kinsmen to keep them warm in the underworld. This is a final observance during Xantolo (Day of the Dead).

PLATE 10. A Nahua shaman pours a cane-alcohol offering on paper images of *ejecatl* spirits. The shaman is ridding a pre-Hispanic ruin of disease-causing spirits. Ruins are believed to be entranceways to the underworld.

PLATE 11. A Nahua shaman chants over an array of *ejecatl* images as her patient sits nearby (Figs. 1–7).

PLATE 12. A bark-paper image of the Otomí spirit Lord of the Night (Fig. 64). Photo courtesy of James Dow.

PLATE 13. A bark-paper image of the Otomí Spirit of the Grape (Fig. 129).

PLATE 14. A bark-paper image of the Otomí Child of the Mountain, also called Flower of Heaven (Fig. 138). The figure consists of two circles of alternating good Otomí men and women.

(Dow, personal communication). The images are brought to life by breathing into their mouths (Dow 1975, p. 64), holding them in copal smoke, or sprinkling them with *aguardiente.* Once sacralized, they become ritually powerful and potentially dangerous to nonshamans (see Galinier 1979c, p. 213 for a semantic analysis of the Otomí concepts of skin and putrescence as they relate to bark paper and the casting out of the images following a ritual). Just as among the Nahuas, the Otomí images do not represent the total spirit but rather its life-force or animating principle. When asked in Spanish about the paper images, Otomí shamans are likely to respond that they represent *espíritus* (spirits) or, in the case of seeds, *dioses* (gods). However, Dow has discovered that the term used in the Otomí language is *zaki,* which is better translated as "life-force" (Dow 1982, p. 632; 1974, p. 95). Galinier transcribes it *nzaki* (1976c, p. 161). Dow further states that *zaki* is one manifestation of the shadow-soul concept common among Middle American Indians. Fitl (1975, p. 105) uses the concepts of *zaki* and *na xudi* (shadow) to describe the life-force embodied by the paper images. Galinier states that the shadow (*shuti* in his transcription) is equivalent to the *notonal,* a Nahuatl term used widely in Middle America for "soul" (Galinier 1980b, p. 27; see also Adams and Rubel 1967, p. 336). Thus, the Otomí concept of spirit, which the paper images are cut to represent, appears to be identical to that of the Nahuas.

The Otomís, like the Nahuas, are animistic in that they attribute basic processes and events in the world to spirit beings. Dow (1982, p. 645) places the Otomí *zaki* in six fundamental categories: gods, the saints, animal companion spirits, malevolent beings, human beings, and common plants and animals. In another classification scheme seven categories are recognized: beneficial spirits; Christian saints; companion spirits; lords that are *judíos* (malevolent spirits); human beings; lords of the seeds; and lords of the mountain (Sandstrom 1981, pp. 16–19). These classifications hint at the enormous number of spirits that inhabit and animate the Otomí universe. We will discuss only the most prominent of these.

Among the more important spirits associated with the sky realm in San Pablito is Dios de Antigua, the Ancient God. This spirit is mentioned by Lopez in his description as the companion, or perhaps wife, of the Earth Mother (Sandstrom 1981, pp. 51ff.). Apparently the Ancient God was more powerful in the past and has now been replaced by Jesus Christ in the spirit hierarchy. Published sources do not specify how the Ancient God is related to other spirits in the Otomí pantheon although it is likely that he is the Dios de Sol (Sun God). Called Maka Hyadi in Otomí (Dow 1974, p. 97; 1982, p. 645), the Sun has a role in plant growth and apparently acts as a protector of the Otomís during the daytime (Lenz 1973 [1948], p. 122; see figure 150). The Sun and Jesus Christ have become thoroughly syncretized among the Otomís, and the cross symbol now strictly signifies the Sun in rituals. The Ancient God-Sun-Jesus Christ complex is remarkably similar to the Nahua Toteotsi-Sun-Jesus Christ connection (see also Galinier 1976c, p. 164; 1979a, p. 137).

Another important spirit among the Otomís is Grandfather Fire, called Maka Xita Sibi (Dow 1982, p. 645). According to Otomí belief, Fire carries a walking stick and accompanies the Sun on its daily course. It is associated with the three stones surrounding the household cooking fire and is believed to protect household members (Christensen 1952–53, p. 267; Lenz 1973 [1948], p. 126; Dow 1974, p. 99; 1975, p. 61; 1982, p. 645). An alternate name for Grandfather Fire is Dios de Tequil, Hearth God. Dow sees a connection between this spirit and the Aztec deity Huehueteotl (1974, p. 99). In some Otomí villages, however, the fire spirit apparently is believed to be associated with death and evil (Galinier 1976c, pp. 164, 169). The Otomís also recognize a moon spirit, although no published reports detail its character or connection to other spirits (Dow 1982, p. 645). It is likely that the moon is associated with fertility, menstruation problems, and dangerous spirits of the night (Lenz 1973 [1948], p. 122; Galinier 1976c, p. 164; 1980b, p. 27). The Otomís also recognize Oja, a high god that is clearly of Christian origin (Dow 1974, p. 97).

In most Otomí villages an inventory of Catholic saints has been added to the traditional pantheon. Saints are often syncretized with Otomí spirits, making it difficult to separate the two. Probably most Otomís do not perceive Christianity to be antithetical to their traditional beliefs, but rather see it as a parallel system of *costumbres* (rituals). Catholic saints are called *zidāhmū*, "revered great lords" (Dow 1974, pp. 104ff.). Images of the saints are displayed in churches, in small shrines called *oratorios*, or on home altars (see Galinier 1976c). The priest, who may visit a village once a year, is viewed as a ritual specialist who has power and knowledge in a different system. In fact many Otomís refer to the celebration of the Mass as simply the *costumbre para iglesias* or "ritual for churches" (Fitl 1975, p. 199).

Christian practices in San Pablito surround the saints' statues in the local church. In smaller Otomí villages (the population of San Pablito is about seventeen hundred) the celebrations may center on the individual shrines. The saints' days are celebrated in San Pablito with feasting and ritual activity sponsored by village volunteers. Three or four sponsors called *mayordomos* support each saint. Their term of office lasts for one year, and they are expected to pay all expenses for the proper celebration of their saint. The focus of each celebration is a villagewide feast provided by the *mayordomos*, the primary purpose of which is to seek the blessing and protection of the saints. Obligations and expenses that the *mayordomos* share are called the *cargo*, and the more onerous the *cargo*, the greater the prestige attached to it. One of the major means of increasing one's prestige in San Pablito is through the *mayordomo* system. For more on the cargo system of San Pablito see Kaupp (1975), Christensen (1942), and Sandstrom (1981).

The Otomís, like the Nahuas, have a complex view of the earth and its associated spirit pantheon. In its positive aspect, the earth is called Madre de la Tierra (Earth Mother) or Reina de la Tierra Buena (Queen of the Good Earth or Hmuho'i in Otomí according to Galinier 1976c, pp. 164, 169; 1979a, p. 137; Sandstrom 1981, pp. 49ff.). In this guise the earth nurtures the crops and makes life possible. Kaupp (1975, p. 189) reports that the Earth Mother is married to the Ancient God mentioned earlier. On the negative side, the earth's sister or alter ego, called in Otomí Mū Ximhäi (Reina de la Tierra Mala or Queen of the Bad Earth), is jealous of their marriage and takes her vengence on human beings (see figure 60). Moctezuma, called Maka Häi in Otomí (or the Spanish Tierra Sagrada, Sacred Earth, or Santosoma in some other highland Otomí villages), is another dangerous aspect of the earth (Dow 1974, p. 97; Galinier 1976c, p. 165; see figure 67). Moctezuma demands payment from farmers and others who use the earth and consumes the corpses of the newly buried. Among the Otomís, Moctezuma leads disease-causing spirits and represents a constant danger to the human community (Dow 1974, p. 97; 1982, p. 645; see also citations following figure 67). One offering associated with Moctezuma is the live burial of a sacrificial fowl (Dow 1975, p. 68; 1974, p. 97).

Another spirit associated with the earth is Maka Me (Sacred Lady). According to Dow (1974, p. 97), the spirit is identified with the Virgin Mary and generalized fertility, and it may thus be equivalent to the Nahua Tonantsi. Living in sacred caves and obviously related to Maka Me are the spirits of the seeds (Lenz 1973 [1948], p. 126). These spirits control crop growth and are arranged in a loosely structured hierarchy, with the Spirit of Corn ranked first (Fitl 1975, p. 106; Dow 1982, p. 645; Christensen 1963, pp. 365–66). Other spirits connected with the earth include the Spirit of the Field, which is associated with the growing crops (Christensen 1952, p. 267; 1963, p. 364; 1971, p. 29); the Spirit of the House, which may be connected to the Hearth Spirit of the celestial realm (Christensen 1952, p. 267; 1963, p. 364; 1971, p. 31); Ma Yoho Nija (Two-Shrine), who lives in a cave and sends rain (Sandstrom 1981, pp. 58ff.; Galinier 1976c, pp. 169–70); Yogi, Nyogi, or Bo'mëti (Antiguos or Ancient Ones), terms that are applied to major non-Christian spirits but which also apply to small, prehistoric figurines that represent the lesser spirits (Dow 1974, p. 99; 1975, p. 67; Galinier 1976c, p. 162); and Señor del Monte, the Lord of the Mountain and his bird messengers.

The Otomís also share with many other Indian groups in Middle America the belief that each person has an animal companion. Called *rogi* in Otomí, the animal and its human partner are believed to have identical destinies; whatever happens to one will also befall the other. This belief is called *tonalism*, a term derived from the Nahuatl word *notonal* (refer to chapter 4). Most humans are unable to identify their own *rogi*, even if they should catch a glimpse of it in the forest. Ritual specialists, however, are able to recognize and even control their animal companions. The cougar, jaguar, and eagle are typical companion spirits of shamans, while the fox and owl are companions of sorcerers. If sorcery is suspected in an illness, the shaman will magically send out his *rogi* to do battle with the sorcerer's *rogi*. In some cases the shaman cuts an image he identifies as the patient's *rogi* from paper and includes it in the curing ceremony (Dow 1974, p. 102; 1975, pp. 60ff.; 1982, p. 646; see also figure 148). A similar idea has been reported among the Nahuas of the region, but apparently it is not found among the Tepehuas.

The Otomís also conduct rituals to placate spirits associated with the water realm. The most important of these is Maka Xumpö Dehe, the Lady of the Water (Dow 1982, p. 645; 1974, p. 98; see Galinier 1976c, p. 165 for an alternate name). This spirit is probably the same as the Sirena de la Laguna (Siren of the Lake) and the Spirit of the Well, both of which are reported from San Pablito. The Lady of the Water controls aquatic animals and brings rain and fertility to the fields. It is also associated with the seed spirits, although the precise connection is unclear (Dow 1974, p. 99). The ritual described by Frederick Starr in which a pilgrimage was made to a sacred lake apparently was held to placate the Lady of the Water (see chapter 1). This spirit is related to Mahā The, the Sirena Mala (Wicked Siren) who controls the spirits *(zaki)* of people who suffered unfortunate, water-related deaths. The Sirena Mala demands offerings in return for withholding the vengeance of these disease-causing spirits (see figure 68). Another spirit apparently associated with both the good and bad aspects of the water is Santa Rosa (Sacred Rose), which is synonymous in the region with marijuana (Knab 1979b, pp. 224ff.; Galinier 1976c, p. 169; see figure 153). Water spirits are often implicated in curing rituals since they can both capture people's souls and send out disease-causing spirits.

In the underworld the *zaki* of people who die natural deaths live alongside a series of malevolent spirits of somewhat higher rank called the jews *(judíos)*. For the most part, people who die peacefully and naturally pose no threat to the living if they are given their due compensation during Todos Santos. Those who die unnatural deaths, for example by being murdered, are doomed to wander about the earth like rabid animals, wreaking vengeance upon the living. The unfortunates are called *los aires* (the airs), and they are among the primary causes of disease (Dow 1974, pp. 100–101; 1982, p. 646). The appellation "jew" is obviously a legacy of the nearly five centuries of teaching by Christian missionaries who portrayed historic Jews as evil beings. The Indians are clearly unaware that there are contemporary people who call themselves Jews. For this reason we write the Otomí term for these spirits in lower case. The jews are sometimes labeled *diablos* (devils), and at other times they are called *malos aires* (bad airs) (Fitl 1975, p. 118; Lenz 1973 [1948], p. 122). More will be said about the nature of these spirits in the section immediately following.

The Otomí pantheon is complex and difficult to classify. The problem is exacerbated by the incomplete and scattered nature of the ethnographic reports available. Table 5 summarizes the information presented here and, as previously mentioned, is largely based on data from San Pablito. The list of spirits has an Otomí stamp, but it is difficult to overlook the remarkable similarity to the Nahua pantheon (summarized in table 2). Specific correspondences between the two religious systems will be discussed in the concluding chapter. Examination of Otomí paper images reveals additional similarities between these groups.

TABLE 5. The Otomí Pantheon

Realms of the Universe and Associated Spirits
(Predominantly from San Pablito)

(Sky)

    Maka Hyadi (Sun, Jesus); also
        Dios de Antigua (Ancient God)
        Oja (Christian God)
    Maka Xita Sibi (Grandfather Fire); also
        Dios de Tequil (Hearth God)
    Zidāhmū (Catholic saints)
    Moon

(Earth)

    Hmuho'i (Queen of the Good Earth); also
        Madre de la Tierra (Earth Mother)
    Maka Häi (devouring Earth, Moctezuma); also
        Tierra Sagrada (Sacred Earth)
    Maka Me (Sacred Lady)
    Seeds
    Spirit of the Field
    Spirit of the House
    Ma Yoho Nija (Two-Shrine)
    Mū Xandöhu (Lord of the Mountain)
    Yogi (Ancient Ones)
    Rogi (companion spirits of human beings)

(Underworld)   According to San Pablito Otomí myth the jews currently live in the underworld, although it is clear that some originated in other realms

    Judíos (devils, *malos aires*)
        Mū Ximhäi (Queen of the Bad Earth) (associated with the earth)
        Ra Ze'mi Nge Ra Nitū (President of Hell)
        Ra Zitū (Devil or Lord Devil)
        Ra Hāi Nge Ra Juda (Lord Jew or Jew Person)
        Mū Xūi (Lord of the Night)
        Mū Huei (Lord of Lightning)
        Mū Ngäni (Lord of Thunder)

TABLE 5. *Continued*

Ra Mantezoma (Montezuma) (associated with the earth)
Mahā The (Water Lady or Wicked Siren) (associated with the water)
Mū Behkuni (Lord Rainbow or Rainbow)
Ra Puni (Nagual or Lord Nagual)
Ra Nedäni Nge Hin Bi Yö Ra Ñā (Bull Snout
  that Does Not Respect [Parents])
Ra Nefani Nge Hin Bi Yö Ra Ñā (Horse Snout
  that Does Not Respect [Parents])
Ya Yägi (Lightning Bolts or Lord of Lightning Bolts)
Zaki (Life-force, Spirits of the dead)

(Water)

Maka Xumpö Dehe (Lady of the Water); also
  Sirena de la Laguna (Siren of the Lake)
  Spirit of the Well
Santa Rosa (Marijuana)
Zaki (Life-force, Spirits of the dead)

OTOMÍ DISEASE-CAUSING SPIRITS

Disease among the Otomís is attributed to many different causes (see Sandstrom 1981, pp. 11ff.), the most common of which is attack by malevolent spirits. People may be attacked by the *aires,* spirits of people who died unnatural deaths, or by the class of spirits called *judíos.* The *judíos,* in fact, are even called *espíritus de ataque,* "attack spirits," and they are believed to cause a category of illness called "attack diseases" *(ataques)* (Sandstrom 1981, p. 26). The precise status of the *judíos* relative to the *aires* is not clear. Dow (1982, p. 646) indicates that the *judíos* lead the *aires,* while Lenz (1973 [1948], p. 122) implies that at least some *judíos* are the *aires* themselves. In fact, several of the *judíos* are the spirits of people who died unnatural deaths (see figures 69, 71, and 72). Other *judíos,* however, appear actually to lead or control *aires* (see figures 61, 64, 65, and 67). One *judío,* called Lord Nagual (figure 70), stands out from the rest since it is considered to be a human sorcerer transformed into an animal or, alternatively, the *rogi* of a sorcerer (Dow, personal communication).

The diversity of the *judíos* can be explained if it is kept in mind that the category in which they are included is the creation of a single shaman, Santos García. He seems to have taken traditional spirits from the Otomí pantheon and grouped them according to their malevolent attributes. He called this category Señores de los Judíos (Lords That Are Jews), and his innovation has been carried on by his son and other shamans in San Pablito. His manner of portraying the *judíos* also appears to be highly innovative since they have features not found in any other of the paper cuttings from the region. There are fourteen malevolent *judíos* in a complete set. They are reproduced in figures 60–73. Like the *ejecatl* among the Nahuas, each individual spirit has its own story and symbolic representation. In the case of the *judíos*, however, the conceptions are particularly elaborate and detailed.

Figure 60
Mū Ximhäi, Reina de la Tierra Mala,
    Queen of the Bad Earth
Bark paper
21× 14.5 cm

This dangerous, disease-causing spirit is surrounded by four serpents who are her spirit helpers. Her sister is the beneficent Madre Tierra, Earth Mother, who is married to the powerful Otomí deity Dios de Antigua, Ancient God. Jealousy over her sister's marriage has caused the Queen of the Bad Earth to vent her rage on human beings. It has been suggested that this spirit is a modern Otomí version of the classical Aztec deity Coatlicue (She of the Serpent Skirts), who was associated with the earth (Fitl 1975, p. 143; Dow 1982, p. 645; Kaupp 1975, p. 189).

Figure 61
Ra Ze'mi Nge Ra Nitū, Presidente
  del Infierno, President of Hell
Bark paper
21 × 14.5 cm

The spirit portrayed in figure 61 is the leader of all the harmful
and dangerous spirits who inhabit the underworld. As such it
is the most powerful among them and is distinguished from the
others by its wings. In addition, the spirit is cut with a single
horn protruding from the forehead, a hideous beaklike mouth,
and pointed tongue. The tail signifies the animallike nature of
the President of Hell. Lord Devil, Señor de Judío, and Lord
of the Night are the spirit's most important assistants (Fitl
1975, p. 134; Sandstrom 1981, p. 34; Kaupp 1975, p. 190).

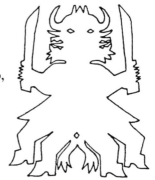

Figure 62
Ra Zitū (Devil), Señor Diablo,
  Lord Devil
Bark paper
21 × 15.5 cm

This figure is the companion of Señor de Judío (figure 63) and
is portrayed with horns above the nose, a tail, and a machete
in each hand. Lord Devil, along with his companions, searches
out people who like to fight. Should death result from a fight,
Lord Devil dines on the flesh of the victim. His sharply pointed

tongue encourages people who like to fight to destroy each other (Fitl 1975, p. 140; Kaupp 1975, p. 191; Dow 1975, p. 62; Sandstrom 1981, p. 34).

Figure 63
Ra Hāi Nge Ra Juda (Jew Person),
    Señor de Judío, Lord Jew
Bark paper
15.5 × 10.5 cm

Lord Jew accompanies Lord Devil (figure 62) in his quest for people who are fighting. This spirit is particularly happy if the row involves knives or machetes because of the increased possibility of death. When there is a death, Lord Jew drinks the blood of the victim. He is portrayed with a bald head, an upturned pointed nose, a goatee, a tail, and a machete. His stomach is distended by numerous grisly feasts (Fitl 1975, p. 139; Kaupp 1975, p. 189 [calls this spirit Judas]; Sandstrom 1981, pp. 34–35).

Figure 64
Mū Xūi, Señor de la Noche,
    Lord of the Night
Bark paper
20.5 × 15 cm

This frightening figure guards the doorway to the underworld where the malevolent spirits live. Between 11:00 P.M. and 1:00

A.M. he discharges these spirits to wander over the earth in search of victims. The harmful nature of the Lord of the Night is indicated by pointed teeth, a tongue, and the beard. The tail, the heavy boots he wears, and the machete attached to the wrists give further proof of his dangerous character (see color plate 12) (Fitl 1975, p. 144; Kaupp 1975, p. 190; Dow 1982, p. 646; Sandstrom 1981, p. 36).

Figure 65
Mū Huei, Señor de Relámpago,
    Lord of Lightning
Bark paper
20.5 × 15 cm

The tail and fingertips of this figure symbolize lightning bolts, and the protrusions from each side represent thunderclaps. This dangerous spirit is the companion of the Lord of Thunder (figure 66), which is why thunder and lightning always accompany each other. The Lord of Lightning has a bet with the Lord of Thunder that the latter can not catch up with him. Should he be caught, the Lord of Lightning will destroy all of the people on earth. This wager explains why a lightning flash always precedes a thunderclap. When not playing deadly games, this spirit lights the way for other malevolent spirits (Fitl 1975, p. 131; Kaupp 1975, p. 191; Dow 1975, p. 62; Sandstrom 1981, p. 37).

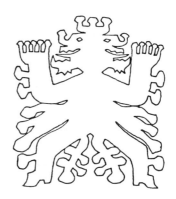

Figure 66
Mū Ngäni, Señor de Trueno,
  Lord of Thunder
Bark paper
20.5 × 14.5 cm

Companion to the Lord of Lightning (figure 65) and the Lord
of Lightning Bolts (figure 73), this spirit is portrayed surrounded
by ball-like thunderclaps. Even the fingertips, the three-pronged
crown, and the end of the nose are rounded as a symbolic
device to represent thunder. The Lord of Thunder chases the
Lord of Lightning, trying to catch him and win their bet.
If he succeeds, human beings will be destroyed. The spirit
scares people with his booming voice (Fitl 1975, p. 133; Kaupp
1975, p. 191; Dow 1975, p. 62; 1982, p. 646; Lenz 1973
[1948], p. 126; Sandstrom 1981, p. 37).

Figure 67
Ra Mantezoma, Moctezuma, Montezuma
Bark paper
21.5 × 14.5 cm

The spirit in figure 67 may derive from the historical figure
of Moctezuma Xocoyotzin, one of the last Aztec emperors.
While emperor, he conquered many surrounding Indian groups,
including several in the Huasteca region (see chapter 3). The

historical person may have symbolically entered the Otomí
religious system as a dangerous spirit. Portrayed as bald and
carrying a machete, Moctezuma commands all of the diseases
conveyed by the Wicked Siren (figure 68) and Rainbow (figure
69). This spirit lives underground and is closely associated with
the earth in one of its dangerous, devouring aspects. Sometimes called Maka Häi in Otomí or Santasoma in Spanish,
this figure is cut by shamans for use in curing and cleansing
ceremonies (Fitl 1975, pp. 135, 160; Kaupp 1975, p. 186; Dow
1975, pp. 61–62; Lenz 1973 [1948], pp. 122ff.; Sandstrom
1981, p. 38).

Figure 68
Mahā The (Water Lady), Sirena Mala,
    Wicked Siren
Bark paper
15 × 10.5 cm

The Wicked Siren lives in the rivers and is responsible for all
water-related accidents or diseases. She has the habit of knock-
ing people down when they try to cross rivers or streams, and
drowning victims are often said to have gotten tangled in her
bushy tail. She is in league with Thunder (figure 66) and
Lightning (figure 65) and is believed to consume all of the
offerings thrown out after a cure. She is portrayed with flipper-
like hands, an upturned nose, and grossly exaggerated lips,
tongue, and teeth (Fitl 1975, p. 129; Kaupp 1975, p. 189;
Sandstrom 1981, p. 41).

Figure 69
Mū Behkuni (Lord Rainbow),
   Arco Iris, Rainbow
Bark paper
20.5 × 14.5 cm

This paper cutting represents the spirit of a woman who died in childbirth. Angry at having lost her life, she roams about inflicting sickness on pregnant women. An Otomí woman expecting a child will call a shaman to protect her from attacks by Rainbow. The arch over her head contains a crown and oval-shaped symbolic thunderclaps, and the small figures on either side of the arch are ungrateful, troublesome children, the products of a difficult birth. These figures are sometimes interpreted as bad children who have become Horse Snout spirits (see figure 72). Thunderclaps protrude from her sides. Shamans are careful to include this spirit in all cures so it will not feel neglected and attack birthing women (Fitl 1975, p. 128; Kaupp 1975, p. 191; Dow 1975, p. 62; 1982, p. 646; Sandstrom 1981, p. 39).

Figure 70
Ra Puni (Nagual), Señor Nagual,
   Lord Nagual
Bark paper
15.5 × 10 cm

Lord Nagual is a flying sorcerer who attacks people walking

on trails at dusk or at night. It is sometimes called a transforming sorcerer because of the widespread belief that human
sorcerers can turn themselves into *naguals* at will. This dangerous spirit is sent by the President of Hell to suck the blood of a
newborn infant. To protect their infants, parents hang a pair
of scissors over the house entrance or place two crossed needles
over the baby's cradle. When the spirit approaches, it will
impale itself on the trap and die. Lord Nagual is portrayed with
wings, an upturned nose, and exaggerated lips, teeth and tongue
(Fitl 1975, p. 141; Kaupp 1975, pp. 157, 191; Dow 1974, p.
101; 1982, p. 646; Sandstrom 1981, p. 40).

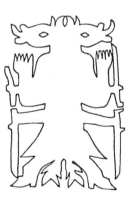

Figure 71
Ra Nedäni Nge Hin Bi Yö Ra Nā
   (Bull Snout That Does
   Not Respect Parents),
   Trompa de Toro que No Respeta,
   Bull Snout that Does Not Respect
Bark paper
15 × 10.5 cm

The Bull Snout is the spirit of a man who did not show respect for anyone, particularly his mother and father. His lack
of respect caused him to die of a terrible disease and his spirit
to wander about as the Bull Snout. Before dying his nostrils
enlarged, his tongue stuck out, and his eyes bulged, thus producing this ugly spirit. Difficult children, thieves, and mur-
derers can also be represented by cutting this figure. The spirit
is portrayed with an animal's head and four machetes to indicate the danger it poses to all humans (Fitl 1975, pp. 137,
150; Christensen 1971, p. 23; Kaupp 1975, p. 192; Sandstrom
1981, p. 42).

Figure 72
Ra Nefani Nge Hin Bi Yö Ra Ñā
  (Horse Snout That Does
  Not Respect Parents),
  Trompa de Caballo que No Respeta,
  Horse Snout that Does Not Respect
Bark paper
21 × 14.5 cm

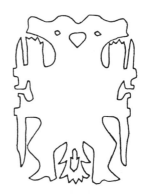

The Horse Snout is the spirit of a woman who did not show respect to her parents. During her death agony, her tongue and eyes stuck out and she took on the appearance of a horse. Her spirit wanders around in this form, causing disease and death. The spirit is portrayed as a human figure with the head of a horse (Fitl 1975, pp. 138, 150; Kaupp 1975, p. 192; Sandstrom 1981, p. 43).

Figure 73
Ya Yägi (Lightning Bolts), Señor de
  los Rayos, Lord of Lightning Bolts
Bark paper
21 × 14.5 cm

This spirit is related to the Lord of Lightning (figure 65), although why the Otomís have different spirits for lightning bolts and lightning is unclear. The harmful nature of the Lord of Lightning Bolts is indicated by the goatee, exaggerated tongue and teeth, the animal tail, and the boots and machetes. It provides light for other bad spirits, and helps Thunder (figure 66) by cutting a course through the sky with its machetes (Fitl 1975, p. 132; Kaupp 1975, p. 189; Dow 1982, p. 646).

Taken as group, the *judíos* represent virtually the gamut of antisocial characteristics: jealousy, fighting, and disrespect; feasting on human blood and flesh; attacking infants and pregnant women; and delivering disease into the village. The *judíos* both manifest and are stimulated by behavior that contradicts the norms of Otomí society. In this sense they are remarkably like the Nahua *ejecatl* spirits who pollute an otherwise harmonious world. Like the *ejecatl*, they are closely associated with spirits of the dead. At night they emerge from the underworld (*infierno*), loosed upon the earth by the Lord of the Night. The curing ritual through which the *judíos* are dispelled is called the *hokwi* or *maxi*, which means "cleansing" or "sweeping clean" (Dow, personal communication). In short, they are conceived of and symbolically manipulated in much the same way as the Nahua *ejecatl* spirits.

What is remarkable in these figures is the way the shaman communicates the dangerous and alien character of the *judíos*. Some are symbolically connected to powerful natural phenomena such as thunder and lightning. Others have animal heads, tails, or wings attached to human bodies, thus creating half-human monsters. Even more interesting is the way the shaman uses frightening interethnic relations to define these dangerous spirits. Each figure wears heavy boots associated with the world of the *mestizo*. This is reinforced by the bald heads and the goatees, which occur far more commonly among outsiders than among the Indians. So that no ambiguity remains in communicating the threatening nature of these spirits, the shaman portrays them with machetes and grossly exaggerated teeth, tongues, and lips. Unlike the *ejecatl* cutouts, the danger is graphically represented here. Perhaps for this reason, the duplication often found in Nahua images is absent in the Otomí ones. Also the double profile of each figure is probably meant to signify that these spirits are ever-watching (compare with figures 75–80, the intermediary or messenger spirits). With the exception of the lion (figure 148), these are the only specimens we have that are cut in profile; all others are *en face*. The bodies of the *judíos* appear front faced, although there is a degree of ambiguity in this. Figures 61 and 62 have four legs, and several others have two tails, which implies that the bodies are meant to be in profile like the heads. (For information on the topic of frontality in pre-Hispanic art see Klein 1976, and for a further discussion of frontality as it relates to the paper images see chapter 7.)

Unfortunately we do not have sets of disease-causing figures cut by other Otomí shamans to compare with the one presented here. While it may be premature to generalize about the *judíos*, several observations can be made. First, it is interesting to note the greater degree to which Christianity has influenced these images compared with those cut by the Nahuas. The identity of the Devil, Señor de Judío, and the President of Hell undoubtedly came from the Christian tradition. Second, the *judíos* are cut from bark paper, which makes the use of color symbolism impossible. Even the pattern witnessed in the past of reserving dark paper for dangerous spirits and light paper for beneficial ones is not followed consistently. Finally, as mentioned earlier, the *judíos* have elaborate histories which the shaman recites, whereas among the Nahuas only a few words are said about each cutting. It is likely that the introduction of Christian elements, the indiscriminate use of both light and dark paper, and the more elaborate stories told about each paper image result from attempts to sell the images to tourists. In sum the spirits represented by the paper images are authentically Otomí, but the portrayal may have been influenced by the desire to make them more comprehensible to potential customers.

AN OTOMÍ RITUAL

To illustrate how the paper images are used, we include the following description of an Otomí curing ritual. The major description is provided by Señor Antonio Lopez, an Otomí shaman from San Pablito. He and Alfonso García write descriptions of cures, rain ceremonies, and other rituals in small books they make from bark paper and offer for sale in the tourist markets. What follows is an exerpted version of a cure taken from Lopez's manuscript entitled "La historía de la cura-

ción antiguo de San Pablito, Pahuatlan, Pue." ("An Account of
Ancient Curing Practices of San Pablito, Pahuatlan, Puebla").
For a complete account of this and another ritual, see Sandstrom
(1981). Additional information on curing procedures from the
published works of several ethnographers supplements the following account (also see Lenz 1973 [1948], pp. 123ff. for a
description of another San Pablito curing ceremony).

Religious Ceremony to Counteract Sorcery

Lopez begins his account with a statement about one cause of
disease and the first steps necessary to a successful cure. "The
people who truly believe in the ancient customs hold a ceremony to counteract diseases caused by sorcery. Such diseases
are called [spirit] attacks. To treat the disease, one has to
call a curer *(curandero)*, who will perform a divination."

The Divination and Preparation

"The curer goes to ask the Heart of the Mountain which type
of sorcery is causing the disease. He counters the sorcery by
making an offering. First he cuts out 24 bark paper beds
[figures 144–45]. Then he cuts out 24 harmful spirits of people
who were violently killed either by pistol, machete, or knife
[figure 146]. Next he cuts out 24 good spirits of people who
died from fever, vomiting, or dysentery [figure 147]. Finally,
he cuts out 24 harmful spirits called *judíos* [see figures 60–73]."

The Cleansing

Lopez goes on to describe some major features of a cure in
the village of San Pablito.

First, the curer lays out some of the beds in a square inside the
patient's house. Next, he lays out some of the paper images on the
beds. He sprinkles four drops of *aguardiente* over the paper and lights
four cigarettes for the *judíos* to smoke. He pricks a live chicken and
the blood falls on the paper images. Next, he pours out more
aguardiente to baptize the jews and then he begins to chant. The

curer then lights four candles to illuminate the way for all the jews and other spirits who will be driven from the house.

Next, the curer makes a small chair-like altar out of wood called a *tlapexque*. He places a candle at each of the four corners of the *tlapexque* and then lays out 12 bark paper beds between them. Upon these he lays cutouts of harmful spirits including the jews. Then he baptizes the jews with *aguardiente*, after which he places some of them outside of the house.

Now the curer makes a hoop from a wooden rod [called a *rueda de ataque*, "attack wheel"; see Christensen 1952, p. 266] and ties paper cutouts of the jews to it. He instructs the violinist and guitarist to begin playing, which they will do until the ceremony is completed. Then he hangs the hoop from the roof by a cord. As the curer sings [chants] to it, a helper lowers the hoop four times to the patient who is lying on the floor. Next, the curer cleanses the patient after which the hoop is raised up. This signals the end of this part of the ritual.

Two assistants now roll up the spirit beds and form a bundle. This bundle is placed on the *tlapexque* before the curer takes it and throws it into the ravine. Everything causing the patient's illness remains in the bundle. Upon leaving the patient's house to dispose of the bundle the curer begins to sing and the musicians accompany him to the ravine.

Lopez skips over several important features of the curing ritual, perhaps because they seem too obvious to mention. For example, a common means by which Otomí shamans divine the cause of an illness is to read patterns in copal incense smoke (Christensen 1942, p. 114; Fitl 1975, p. 173; Kaupp 1975, pp. 142–43). Copal smoke for the Otomís, as for the Nahuas, is an important sacralizing agent used throughout a ritual (Lannik, Palm, and Tatkon 1969, p. 14). Lopez also neglects to mention the food offering that forms part of all curing procedures (Fitl 1975, p. 173). While he does mention baptizing the *judíos* with *aguardiente*, he does not indicate that it is drunk by the participants during the cure (Spranz 1961, p. 54) nor that it is sprayed from the mouth of the shaman over the paper images at the four corners of the home (Fitl 1975, p. 173). The shaman also dances and jumps over the display of paper images (Christensen 1942, p. 114; 1963, p. 364; 1971, p. 28; Fitl 1975, p. 173; Lannik, Palm, and Tatkon 1969, p. 14). In addition, the bundle of paper images, offerings, and adornments is rubbed over the patient and taken around the house to absorb the bad spirits (Christensen 1942, p. 114; Fitl 1975, pp. 173, 176). Finally, Lopez does not mention the thorny twig, which is a common offering to the *judíos* (Kaupp 1975, p. 147; Fitl 1975, p. 176).

Ceremony to the Lord of the Mountain

This ritual is usually part of a major cure, although it can also be held independently. The ceremony is addressed to the Lord of the Mountain (figure 74), the Lord of the Tree, and the Queen of the [Good?] Earth, all of whom help people who make offerings to them. The curer must first divine a good day for the offering. The patient provides the bark paper, and the curer cuts the figures four days before the ritual. On the day of the ritual, the curer goes into the forest and makes two small altars.

In his manuscript Lopez does not describe the ritual itself, but he does list the items required: twenty-four bark paper beds (like figure 145); two Little Birds of the Mountain (figure 76); twenty-four shirts of the Lord of the Tree; Napkins of the Mountain (figures 140–41); *tlapanco* flowers; two Spirits of the Water; one Spirit of the Patient (figure 149); twenty-four bunches of marigolds *(cempoalxochitl);* eight lions (figure 148); tortillas; cornmeal figures of marbles (?), stars, and eagles; four candles; incense; two chicken eggs; and a cornmeal figure of a turkey.

The following brief description of the Ceremony to the Lord of the Mountain is provided by Fitl.

> [The shaman] leaves the village with the *"muñecos"* and the offerings to visit the place of sacrifice for the "Lord of the Mountain" in the forest. Once there he builds a *"tlapexque"* [from the Nahuatl *tepextli,* "bed"] over which he spreads the Napkin of the Mountain. He places the offerings, the *"camas,"* the *"leones"* and the figure *"hombre"* [Spirit of the Patient] on the "Napkin." He stretches a string between the trees around the altar and fastens the "Little Birds of the Mountain" to it. The [Little Birds] have

the task to keep all the *"aires"* and evil spirits from the place of sacrifice. Then [the shaman] reaches for the [live] chickens and cuts their throats and allows the blood to drip on the figures and the offerings. He implores the "Lord of the Mountain" to protect the [patient] in his life and to accept the offerings as consideration. This ends the ritual and [the shaman] returns to the village (1975, p. 179).

Other ethnographers report that this ritual also includes a trip to the top of the mountain, where additional offerings are made to the Lord of the Mountain (Lannik, Palm, and Tatkon 1969, p. 15; Christensen 1971, p. 34).

Lopez explains that the Lord of the Mountain is a "true god" who guards the spirits of all people. He particularly protects humans from hunger and from falling. He also has messengers who help people and who watch over babies from the time they are born. If the proper offerings are not made, however, the Lord of the Mountain will become angry and will send diseases via his messengers. A curer must then be consulted in order to placate him.

Ceremony to the Earth Mother

Another ritual sequence Lopez refers to in conjunction with a curing is the ceremony to the Earth Mother. "The ceremony for making offerings to the Earth Mother begins with a Catholic prayer, 'In the name of the Father, and of the Son and of the Holy Spirit, so said my Lord Jesus Christ. Pardon us here on earth for we are about to offer a little cornmeal and bark paper to the Earth Mother.'"

According to Lopez, offerings to the Earth Mother include twenty-four beds, a little chocolate *atole*, some cacao *atole* with raw sugar, two roasted chickens, a few sweets, cooked eggs, and peanut *mole*. Lopez states, "The shaman paints the spirit bed with turkey blood for the Earth Mother. She will deliver some of it to the Ancient Lord who sends the rain for the crops. A long time ago the Ancient Lord and Earth Mother were rulers but that was before the birth of Our Lord Jesus Christ, who usurped their power [*lo quito el poder*]."

Lopez continues, "Thus the Lord Jesus Christ now rules all of the earth and commands everything. But, to cure disease, the curer adorns the altars of the Earth Mother and the Ancient Lord, because it is the Earth Mother who still commands disease. The shaman does it also to remember the old gods who supported us for all the times past, for so many years."

Interestingly, Fitl includes an account from Alfonso García of the ceremony to the Earth Mother that is almost identical to Lopez's description (1975, pp. 198–99). A prominent part of the description she records also includes reference to Christian elements and to the power of the Earth Mother to send disease if she is neglected. According to Fitl's information, this ritual is seldom practiced any longer.

Unfortunately no detailed description and analysis of a curing ritual from San Pablito has been published. There are several general descriptions, however, and it is from these that we have supplemented the account of Antonio Lopez. We wanted to include a ritual from San Pablito because it was here that Starr first saw the paper images and because most of the images included in this chapter are from the village. Although Lopez appears to present three separate rituals, it is clear that they go together, just as the Nahua ritual described earlier is composed of two sequences. Here, just as among the Nahuas, a cleansing episode precedes the offering made to beneficial spirits.

Paper Images and the Ritual

In addition to similarities in the structure of the Otomí and Nahua rituals described, the Otomís also share with the Nahuas the list of basic ritual components: paper images are the focus of ritual activity; the images are arranged on altars that are set up as appropriate places for the spirits; offerings are communicated to the spirits by manipulating the appropriate paper images and through chanting by the shaman; and, finally, spirits are controlled using the strategy of obligating them through offerings. The basic technique for removing the *judíos* can be reduced to three steps: first, the paper images are arranged on the altar; second, offerings are dedicated to them; and third, the images are physically removed.

While the fundamental structures and elements of Otomí and Nahua rituals are remarkably similar, there are differences between the two groups. For one thing, the Otomís do not appear to destroy the paper images of the *judíos*. The images are wrapped up in a bundle for cleansing the patient and his surroundings, and afterwards the shaman simply casts the bundle into a ravine. The Nahuas by contrast destroy the images of the *ejecatl* spirits following a curing ceremony. A second difference is that the Otomís apparently do not have witness spirits per se, but rather make offerings directly to mountain spirits. These are the Lord of the Mountain and his messengers. Nahua shamans make offerings to guardian ancestors (Itecu) via witness spirits who act as intermediaries. The Otomís, in contrast, do not seem to regard ancestors as guardian spirits, and, in addition, they address the Lord of the Tree and the Queen of the [Good] Earth in curing rituals, neither of whom is part of the Nahua curing ritual. Finally, the Otomí shaman uses the "attack wheel" and small images made from cornmeal, ritual features that are not shared by the Nahuas.

Many of these apparent differences, however, probably are the result of innovations of individual shamans and, thus, do not indicate a radical departure from a shared world view. It is likely that spirits addressed by the Otomís are found among Nahuas but by different names, even in Spanish. Both the Otomís and the Nahuas look to hill spirits as protectors, and the rituals of both groups suggest a close association between disease-causing spirits and the earth. The Nahua shaman pours offerings into a hole dedicated to the earth, and the Otomí describes an offering to the Earth Mother. Although the *judíos* and the *ejecatl* spirits are not precisely equivalent, both are associated with, or are actual spirits of, the dead. The lack of detail in Lopez's description obscures other similarities with the Nahuas. For example, the use of the marigold hoop to cleanse patients is a technique used by Otomí shamans. The ritual described in chapter 2, led by an Otomí, includes this technique.

One interesting feature of Lopez's description is the way he writes about the influence of Christianity in Otomí religion. Lopez sees the coming of Christianity as a supplanting of the traditional deities by Jesus Christ. The old spirits are less powerful now, but they still should be propitiated. Undoubtedly the missionaries told the Indians that the old gods are devils, and so spirits like the Earth Mother in this ritual are reduced to controlling disease-causing spirits of the dead. It is worth repeating here that despite the seemingly greater impact of Christianity upon the Otomís, they have a reputation in the whole region for being masters of shamanic techniques.

Table 6 contains additional Otomí rituals. Just as among the Nahuas, a complete listing is impossible because the shamans continually create new rituals and add innovations to older ones. The table suggests the range of rituals among the Otomís and indicates the paper images associated with each one.

TABLE 6. Major Otomí Rituals

Maxi or Hokwi: Curing/cleansing ritual of variable complexity and duration. Paper images: *judíos,* mountain spirits, beds, large cutouts of guardians, companion spirits, spirit of the patient, Otomí man and woman (Christensen 1942, pp. 114ff.; 1952, pp. 264ff.; Dow 1982, pp. 636ff.; Fitl 1975, pp. 172–73, 179–81; Lenz 1973 [1948], pp. 132ff.; Sandstrom 1981, pp. 25ff.).

Ofrenda Completa: Ritual held to cure soul loss. Paper images: *judíos,* beds, good spirits of the dead (Otomí man and woman), bad spirits of the dead (Otomí man and woman), attack wheel figures (Christensen 1952, p. 266; Fitl 1975, pp. 173–76).

Su Dia del Monte: Rite to regain spirit of the patient from Lord of the Mountain. Paper images: mountain spirits, beds, spirit of the lion, Otomí man (Christensen 1952, p. 266; Fitl 1975, pp. 177–78; Lannik, Palm, and Tatkon 1969, pp. 15ff.).

Costumbre al Cerro: Offering to hill spirits to prevent disease. Paper images: spirit of the hill (Christensen 1942, p. 116; 1971, p. 34; Fitl 1975, pp. 181–82; Kaupp 1975, p. 188).

Costumbre para la Milpa: Offering to field spirit to increase crop yields. Paper images: spirit of the field (Christensen 1942, pp. 114ff.; 1971, p. 29; Fitl 1975, p. 181).

TABLE 6. *Continued*

Costumbre para las Semillas: Ritual for seeds to insure bountiful harvests. Paper images: seed figures, mountain spirits, preliminary cleansing using figures of *malos aires* (Christensen 1942, pp. 117ff.; 1963, pp. 365ff.; 1971, pp. 42ff.; Fitl 1975, 190-94; Kaupp 1975, p. 188; Lenz 1973 [1948], pp. 126ff., 130).

Costumbre a Moctezuma: Offering to Moctezuma in payment for planting fields. Paper images: Moctezuma (Fitl 1975, pp. 182-84; Lannik, Palm, and Tatkon 1969, p. 16; Lenz 1973 [1948], pp. 122ff.).

Costumbre al Espíritu del Agua: Offerings are cast into the lake home of Maka Xumpö Dehe to control rain. Paper images: figure of a woman, mountain spirits, altar mats (Flower of Heaven, Gate of Heaven?) (Christensen 1942, pp. 116ff.; 1963, p. 365; 1971, pp. 35ff.; Fitl 1975, pp. 195-97; Sandstrom 1981, pp. 54ff.).

Costumbre para la Fuente: Offering to remove harmful spirits from the village water supply. Paper images: figure of a man, mountain spirits, altar mats (Flower of Heaven, Gate of Heaven?) (Christensen 1942, p. 115; 1971, pp. 34ff.; Fitl 1975, pp. 194-95).

Pagar Algo: Offering to a variety of spirits as compensation for human offenses. Paper images: harmful spirits *(malos aires?)*, figures from white paper (witnesses?) (Fitl 1975, pp. 185-86; Kaupp 1975, p. 188; Lenz 1973 [1948], pp. 127ff.).

Ofrenda de la Tierra: offering to the earth as compensation for human disturbances. Paper images: beds, other unidentified figures (Fitl 1975, pp. 198-99; Galinier 1976c, p. 169; Kaupp 1975, p. 188; Lenz 1973 [1948], pp. 127ff.).

Ofrenda de Dios de Tequil: Offering to guardian hearth spirit to protect household members. Paper images: no information (Fitl 1975, p. 198).

Costumbre para la Casa: Ritual for a newly built house to placate its spirit. Paper images: beds, Otomí man (Christensen 1942, pp. 115ff.; 1963, pp. 364ff.; 1971, pp. 31ff.; Fitl 1975, pp. 188-89; Kaupp 1975, p. 188).

Ofrenda para Enamorarse: Love magic rite. Paper images: spirits of lovers (Christensen 1963, p. 365; 1971, pp. 37-38; Fitl 1975, pp. 208-209; Kaupp 1975, p. 188; Lenz 1973 [1948], p. 129).

TABLE 6. *Continued*

Todos Santos: Ceremony to feed the souls of ancestors; syncretized with All Souls. Paper images: no information.

Navidad: Christmas. Paper images: no information (Christensen 1942, pp. 121ff.; Lenz 1973 [1948], p. 134).

Año Nuevo: New Year's. Paper images: no information (Christensen 1942, p. 121).

Carnaval: Dancers in various guises perform throughout the village, the Devil prominent among them; syncretized with the Christian celebration of Carnival. Paper images: no information (Boiles 1971; Williams García 1960).

Rentgó Ojo: Called the "people's feast," this ritual is held following Easter. Paper images: no information (Lenz 1973 [1948], pp. 134ff.).

Costumbre al Sēnor del Monte: Offering to the mountain spirit upon the birth of a child. Paper images: mountain spirits, Otomí man, spirit of the lion, beds, altar mats (Napkin of the Mountain) (Fitl 1975, pp. 178–79).

Limpia a la Partera: Cleansing performed by a midwife at the birth of a child. Paper images: no information (Kaupp 1975, p. 188).

Costumbre para Difunto: Funeral rite to prevent return of the dead person's spirit. Paper images: Otomí man, spirit of the lion, other unidentified figures (Christensen 1942, pp. 119ff.; 1963, p. 365; 1971, pp. 36ff.; Fitl 1975, pp. 186–87; Kaupp 1975, p. 188; Lenz 1973 [1948], 131ff.).

OTOMÍ MOUNTAIN SPIRITS

In the ritual just described, an important role was played by a series of spirits called Señores del Monte or Lords of the Mountain. Chief among these is Mū Xandöhu, Lord of the Mountain, also called Döhandöhö, Heart of the World (Dow 1974, p. 98; 1982, p. 645). This protector spirit is assisted by seven helper spirits which take the form of multiheaded birds (figures 75–80). Birds have been used to represent messenger spirits among Indians in Middle America since pre-Columbian times (Hunt 1977, pp. 57ff.). These bird spirits watch over people and report back to the Lord of the Mountain. The multiple heads symbolize watchfulness since they are able to look in more than one direction at once. The little birds tell their master if someone is ill so he can intervene and help in the cure. However, the little birds also report back if someone has forgotten to give the master his due. In this case the Lord of the Mountain becomes angry and aggressive. Following is a complete set of paper images of mountain spirits used in San Pablito.

Figure 74
Mū Xandöhu, Señor del Monte,
    Lord of the Mountain
Bark paper
21.5 × 16 cm

According to Otomí informants, this was one of the most powerful spirits before the coming of Jesus Christ. Today he guards over people, ensures that there is no hunger, and prevents injuries from falls. Because of his role as protector, he is often cut in conjunction with curing rituals. He sends out messengers to obtain information about people who neglect him and to give warning to people when something is about to happen. The spirit lives on the mountain and moves on the air when he travels. Because of his association with the air some ethnographers classify him as an attack spirit, although his function is sufficiently different to warrant a separate category. While generally viewed as a beneficent protector, the Lord of the Mountain will nevertheless send disease to people, particularly a newborn infant, if he feels neglected by the villagers. The spirit is portrayed with a rainbow, and the branches and leaves of the forest form a canopy over his head. Circular cuts over the head represent thunder. Two animal spirit helpers are cut by his legs, and the two infants emerging from his arms symbolize his role as protector. These infants are sometimes interpreted as the weakened spirits of sick people that he guards over. Offerings are made to the Lord of the Mountain in a special place in the forest visited often by shamans (Fitl 1975, pp. 119ff.; Christensen 1952, p. 266; 1971, p. 34; Dow 1974, p. 98; 1975, p. 62; 1982, p. 645; Lenz 1973 [1948], preceding p. 97; Lannik, Palm, and Tatkon 1969, p. 15; Kaupp 1975, p. 190; Spranz 1969, p. 66; Sandstrom 1981, pp. 44ff.).

Figure 75
Nxūni Nge Goho Ra Hyā, Aguila
    de Cuatro Cabezas,
    Eagle with Four Heads
Bark paper
20.5 × 14 cm

This paper image is cut by Otomí shamans to represent a powerful guardian spirit who acts as a messenger for the Lord of the Mountain (figure 74). It is portrayed as a single bird's body with four heads attached. The four heads are able to look in all directions at once for approaching danger and to spot people who have failed to make offerings to the Lord of the Mountain. The cutout may be hung in people's houses as a protection against trouble (Fitl 1975, p. 122; Lenz 1973 [1948], p. 126; Kaupp 1975, p. 191).

Figure 76
Zinzu Nge Ra Mū Xandöhu
   (Bird of the Mountain Lord),
   Pajarito del Monte,
   Little Bird of the Mountain
Bark paper
15.5 × 11 cm

The spirit portrayed here is one of the messengers associated with the Lord of the Mountain. Little Bird of the Mountain wards off bad spirits from wherever it is situated. It also has the ability to prevent fights from occurring. People in San Pablito often hang this image in their homes as protection against disease-causing *judíos* and other dangerous spirits. Cut with two heads to symbolize watchfulness, it wears a crown of two small bird-companion spirits (Fitl 1975, p. 124; Kaupp 1975, pp. 189–90; Lannik, Palm, and Tatkon 1969, p. 15; Christensen 1952, p. 266; Lenz 1973 [1948], p. 130).

Figure 77
Zinzu Nge Ra Pāse (Bird of the
   Monkey), Pajarito de Mono,
   Little Bird of the Monkey
Bark paper
15.5 × 10.5 cm

The Little Bird of the Monkey is the protector of the sick and is cut by shamans as part of curing procedures. It is portrayed as a two-headed bird accompanied by two smaller birds and by two monkeylike figures that are interpreted as the weakened spirits of small children. The small birds carry the spirits of sick people to the Lord of the Mountain to be cured. Often the shaman will leave a paper image of this spirit along with food offerings on top of a sacred mountain to aid in the curing process (Fitl 1975, p. 125; Kaupp 1975, p. 191).

Figure 78
Zinzu Nge Ra Zö (Bird of the Star),
    Pajarito de Estrella,
    Little Bird of the Star
Bark paper
15 × 10.5 cm

Another messenger from the Lord of the Mountain, this two-headed bird spirit is cut with a crown of stars. The Otomís say that the spirit is a link between the heavens and earth. Its head is among the stars and its tail connects to humans down below. The Little Bird of the Star announces things that are about to happen and is often a harbinger of misfortune (Fitl 1975, p. 126; Kaupp 1975, p. 190).

Figure 79
Zinzu Nge Ra Nxūni (Bird of the Eagle),
    Pajarito de Aguila,
    Little Bird of the Eagle
Bark paper
14.5× 10.5 cm

The Little Bird of the Eagle reports to the Lord of the Mountain when someone is sick. Provided the proper food offerings are made, it may actually take the spirit of the patient back to the master to plead on its behalf. Sometimes this spirit can effect a cure by causing the patient to vomit up his sickness; vomiting is taken as a sign that the patient's spirit has been taken to the Lord of the Mountain. The spirit is portrayed as a two-headed bird with small eagles cut above its head. These smaller birds help the Little Bird of the Eagle by watching for people who are sick. The image is cut as part of an offering to the Lord of the Mountain (Fitl 1975, p. 127; Kaupp 1975, p. 190).

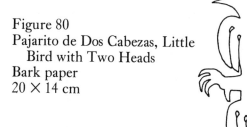

Figure 80
Pajarito de Dos Cabezas, Little
   Bird with Two Heads
Bark paper
20 × 14 cm

The Little Bird with Two Heads is yet another messenger and helper of the Lord of the Mountain. Two heads help this spirit keep track of events in both the celestial and earthly realms. This cutting often adorns Otomí religious altars and is sometimes referred to as the Guardian of the Sky (Fitl 1975, p. 123; Christensen 1942, p. 115; Lenz 1973 [1948], p. 125).

These spirits bear no physical resemblance to the witnesses and guardians cut by the Nahuas, and yet they seem remarkably similar in conception. The idea of messengers or intermediaries between powerful mountain spirits and human beings is found in both sets of paper cuttings. The Lord of the Mountain is portrayed as a barefoot human figure surrounded by spirit helpers. Although the Otomís must view this spirit with some ambivalence because of its role in causing disease, it is still portrayed as a benevolent being which resembles a seed spirit. The thunderballs over its head may give a hint about its potential danger. The little birds are portrayed in a fairly naturalistic style except for the multiple heads. Just as in Nahua cuttings, crowns are used to identify the particular spirit.

OTOMÍ SEED SPIRITS

Some of the best-known and best-selling paper cuttings of the San Pablito Otomís are the images of seed spirits which follow. Although the Otomís themselves call these figures *dioses* or "gods," it is clear that they represent the *zaki* of each crop. That they are also called *semillas*, "seeds," indicates that they represent the potential for fertility and growth of each plant. Like their Nahua counterparts, Otomí shamans conduct private and public rituals to increase the *zaki* of the crops and thereby improve yields. The images are cut out of bark paper or industrially manufactured tissue paper (*papel de China*). Seed spirits are portrayed anthropomorphically in a characteristic pose: front faced with hands upraised by the sides of the head. Clearly identifiable images of the mature fruit or vegetable, with or without accompanying leaves, protrude from each side of the figure and occasionally from the top of the head. In most of the images the spirit wears a crown headdress and has roots emerging from the bottoms of bare feet. Bark paper images are usually single ply; tissue paper images are cut from variously colored sheets of paper which are then sewn together in layers. In the latter case, the top sheet, usually a light green or blue, is cut to reveal the differently colored paper underneath. Thus the crown of the figure or the fruits which project from the sides show as different colors from the body.

As mentioned previously, the San Pablito Otomís are unusual in that they cut a different image for each crop grown. Both the Nahuas and Tepehuas cut images of only a few crops, such as maize or chiles. The proliferation of seed images in San Pablito may be linked to the demands of the tourist market.

Like the Nahuas, the Otomís keep a permanent collection of seed images sealed in a wooden cabinet that is kept on the altar of a special shrine (Christensen 1963, p. 366; Lenz 1973 [1948], p. 130; Sandstrom 1981, p. 73; Galinier 1976c, p. 161). The figures are dressed in miniature clothes with tiny hats, necklaces, earrings, combs, and other furnishings. The figures are removed annually and used in a ceremony dedicated to crop increase, after which they are returned to the cabinet (see chapter 2). Throughout the year small offerings may be placed in front of the cabinet in hopes of further influencing crop yield. In some cases paper images of the *zakis* of domesticated animals such as turkeys, chickens, and pigs are cut along with the seed spirits. They too are called *semillas* (seeds). Except for information on honeybees (figures 116–18), however, no ethnographic information is available on how they are used or even what they look like (Lenz 1973 [1948], p. 126).

The seed spirits that follow were all cut in the village of San Pablito and have been grouped according to the crop represented. Otomí names of the cutouts have been included where they are available; otherwise only the Spanish and English labels are provided. Translation of the Otomí and Spanish varietal names has proven extremely difficult because of regional variations in folk taxonomy. Whenever there is a doubt about the variety of plant portrayed we have simply translated the broadest category possible. Thus the Dios de Jitomate Arribeño is translated simply as "Spirit of the Tomato," since "*jitomate arribeño*" or "highland tomato" may not denote the same variety of tomato in each village.

Figures 81–84 are used in crop fertility rituals to represent some of the varieties of maize grown by Otomí villagers. The Spanish word *mazorca*, which appears in figures 81 and 84, means ear of corn or the female spike of the corn plant. The Otomís sometimes use this word to mean the entire corn plant, and so the name Dios de Mazorca has been translated as simply Spirit of Maize.

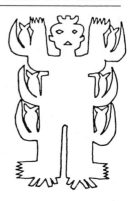

Figure 81
Ra Mūtä Nge Ra Tha, Dios de Mazorca,
    Spirit of Maize
Bark paper
20 × 12.5 cm

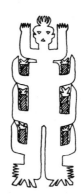

Figure 82
Dios de Maíz Negro, Spirit of
    Black Maize
Blue with purple ears
31 × 11.5 cm

Figure 83
Dios de Maíz Amarillo, Spirit of
    Yellow Maize
Blue with yellow ears
16.5 × 8 cm

Figure 84
Dios de Mazorca Amarillo, Spirit
    of Yellow Maize
Blue with orange ears
26 cm tall
After Spranz (1961, p. 65)

Figures 85-89 represent the spirits of some of the varieties of beans cultivated by the Otomís. Most villagers can readily identify the variety of bean represented by the shape and color of the cutout image.

Figure 85
Ra Mūtä Nge Ra Boju, Spirit
    of the Black Bean
Bark paper
15.5 × 10.5 cm

Figure 86
Ra Mūtä Nge Ra Maju, Spirit
    of the Crawling Bean
Bark paper
21 × 15 cm

Figure 87
Dios de Frijol de Mata Colorado,
    Spirit of the Red Bush Bean
Green with red pods
31.5 × 11.5 cm

Figure 88
Dios de Frijol Torito Blanco,
    Spirit of the White Bean
Green with purple pods
31.5 × 11.5 cm

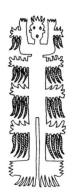

Figure 89
Dios de Frijol Delgado, Spirit
    of the String Bean
Green with purple pods
26 cm tall
After Spranz (1961, p. 64)

Figures 90 and 91 are two versions of the Spirit of the Garbanzo Bean (chick pea) cut by Otomí shamans.

Figure 90
Dios de Garbanzo, Spirit of
   the Garbanzo Bean
Green with white beans
Size of original unknown

Figure 91
Dios de Garbanzo, Spirit of the
   Garbanzo Bean
Bark paper
15.5 × 11 cm

Figures 92-97 portray the spirits of several of the many varities of tomatoes planted by the Otomís.

Figure 92
Ra Mūtä Nge Ra Xitha Temäxi,
   Dios de Tomate,
   Spirit of the Tomato
Bark paper
20.5 x 15.5 cm

Figure 93
Ra Mūtä Nge Ra Temäxi, Dios de
    Jitomate, Spirit of the Tomato
Bark paper
15.5 × 10.5 cm

Figure 94
Dios de Jitomate Arribeño,
    Spirit of the Tomato
Blue with red tomatoes
31.5 × 11.5 cm

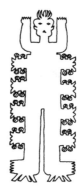

Figure 95
Dios de Cuatomate Amarillo,
    Spirit of the Yellow Tomato
Blue with yellow tomatoes
31.5 × 11.5 cm

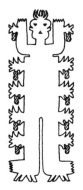

Figure 96
Dios de Tomate Grajillo,
    Spirit of the Tomato
Green with red tomatoes
Size of original unknown

Figure 97
Dios de Jitomate, Spirit of
    the Tomato
Green with red tomatoes
26 cm tall
After Spranz (1961, p. 64)

Figures 98–101 are the spirits of some of the several dozen varieties of peppers grown by the Indians.

Figure 98
Ra Mūtä Nge Ra Ngi, Dios de Chile,
    Spirit of Chile
Bark paper
20 × 14 cm

Figure 99
Dios de Chile Grande, Spirit
   of Large Chile
Blue with red chiles
31.5 × 11.5 cm

Figure 100
Dios de Chile Colorado, Spirit
   of Red Chile
Blue with red chiles, leaf tips white
26 cm tall
After Spranz (1961, p. 64)

Figure 101
Dios de Chile de Hoja,
   Spirit of Chile
Blue with yellow chiles
25 cm tall
After Spranz (1961, p. 64)

Some of the varieties of bananas grown by Otomí farmers are portrayed in figures 102–105.

Figure 102
Ra Mūtä Nge Ra Mūza, Dios de Plátano,
   Spirit of the Banana
Bark paper
21 × 12 cm

Figure 103
Dios de Plátano Chaparro,
   Spirit of the Banana
Green with yellow bananas
33 × 11.5 cm

Figure 104
Dios de Plátano Largo,
   Spirit of the Long Banana
Green with peach-colored bananas
16.5 × 8 cm

Figure 105
Dios de Plátano Amarillo,
   Spirit of the Yellow Banana
Green with yellow bananas; leaf
   tips above feet are yellow
26 cm tall
After Spranz (1961, p. 65)

Sugarcane is an important crop for the Otomís. Figures 106–108 represent some of the varieties grown.

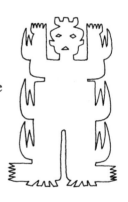

Figure 106
Ra Mūtä Nge Ra Yumpö, Dios de
   Caña, Spirit of Sugarcane
Bark paper
20.5 × 12 cm

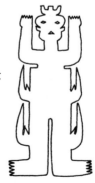

Figure 107
Dios de Caña Jalapeño, Spirit
   of Jalapan Sugarcane
Purple
16.5 × 8 cm

Figure 108
Dios de Caña Blanca, Spirit
  of White Sugarcane
Blue with white tips protruding
  from the body
26 cm tall
After Spranz (1961, p. 65)

Figures 109 and 110 are two of the several varieties of peanuts
grown by Otomí farmers.

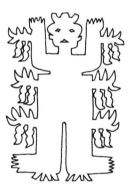

Figure 109
Ra Mūtä Nge Ra Jumhäi, Dios de
  Cacahuate, Spirit of the Peanut
Bark paper
20.5 × 14 cm

Figure 110
Dios de Cacahuate Serrano, Spirit
  of the Mountain Peanut
Blue with brown peanuts
32.5× 11.5 cm

Figure 111 is an image of the potato, and figures 112 and 113 are two different paper images of the Spirit of the Camote plant.

Figure 111
Dios de Papa Blanca, Spirit
  of the White Potato
Green with pink potatoes
31 × 11.5 cm

Figure 112
Dios de Camote Dulce Blanco, Spirit
  of the Sweet White Camote
Green with pink camotes
31 × 11.5 cm

Figure 113
Dios de Camote, Spirit of
  the Camote
Bark paper
23 × 14 cm

Figures 114 and 115 are two representatives of the jícama plant.

Figure 114
Ra Mūtä Nge Ra K'apaxā, Dios
    de Jícama, Spirit of the Jícama
Bark paper
20.5 × 14 cm

Figure 115
Dios de Jícama, Spirit
    of the Jícama
Green with white jícamas
26 cm tall
After Spranz (1961, p. 64)

Figures 116–18 are different paper images depicting the tropical honeybees. Honey is a luxury item produced by many households.

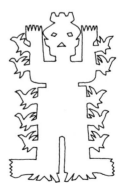

Figure 116
Ra Mūtä Nge Ra Tatha (Spirit of the Bee),
    Dios de Enjambre
    Spirit of the Bee Swarm
Bark paper
21 × 13 cm

Figure 117
Dios de la Colmena de Enjambre,
    Spirit of the Beehive
Yellow
30 × 11.5 cm

Figure 118
Dios de Enjambre,
    Spirit of the Bee Swarm
Yellow
26 cm tall
After Spranz (1961, p. 65)

Figures 119 and 120 are two versions of the coffee plant cut by
Otomí ritual specialists.

Figure 119
Ra Mūtä Nge Ra Kafe, Dios de Café,
    Spirit of Coffee
Bark paper
20.5 × 14.5 cm

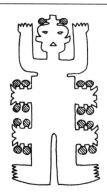

Figure 120
Dios de Café, Spirit of
   Coffee
Green with red coffee beans
16.5 × 9 cm

Some of the varieties of pineapple grown by the Otomís are
represented in figures 121-23.

Figure 121
Ra Mūtä Nge Ra Hwatā, Dios de Piña,
   Spirit of the Pineapple
Bark paper
21 × 14.5 cm

Figure 122
Dios de Piña Serrana, Spirit
   of the Mountain Pineapple
Blue with a brown pineapple crown
31 × 11.5 cm

Figure 123
Dios de Piña, Spirit of the
    Pineapple
Blue with yellow pineapples;
    leaves of the pineapples are red
26.5 cm tall
After Spranz (1961, p. 65)

Figures 124 and 125 are different depictions of the Spirit of
the Papaya.

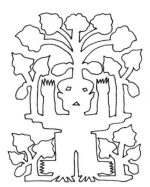

Figure 124
Ra Mūtä Nge Ra Papaya, Dios
    de Papaya, Spirit of the Papaya
Bark paper
15.5 × 11 cm

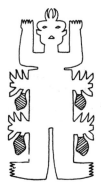

Figure 125
Dios de Papaya Erial, Spirit
    of the Papaya
Light blue with peach-colored
    papayas
16.5 × 9 cm

Figure 126
Dios de Espinoso, Spirit of
   the Thorn Plant (?)
Bark paper
21.5 × 16.5 cm

The following paper cutouts depict the great diversity of fruits
cultivated by the Otomís.

Figure 127
Dios de Naranja, Spirit of
   the Orange
Bark paper
21 × 16 cm

Figure 128
Dios de Granada Cordelina,
   Spirit of the Pomegranate
Green with red pomegranates
Size of original unknown

Figure 129 (see color plate 13)
Dios de Uva, Spirit of the Grape
Bark paper
33.5 × 25 cm

Figure 130
Dios de Manzana, Spirit of
the Apple
Bark paper
15.5 × 10.5 cm

Figure 131
Dios de Palma, Spirit of the
Palm Nut
Bark paper
15.5 × 10.5 cm

Figure 132
Dios de Aguacate, Spirit of the
    Avocado
Bark paper
15.5 × 10.5 cm

Figure 133
Ra Mūtä Nge Ra Xamū, Dios de
    Chayote, Spirit of the Chayote
Bark paper
20.5× 15 cm

Figure 134
Dios de Mango, Spirit of the
    Mango
Bark paper
15.5 × 10.5 cm

Figure 135 is unusual in that two crops are depicted simultaneously; the meaning of the juxtaposition is not clear.

Figure 135
Dios de Plátano con Frijoles,
   Spirit of Banana with Beans
   or Seedy Banana?
Bark paper
21.5 × 16 cm

Four major sources of variation determine the styles displayed by the seed spirits. The first is the material out of which they are cut, either bark paper or tissue paper. Generally speaking, the tissue paper figures are larger and taller than those cut from bark paper. This is because traditional bark paper is made only in smaller sheets. Often, tissue-paper images are somewhat more intricate in design, which may reflect the greater ease of cutting the thinner paper. This is not a rule, however, since some of the images cut from bark paper are also quite elaborate. Another impetus for variation is the need for ritual specialists to distinguish themselves from their colleagues. A third source is the need to portray the sometimes large number of varieties of any single crop grown by the villagers. Finally, some of the variations, particularly the extremely decorative ones such as figures 129 and 130, are clearly influenced in their design by considerations of the tourist trade.

OTOMÍ MISCELLANEOUS PAPER CUTTINGS

Figures 136–43 are a sample of altar mats cut by shamans in San Pablito. The ornate images are cut primarily to make the altar a beautiful place for the spirits, but in some cases they are also cut to ward off dangerous spirits. These large cutouts often depict watchful birds or good Otomí men and women who will create an impenetrable barrier to the *judíos* and *malos aires*.

Figure 136
Niño del Monte, Child of
    the Mountain; also
    Vigilante, Watchful One
Bark paper
41 × 30 cm

This large paper image is cut by Otomí shamans to prevent fights and accidents perpetrated by dangerous spirits. During rituals it is hung inside the shrine to prevent violence that might flare up as a result of the heavy consumption of *aguardiente*. The central feature is a circle composed of four good Otomí men alternating with four good Otomí women. A pair of watchful birds is cut at each corner (Fitl 1975, p. 161; Lenz 1973 [1948], p. 131).

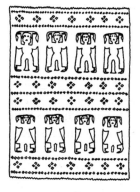

Figure 137
Niño del Monte, Child of the
    Mountain; also Centinela,
    Sentinel
Bark paper
41 × 30 cm

Otomí shamans cut this image to turn back dangerous spirits who try to enter a house where a ritual is being held. Undesirable spirits are sometimes attracted to the music, offerings, and activities of a ritual, and they must be prevented from spoiling the affair. The top row of figures are good Otomí men and the bottom row, good Otomí women. The cutout is hung in the doorway of the house so that the good Otomís can overpower dangerous spirits and incarcerate them in escape-proof caves (Fitl 1975, p. 161; Lenz 1973 [1948], p. 131).

Figure 138
Niño del Monte, Child of the Mountain;
    also Flor del Cielo, Flower of Heaven
Bark paper
42 × 29 cm

This cutting is a variation of figures 136 and 137. It consists of two circles of good Otomí men who alternate with good Otomí women (see color plate 14). The image is placed on the altar during rituals to turn away dangerous spirits who are attracted by the offerings (Christensen 1942, following p. 114).

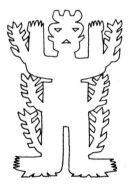

Figure 139
Niño del Monte, Child of the Mountain
Bark paper
16.5 × 10 cm

This unusual portrayal of the Child of the Mountain is placed on the main altar during Otomí rituals. Foliage grows out the figure's sides, and roots extend from its feet.

Figure 140
Servilleta del Monte, Napkin of the
    Mountain; also Escobetilla del Monte,
    Broomstraw of the Mountain
Bark paper
61 × 40.5 cm

Figure 141
Servilleta del Monte, Napkin of the
    Mountain
Bark paper
59.5 × 43 cm

Otomí altars are designed to be beautiful places, appropriate settings for beneficial spirits to receive offerings. These paper cuttings serve the dual function of beautifying the altar and keeping dangerous spirits away. Figure 140 is the more standard adornment; figure 141 is a variation. Double bird motifs, which symbolize watchfulness, are found in both figures. Figure 140 has a rosette as its central feature. The rosette is sometimes interpreted as a series of upraised arms and sometimes as the broomstraw plant. Both images are placed on the altar to sweep it clean of dangerous spirits. It is specially cut for the Costumbre del Monte, Ritual for the Mountain (Fitl 1975, p. 151).

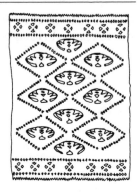

Figure 142
Servilleta de Estrella de la Montaña,
    Napkin of the Star of the Mountain
Bark paper
41 × 30 cm

Figure 143
Servilleta de Estrella de la Noche,
    Napkin of the Evening Star
Bark paper
42.5 × 31 cm

Otomí shamans use both of these cuttings as altar adornments. Figure 142 is cut with the watchful-birds motif, while figure 143 is decorated with star designs. Both of these napkins are used in conjunction with rituals directed to the spirit Ma Yoho Nija (Two-Shrine) to ask for rain (Sandstrom 1981, pp. 66, 94; Galinier 1976c, pp. 169–70).

Lenz photographed similar mats in the 1940s. Since the mats appear to be the same as those cut today, it seems that demands of the tourist trade have not had much of an effect on their design. Today's mats are cut from extra large sheets of bark paper. They thus represent an additional expense for the sponsor of the rituals in which they are used. Compared to other relatively simple Nahua altar mats, these altar mats are masterpieces of complexity.

The final group includes some miscellaneous paper images cut for special rituals.

Figure 144
Cama de Ataque, Attack Bed; also,
    Cama de Antigua, Ancient Bed
    or Bed of Ancient Ones,
    plus many other names
Bark paper
24 × 11.5 cm

Figure 145 Cama de Ataque, Attack Bed;
    also Silla, Seat
Bark paper
21 × 13.5 cm

The Otomís call these images *pepechtli* or *tlapexque*, taken from the Nahuatl *tepextli*, meaning "bed." Paper images of spirits are displayed on top of these cutouts during rituals. The term "attack bed" refers to the attack spirits (those disease-causing spirits of people who died tragically) that are placed on them. Dozens of the figures and beds may be cut for a single ritual, and all of them are disposed of afterwards. The significance of the two styles of bed is not known. Spranz has suggested that the cloverleaf cuts in figure 145 represent crossroads or the four directions. (Spranz 1961, pp. 60–61; Fitl 1975, pp. 145–46; Christensen 1971, pp. 25–26; 1942, 113; Lenz 1973 [1948] p. 132; Lannik, Palm, and Tatkon 1969, p. 13).

Figure 146
Gente Mala, Spirit of Bad People
Bark paper
Size of original unknown
After Christensen (1971, p. 22)

Figure 147
Gene Buena, Spirit of Good People
Bark paper
Size of original unknown
After Christensen (1971, p. 24)

A common theme in Otomí rituals is the juxtaposition of good and bad spirits. The spirit of a good person, one who had a good death, can protect the living from attacks by harmful spirits. There is a great deal of variation in how the spirits of good and bad people are portrayed. Figure 146, the Spirit of Bad People, is a female with four arms and heavy boots. Figure 147 is a male with bare feet. As mentioned earlier, boots or shoes on a paper cutting signify danger, while salutary spirits are cut with bare feet (Fitl 1975, pp. 147, 149, 156–59).

Figure 148
Ra Zate, Espíritu del Leon,
   Spirit of the Lion
   (Jaguar or Cougar)
White
Size of original unknown
After Lenz (1973 [1948], following p. 96)

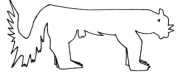

The jaguar is a symbol of power and strength for the Otomís, and its spirit is believed to guard the sick and those who have died. Often a paper image of the jaguar is buried with a corpse to protect the soul from attack by wild animals. The Otomís believe that each person has an animal companion called a *rogi* whose life parallels that of the person. Powerful shamans often have the jaguar as their animal companion. This image is cut for rituals dedicated to the Lord of the Mountain (Fitl 1975, p. 152; Lannik, Palm, and Tatkon 1969, p. 15; Christensen 1952, pp. 266–67; Lenz [1948], pp. 131–32).

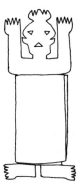

Figure 149
Espíritu del Enfermo, Spirit
   of the Patient
Bark paper
20.5 × 7 cm
Boilès collection

In an effort to cure disease, Otomí curers sometimes cut an image of the patient out of paper. The image will then be manipulated in a ritual in order to effect a cure. Here the patient is portrayed wrapped in a bark paper blanket (Fitl 1975, p. 147; Lannik, Palm, and Tatkon 1969, p. 15; Christensen 1952, p. 266).

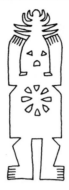

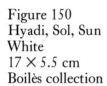

Figure 150
Hyadi, Sol, Sun
White
17 × 5.5 cm
Boilès collection

This image was cut by an Otomí shaman in Tzimatla, Veracruz. It represents the spirit of the sun, the key spirit in the Otomí pantheon, which is symbolized by the circular arrangement of cuts. This figure is used in curing rituals (Dow 1974, p. 97; 1982, p. 645).

Figure 151
Tambor, Drum
White
17 × 6 cm
Boilès collection

The Spirit of the Drum portrayed here was cut in the Otomí village of El Zapote in northern Veracruz. The image of the drum can be seen in the center of the figure's body. For the Otomís, each musical instrument has a kind of force or spirit which animates it. This figure is cut for the propitiation ritual held at the top of a sacred mountain (see Galinier 1976c, p. 162).

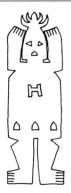

Figure 152
Bidʔih, Spirit of the Slit
    Drum *(teponaztli)*
White
17.5 × 5.5 cm
Boilès collection

The slit drum, known in the literature by the Nahuatl word
teponaztli, is a pre-Columbian instrument that is still played
in some of the more remote Indian villages in Mexico. Portrayed here is the Spirit of the Slit Drum, which was cut in the
Otomí village of El Zapote in northern Veracruz (see Galinier
1976c, p. 162).

Figure 153
Santa Rosa, Sacred Rose or Saint Rose
    of Lima(?); also, La Sirena, the Siren
White
17.5 × 6.5 cm
Boilès collection

This figure represents the spirit of the marijuana plant. The
Sacred Rose, which may be symbolically connected to Saint
Rose of Lima, is identified with a water spirit called the Siren
and is the object of several important Otomí rituals. Marijuana
leaves are eaten during the rituals because to smoke them would
be to mix fire and water. The central cuts represent marijuana
leaves.

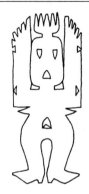

Figure 154a
Spirit of a man for
   love magic
White
23 × 9 cm
Dow collection

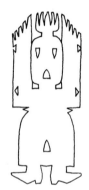

Figure 154b
Spirit of a woman
   for love magic
White
21 × 8.5 cm
Dow collection

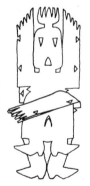

Figure 154c
Spirit of man and
   woman in love-
   making position
White
Dow collection

This group of paper images was cut by a shaman in the Otomí
village of Chicamole, San Bartolo, Tutotepec, state of Hidalgo.

The Otomís use these figures in magical procedures designed to make people fall in love. Shamans cut out paper images of the two people to be affected and place the images in a love-making position. After offerings and chants are delivered to the images, the man and woman who are the subjects of the ritual will be compelled to fall hopelessly in love. According to the Otomís, neither party need be aware of the ritual for it to be effective (Christensen 1963, p. 365; 1971, pp. 37–38).

The variety of paper images in this last category reveals much about the animistic view of the world held by the Otomís. Not only are people, plants, and animals susceptible to ritual manipulation, but objects like musical instruments are also. As far as we know, no other group in the region cuts such a variety of paper images nor uses them in so many different rituals. It is no wonder that the Otomís have the reputation of being masters of the *costumbre* rituals.

Features of Otomí religion generally appear similar to the Nahua religious concepts and practices discussed in chapter 4. The similarity extends to certain paradoxical characteristics concerning the nature of the spirits and the organization of the spirit pantheon. Like the Nahuas, the Otomís appear to have numerous spirits, all existing in multiple manifestations or alter egos. This leads to the confusion of names that is so apparent in ethnographic reports on the Otomís. Furthermore many spirits have what appear to be contradictory attributes. The earth is a beneficient provider and at the same time a devouring monster that leads *malos aires*. These paradoxes, which are also evident when we examine Tepehua religion, are not the result solely of incomplete reportage on the Indian cultures. We will argue in chapter 7 that the paradoxes and the design features of the paper images are keys to a fundamental understanding of the *costumbre* religion.

CHAPTER 6

PAPER CULT FIGURES AMONG CONTEMPORARY TEPEHUA INDIANS

In 1900, while conducting his research on the anthropometry of the Indians of Mexico, Frederick Starr visited the Tepehua village of Huehuetla in the state of Hidalgo. He noted that "at Huehuetla ancient idols and parts of figures are now objects of veneration" (1901, p. 85). This is the first published hint of pre-Columbian survivals among the Tepehuas. In 1937 the French ethnographer Robert Gessain and his wife followed Starr's lead and travelled to Huehuetla, where they planned to conduct a long-term field study of Tepehua culture. Gessain was particularly interested in survivals of the ancient religion and, in fact, was the first to report that the Tepehuas, too, use paper images (1938). In reporting his findings, Gessain notes that up to that time few ethnographers had written about the religious and curative ceremonies, known widely by the name *costumbres*, that were practiced by the Mexican Indians. He also states, "Of equal importance, the *muñecos*, ritual figures of cut paper, have never, to our knowledge, been written about. My wife and I have had the chance to make the first collection known" (1938, p. 343; translation ours). Illness forced an end to the research after only a few weeks, and it was not until twenty-five years later that a study of Tepehua culture was completed. In 1963 the Mexican ethnographer Roberto Williams García published a study of the Tepehua villages of Chintipán and Pisa Flores located in the *municipio* of Ixhuatlán de Madero, Veracruz. Williams García later published a collection of Tepehua myths (1972).

The organization of the paper images in this chapter follows that used in the previous two chapters. First we present disease-causing spirits, then a description of a curing ritual. The ritual

200

is an example of how the paper images are used by Tepehua ritual specialists. Next is a section containing beneficent spirits that are propitiated in large rituals aimed at securing health, rain, fertility, and the like. This section is followed by the images of seed spirits featured in crop increase rituals. The final section contains miscellaneous paper images cut for special, infrequently held rituals. We have selected a total of forty-four paper images as a sample of the many cut by Tepehua shamans. Some of these are from private collections, but the majority are taken from the published works of Williams García and Gessain.

Among the Tepehuas, both males and females are active ritual specialists. Males may be either *curanderos* ("curers") or *adivinos* ("diviners") or both at the same time. The *curandero*, called *hakuch'uunú'* in Tepehua, is a specialist in aspects of medicine such as herbal cures, which have no connection to the religious system. The *adivino*, called *hapapa'ná*, cures by controlling the spirits that cause disease. The *adivino* is the main religious practitioner in Tepehua villages (Williams García 1963, p. 173). Females may be either a *dakunú* (*partera*, or "midwife") or *adivina* ("diviner"). The Tepehuas believe that giving birth offends the earth, and so midwives who help in the birthing process also hold special rituals to make amends to the earth (see Williams García 1966b; 1967). Female diviners are former midwives who have their own set of ritual procedures. The Tepehua term *hat'akuunú'* ("female ritual specialist") can be used for either female diviners or midwives (Williams García 1963, p. 141). Because they specialize in different areas of knowledge, male and female diviners and midwives often work together in curing and propitiation rituals. The similar status of these three practitioners is shown by the fact that the Malaqachanín spirits or "Star Guardians" are considered equally to be the companions of all Tepehua ritual specialists (Williams García 1963, p. 144).

A midwife may become a female diviner if she receives a sign from the spirits. Diviners of both sexes are called to their profession by mystical dreams or by recovery from chronic illness (Williams García 1963, p. 142). Like their Nahua and Otomí counterparts, Tepehua ritual specialists are viewed with some ambivalence. Diviners who become bad and practice their craft to harm people are called *haxkayanán* ("sorcerers"). Such people are greatly feared and are believed to hold secret ceremonies designed to steal people's spirits or spread disease. On the other hand, midwives or female diviners who die become Lak'ainananín ("Great Diviners" or "Great Midwives"), semideified intermediary spirits who live with the sun and stars. Male diviners who die become Lak'aitatanín ("Great Diviners"). They receive the offerings and prayers of their living counterparts and intercede with powerful beneficial spirits on behalf of living humans (Williams García 1963, pp. 141, 145, 173; 1967, p. 303; 1972, p. 42).

Midwives perform a special ritual called the *costumbrita*. The ritual is directed strictly to the earth and to spirits of the dead that live inside of the earth (Williams García 1963, p. 149). Male and female diviners, on the other hand, perform general cleanings or rituals directed to a range of beneficial spirits. Midwives and female ritual specialists do not cut paper images, but instead use the shredded inner bark of the *jonote de hule* tree (genus *Heliocarpus*) to make nonanthropomorphic brushlike images of salutary spirits. These images are formed by wrapping pieces of copal resin, representing the spirit's heart, in small bunches of the shredded fiber. Called *halachint* in Tepehua (*muñecas* in Spanish or "female dolls"), the images are laid in a row to form an altar. Only the male diviner cuts images of the spirits out of paper, and for this reason rituals conducted by men are considered to be more powerful than those conducted by women. The paper images are called *halasítnit* in Tepehua or *muñecos* ("dolls") in Spanish. When speaking Spanish, the Tepehuas use the word *brujos* ("witches") when discussing paper images, with no apparent negative connotation (Williams García 1963, pp. 139, 173, 185–86).

Paper images are cut in large numbers for rituals, and they are laid out on paper beds that are then stacked like a thick book. As the ritual unfolds, the shaman may remove the beds one at a time so that the paper images act as a guide to the chanting and the symbolic acts. The shaman thus uses the paper images in much the same way that the ancient codices were used by the Aztec priests (Williams García 1963, pp. 144, 148, 186). The Tepehuas of this region no longer make bark paper, but instead rely on manufactured paper purchased in the market. As it does among the Nahuas and Otomís, the color of the paper has symbolic significance, with black, yellow, red, or white usually reserved for the more negative spirits and Manila paper used for beneficial ones. The paper out of which the images are cut is called *papel de brujo* ("witch paper") (Williams García 1963, pp. 173, 185–86).

The paper figures, according to Williams García (1963, p. 186), are images of things, objects, persons, or concepts that are named by combining the word *sombra* ("shadow") with the idea represented. Thus an image of a guardian star is called Sombra de la Estrella (Shadow of the Star). He further states that to the Tepehuas the concepts of soul, spirit, and shadow are all the same (Williams García 1963, p. 138). The Tepehua word for shadow is *tukuwín* (Williams García 1967, p. 288). A shadow is conceived of as an "ethereal image" that can be separated from the original object or person and manipulated by shamans. Paper images are not the spirit itself, then, but are merely "copies" of the shadow. The images are sacralized and brought to life when the shaman splashes them with animal blood (Williams García 1963, pp. 138-39). It seems reasonable to say that the Tepehua concept of *tukuwín* is analogous to the Nahua ideas of *noyolo* or *notonal* and the Otomí concepts of *zaki* or *na xudi*. Concepts such as these are always difficult to translate from one culture to another, but it is certain that among the Tepehuas the paper images are more than simple pictures of spirits to be venerated.

The Tepehuas have a complex view of the universe and the spirit entities that inhabit it. Following is a summary of the Tepehua pantheon, which sets the context for the paper images presented later (see also table 7). In the sky lives Wilhcháan, the Sun, which is viewed by the Tepehuas as a paramount deity.

The sun is a Lapanak, or Lord, and it protects human beings and has a major responsibility for making crops grow. In Spanish the sun is called Dios—just as among the Nahuas and Otomís—and it is equated with Jesus Christ. Behind the sun stands an indissoluble pair called Ixpayixnatikinpaydios, which means Father and Mother of Our Lord. In Spanish this pair is called San José and La Virgen (Saint Joseph and the Virgin) (Williams García 1963, p. 192; Gessain 1952–53, p. 209). The stars are the sun's helpers, and at night they take over the sun's role as protector. After the sun goes down, stones threaten to turn into jaguars and devour people. The star guardians, called *stá'ku* in Tepehua, shoot arrows (*aerolitos*, or "meteorites") to kill the stones before they can attack anyone (Williams García 1972, p. 32; 1963, p. 192). Another paramount spirit is Jamanáwin, which means Dueño General or "General Owner" or "Lord." This may be an aspect of the sun or perhaps another spirit entirely (Williams García 1967, p. 289).

Standing in opposition to the sun and stars is another Lapanak, the moon, called Malhkuyú' in Tepehua. The moon is associated with the Devil and with the dangerous spirits of the dead that he leads. It gives rise to demons who feast on blood and terrorize humans. No apparent association is made between the moon and the Virgin Mary as it is among the Nahuas. The moon has also an indissoluble parental pair behind it called Ixpayixnati Malhkuyú'. One of the pair is called the Sereno Amarillo or "Yellow Siren" (*sereno* is the local pronunciation of the Spanish *sireno*). This male aspect is associated with the pale, cold light given off by the moon. The female aspect is called Serena Rojo, or Red Siren, which lives inside of the moon and is responsible for the menstrual cycle. No paper image is made of the moon itself, but the "devils" associated with it are cut from red or yellow paper with hornlike crescents in the headdress (Williams García 1963, pp. 192–93; 1972, p. 34; Gessain 1952–53, p. 209).

The Virgin Mary has multiple manifestations in Tepehua thought. Besides being the mother of the sun, she is also Kinpaxhatnatik'an (the Virgin) and Hachiuxtinín (Patroness of

Women), who controls human fertility. In addition, in her manifestation as the Virgin of Guadalupe, she is linked to the water spirit (Williams García 1963, pp. 140, 195, 197; 1967, pp. 287-88). Accompanying the Virgin in the sky are the Tacunín, water-related spirits of women who died in childbirth. These spirits travel with the clouds and carry rain to the fields. Also in the sky are the Negros (Black Ones), spirits who carry red-hot coals to help evaporate the sea when it threatens to overrun its banks and flood the world. When these coals fall, they are called *texq'óyam* in Tepehua or *bólidos* in Spanish, meaning "fiery meteors" or "shooting stars." This implies that Sacred Fire, called Santa Lumbre, resides in the sky when he is not guarding over families from the three stones around the fireplace. Finally there are the spirits of ritual specialists who watch from overhead and act as intermediaries between the people on earth and the powerful spirits above (Williams García 1963, pp. 98, 140; 1972, pp. 32-34).

The earth is called Xalapanalakat'un (Lord of the Earth), and, just as among the Nahuas and Otomís, it has multiple manifestations. In Spanish the earth is called Santa Tierra (Sacred Earth), and it is thought of as kind of a living being that can become annoyed at the activities of humans. For this reason offerings must be made to the earth on a regular basis. The Mother and Father of the Earth form an indissoluble pair called Ixpayixnatilakat'un, and it is this pair that often becomes annoyed at people. In fact the *costumbrita* held by Tepehua midwives is directed to this pair rather than to Santa Tierra. The earth provides the crops that are the basis of life, but it also consumes dead bodies and contains the underworld within itself. In its devouring aspect the earth is called Señor Mendezuma or Santasoma, both of whom are variations of the name Moctezuma. This aspect of the earth, in league with the moon, Malhkuyú', is in charge of the spirits of those who died tragic deaths (Williams García 1963, pp. 101, 138, 141, 151, 193-94; 1972, pp. 37-39).

The earth is the home of several beneficial spirits. Apparently the Lord of the Wind (Xalapanak'un) lives on earth, although it has no connection to the *malos aires* (spirits of the dead). It is, instead, associated with cool breezes that relieve the heat of the day or foretell of coming rain and that are thought to be caused by sacred children playing in the sky. There is also Xachan'achín, Lord of the Mountain, which seems to be associated symbolically with vegetation. A correspondence is apparent between this spirit and the spirit of the same name found among the Otomís. The seed spirits live on the earth, and they are generally thought to be the children of the Water Spirit. The spirit of maize, however, is conceived of as the offspring of the Deer Spirit and is preeminent among the seeds (Williams García 1972, p. 119). Just as they are among the Nahuas and Otomís, paper images of the Tepehua seed spirits are kept in special wooden cabinets on an altar in the village shrine. They are given occasional offerings in order to increase the harvest. Finally the spirit Santa Rosa (Sacred Rose) is propitiated in Tepehua villages. It is equated with marijuana, but unlike the Otomís and Nahuas, the Tepehuas apparently associate it with the earth rather than with water (Williams García 1963, pp. 196–97, 200–202, 220–21; 1972, pp. 37, 43; see figure 178).

The underworld is called Lak'nín and is the residence of the spirits of those who died natural deaths. These spirits are called *janinín*, and they are thought to live a pleasant life modeled on the one they lived on earth. Before reaching the underworld, however, each spirit passes through a series of trials to expiate sins accumulated during its lifetime. First the newly arrived spirit is cast into a fire so that it will confess any wrongdoings. Then it is passed through a sugarcane press *(trapiche)* to remove all its blood. Following this, the spirit is free to begin its new life. Lak'nin is organized much like a *municipio* with a *presidente* and various political offices. Just as among living people, the spirits must stand before secretaries to get necessary papers filled out. During the celebration of Todos Santos (All Souls), the Tepehuas make offerings to the spirits of their ancestors in Lak'nín so that they will remain satisfied in the underworld. As long as the offerings are made, a spirit will refrain from visiting its living kinsmen to seek revenge. The fate of the spirit is determined, for the most part, by the cause of death rather than by behavior while on earth. However, a person's occupation can also have a role in determining the fate of the soul (Williams García 1963, pp. 197-98; 1972, pp. 37-41).

The spirits of people who were murdered or who died bad deaths come under the power of Moctezuma and Malhkuyú', the moon. They are called *maxkai'un* in Tepehua or *malos aires* ("bad airs") or *malos vientos* ("bad winds") in Spanish, and they sometimes take the form of owls when they return to earth to spread disease. These malignant spirits are doomed forever to wander around with the Devil searching for new victims. The Devil is called Tlakakikuru (from the Nahuatl Tlacatecolotl, Owl Man), and it is this spirit that leads the *malos aires* abroad so that they spread disease and death. Although the Tepehuas have borrowed the word Tlakakikuru from the Nahuas, the latter have a different spirit, Tlauelilo, that they call the Devil. The most dangerous manifestation of the bad winds is the *tamoswilhi'untín* or "whirlwind" that carries off peoples' spirits, leaving them to sicken and die. During the celebration of Carnaval (Carnival), the Devil and his minions, impersonated by masked dancers, visit the villages, causing a commotion and demanding payment from each household. The dancers mock authority and in a joking and irreverent manner violate the norms of everyday village life. Ash Wednesday marks a return to normal life, and the "devils" are banished from the village for another year (Williams García 1963, pp. 193, 197, 244ff.; 1972, pp. 38-40, 43; Gessain 1952-53, p. 210).

In spite of all the sky, earth, and underworld spirits mentioned so far, Williams García claims that the preoccupation of the Tepehuas of Pisa Flores is centered on water (1972, p. 41). The Lord of the Water is Xalapánaak Xkán, and this spirit is considered a more immediate presence than the distant sun and stars or the ambivalent earth. Behind the Lord of the Water stand the indissoluble parental pair Ixpayixnatixkán. They are the caretakers, those that "care for everything we eat." The male aspect is called El Sereno, and he wears green clothes and is the patron of all animals. When angered, El Sereno produces thunder and lightning. The female aspect, called La Serena, also wears green and has feet like a duck. She lives in a distant lake and sends the rain and wind. She is called Reine Pure, Pure Queen, by Gessain (1952-53, p. 209; see also Williams García 1963, pp. 194-96; 1972, p. 35).

Spirits called Papanín (Viejos, or Old Ones) actually produce the rain. These are viewed as small men who wear rubber sleeves on their coats and who travel in the clouds carrying walking sticks (*bastones*). By striking their staffs the Papanín produce thunder and lightning, and if they should encounter ice they cast it down in the form of hail. When not traveling in the clouds, these spirits live in Xakán Papanín, or House of the Old Ones, where they store their coats and walking sticks. One of the Papanín, called Siní in Tepehua and El Sereno or San Juan in Spanish, lives in the ocean and initiates the rainy season each spring. When the sound of distant thunder is heard just before the onset of the rains, the Tepehuas say that Siní is striking his staff. There is an apparent lack of agreement among the Tepehuas over who leads the Old Ones. The average person thinks that they are led by Jesus, while the shamans insist that Xalapánaak Xkán leads them. Some people interviewed said that Jesus and the Lord of the Water are one and the same. Other somewhat ambiguous water spirits include Muchacha del Agua (Girl of the Water), who controls fish and who may be a manifestation of La Serena; Halapanaxkán, also translated as Lord of the Water, but who in this negative manifestation scares people when they cross water so that he can steal their spirits; and the Tacunín, or women who died in childbirth and now carry rainwater to the fields (Williams García 1963, p. 196; 1972, pp. 35-37; 1979, p. 125; Gessain 1952-53, p. 209).

The Tepehuas tell a remarkable myth about the sacred residence of the spirits that helps us understand their pantheon as well as certain aspects of their rituals. They say that at the point on the horizon where the sun rises each morning is a fabulous wonderland called the Cerro de Oro (Golden Hill).

Here, dressed in resplendent robes and surrounded by beauty, live the major Tepehua spirits. The spirits are seated at two tables, the most elegant of which is called the Gran Mesa (Great Table). Here is seated the Sun, surrounded by his helpers, the Stars. The second table is occupied by all of the other spirits of lesser rank, such as the Earth and Water. The tables are covered with iridescent cloths laden with the finest food offerings of every description. The spirits of sacred musicians, called Makanq'achanín, play beautiful melodies continuously, and there are processions of censers, shamans, and dancers to entertain the assembled spirits. The spirits of the newly dead pass before the tables to be judged and to be assigned an appropriate afterlife. Most go to Lak'nín, but some, including male and female diviners, midwives, women who died in childbirth, sacred musicians, and dancers, stay on the Golden Hill to serve the spirits (see table 7 for Tepehua names of these particular spirits and for a general summary of the Tepehua pantheon). Those who died unfortunate deaths go with the Devil (Williams García 1963, pp. 144–46, 197–98).

TABLE 7. The Tepehua Pantheon

Realms of the Universe and Associated Spirits

(Sky)
    Wilhcháan (Sun, Jesus)
    Ixpayixnatikinpaydios (dual caretakers, parents, Joseph and Mary)
    Kinpaxhatnatik'an (Virgin Mary); also
        Hachiuxtinín (Patronness of Women)
    Jamanáwin (General Lord)
    Stá'ku (star guardians)
    Texq'óyam (shooting stars)
    Santa Lumbre (Sacred Fire)
    Malhkuyú' (Moon, associated with Tlakakikuru)
        Ixpayixnati Malhkuyú' (dual caretakers, parents,
            Yellow and Red Sirens)
    Malaqachanín (star guardian companions of ritual specialists)

TABLE 7. *Continued*

Lak'ainananín (intermediary spirits of female diviners and
  midwives)
Lak'aitatanín (intermediary spirits of shamans)
Makanq'achanín (sacred musicians)

(Earth)
  Xalapanalakat'un (Lord of the Earth); also
    Santa Tierra (Sacred Earth)
  Ixpayixnatilakat'un (dual caretakers, parents)
  Moctezuma (devouring Earth)
  Xalapanak'un (Lord of the Wind)
  Xachan'achín (Lord of the Mountain)
  Seeds (associated with Lord of the Water)
  Santa Rosa (Marijuana)
  House Guardian Spirit

Lak'nin (Underworld)
  Tlakakikuru (Devil)
  Janinín (Spirits of the dead)
  Moctezuma (associated with the earth)
  Maxkai'un (bad airs) also
    Tamoswilhi'untín (Whirlwind)

(Water)
  Xalapánaak Xkán (Lord of the Water, associated with Jesus and
    the Virgin of Guadalupe)
  Ixpayixnatixkán (dual caretakers, parents, Sirens)
    El Sereno (male Siren); also
      Siní (San Juan, one of the Papanín)
    La Serena (female Siren); also
      Reine Pure (Pure Queen)
      Muchacha del Agua (Girl of the Water)
  Papanín (rain spirits, associated with Thunder and Lightning)
  Halapanaxkán (negative Lord of the Water)
  Tacunín (Water Bearers, women who died giving birth, associated
    with the sky)

It is to the spirits of the shamans on the Golden Hill that
contemporary shamans direct their offerings. Their deceased

colleagues act as intermediaries by presenting the offerings to the Sun and the lesser spirits that surround him. When conducting rituals, the shamans lay out offerings on three separate squares they call *mesas*. The first two hold offerings to the first and second tables on the Golden Hill, and the third is dedicated to the spirit intermediaries. During their chants the shamans make constant reference to a Señor Santacena, which Williams García interprets as a reference to La Ultima Cena (the Last Supper). It seems likely that the whole image of the Golden Hill with the Sun-Christ surrounded by lesser spirits is taken from descriptions or perhaps a picture of Christ's Last Supper brought to the Indians by missionaries some time in the last 450 years. The concept of the Golden Hill is an extraordinary example of the syncretic nature of Tepehua religion. The major spirits who live on the Golden Hill are called by the general term Los Antiguas (the Ancient Ones). This term also applies to certain of the paper images, such as the seed spirits, and to small prehistoric heads or figurines that shamans place on their altars (Williams Garcia 1963, pp. 144–46, 197–98). See chapters 4 and 5 regarding similar beliefs among the Nahuas and Otomís concerning the Antiguas.

The Tepehuas do not have a particularly elaborate system to propitiate the various Catholic saints. In each village the *agente municipal* or local elected official who represents the village to higher levels of government appoints a *pixcal*, who, with some assistants, cares for the village statues. In a meeting called by the *agente*, villagers select a *mayordomo*, who, along with assistants, organizes the various *costumbres* held in the village. The *agente* is charged with organizing work on the communal field, the proceeds from which are used to finance ritual observances. During certain holidays, for example Todos Santos (All Souls), the saints' statues are carried in a procession to the shrine, which may simply be an official's house, and a ritual is held on their behalf. Often there is more than one shrine in a village. Shrines with a Christian orientation are called the *lakatata* or "place of the priest," while those with a more traditional orientation are called *lakachinchin*, which means "sun place" or "house of Los Antiguas." Masonry churches such as might be found in *municipio* centers are called *tahkín,* meaning "place of the sun." Like other Indian groups, the Tepehuas do not see a fundamental difference between Christianity and the traditional Indian religion since they have syncretized both systems into the unique religion they practice today. They do realize, however, that missionaries and other outsiders may not understand this, and thus they take certain precautions such as building the traditional shrine well off of the most commonly used trails (Williams García 1963, pp. 126ff., 198, 200; 1972, pp. 21–30).

TEPEHUA DISEASE-CAUSING SPIRITS

Like the Nahuas and Otomís, the Tepehuas attribute misfortune, disease, and death to the actions of spirits. There are two ways that spirits cause disease: by stealing a person's *sombra* and through attack by *malos aires.* Surprisingly the spirits most often accused of *sombra* theft are the most prominent members of the Tepehua pantheon. These include the Sun, Water, Earth, and Maize (Williams García 1963, p. 138). In fact any spirit is capable of this act, and the danger of "soul loss" is thus a pervasive concern to the Tepehuas. The *malos aires* or *diablos* ("devils"), as they are sometimes called by the Tepehuas, function much like the Nahua *ejecatl* and the Otomí *judíos.* They are infectious agents that the shaman removes during curing rituals. Tepehua paper images of the *malos aires* resemble those cut by the Nahuas in that their appearance is rather bland and unthreatening. Tepehua shamans cut them out as individual images, never multiple; they are frequently in male and female pairs.

Figure 155a
Lakatikúrulh (from the
  Nahuatl Tlacatecolotl,
  Owl Man), Devil, some-
  times *mal aire*,
  "bad air" (male)
White
17.5 × 5.5 cm
Boilès collection

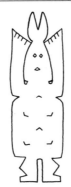

Figure 155b
Lakatikúrulh (from the
  Nahuatl Tlacatecolotl,
  Owl Man), Devil, some-
  times *mal aire*,
  "bad air" (female)
White
17.5 × 5.5 cm
Boilès collection

Williams García believes that the Tepehuas originally had no
concept of the Devil or devils and that the idea was introduced either by Nahuatl speakers or by missionaries (1963, p.
193). In contemporary Tepehua thought the Devil is one of the
malos aires, but it is a particularly powerful one that leads all
the others. These images of the *malos aires* are cut as a pair
by Tepehua shamans. They represent the angry, vengeful spirits
of people who died tragically. There are two possible interpretations of the headdress form. One is that it represents the jaws
of the earth, the powerful force that consumes the bodies of the
dead. This links the paper images to Moctezuma. The second is
that it represents the crescent moon, another negative spirit
in the Tepehua pantheon. The uppermost V cut in the body

stands for the heart, while the lower one represents the stomach. Other cuts are clothing decorations. Figure 155a is cut with pointed knees which represent pants, thus identifying the spirit as male.

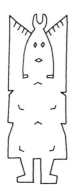

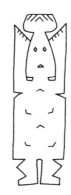

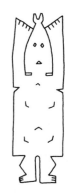

Figure 156a	Figure 156b	Figure 156c
Lakatikúrulh (from the Nahuatl Tlacatecolotl, Owl Man), Diablo, Devil, sometimes *mal aire*, "bad air" (female)	Lakatikúrulh (from the Nahuatl Tlacatecolotl, Owl Man), Diablo, Devil, sometimes *mal aire*, "bad air" (male)	Lakatikúrulh (from the Nahuatl Tlacatecolotl, Owl Man), Diablo, Devil, sometimes *mal aire*, "bad air" (male)
White	White	White
17 × 6 cm	17 × 5 cm	17 × 5.5 cm
Boilès collection	Boilès collection	Boilès collection

These three images are cut as a group by shamans for use in curing rituals. No direct information is available concerning why the two male and single female figure are grouped together, although it is possible that they represent a love triangle. Each is depicted with a heart and stomach in addition to clothing decorations. The female is wearing the two-piece dress typically worn by married women in the region; and the males wear *jorongos*. The headdress on figure 156b may represent the closed jaws of the earth (Moctezuma) (compare figures 163a, b). The bare feet in figure 156c suggest that it represents the spirit of an Indian man rather than that of a *mestizo*.

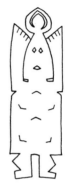

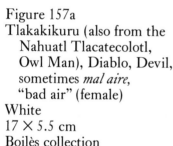

Figure 157a
Tlakakikuru (also from the
    Nahuatl Tlacatecolotl,
    Owl Man), Diablo, Devil,
    sometimes *mal aire*,
    "bad air" (female)
White
17 × 5.5 cm
Boilès collection

Figure 157b
Tlakakikuru (also
    from the Nahuatl
    Tlacatecolotl, Owl Man),
    Diablo, Devil, sometimes
    mal aire, "bad air" (male)
White
17.5 × 5.5 cm
Boilès collection

This is a version of the Devil portrayed as a male and female pair cut with hearts, stomachs, and the usual clothing decorations. The headdresses are simultaneous representations of the full and crescent moon.

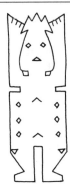

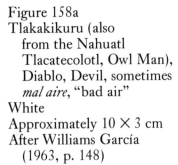

Figure 158a
Tlakakikuru (also
   from the Nahuatl
   Tlacatecolotl, Owl Man),
   Diablo, Devil, sometimes
   mal aire, "bad air"
White
Approximately 10 × 3 cm
After Williams García
   (1963, p. 148)

Figure 158b
Tlakakikuru (also
   from the Nahuatl
   Tlacatecolotl, Owl Man),
   Diablo, Devil, sometimes
   mal aire, "bad air"
White
Approximately 10 × 3 cm
After Williams García
   (1963, p. 148)

This is another Tepehua representation of the Devil. The spirit is depicted as a male-female pair with wavy headdresses that symbolize wind. The ethnographer does not indicate which of the pair is male and which is female. Both are cut with hearts, and figure 158a has an inverted V cut that may represent genitals. The feet are cut to depict either footwear or blowing clothes. The Devil and its minions are thought to crave blood, and this accounts for their attack on human beings. During parts of the curing rituals designed to remove these spirits, animal blood is sprinkled on their paper images. The shaman hopes that the substitute blood will satisfy the spirits and that they will leave the patient alone.

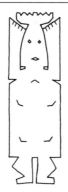

Figure 159
Campo Santo, Graveyard
White
17.5 × 5 cm
Boilès collection

In the animistic view of the world, the graveyard itself becomes a *mal aire*, identified with spirits of the dead and itself capable of causing disease. The Tepehuas see the graveyard as a kind of two-way door between the underworld and the surface of the earth. While most spirits remain in the underworld, particularly if they are ritually fed during All Souls', there are always enough angry spirits lurking on the earth's surface to make the graveyard a dangerous place. The spirit is depicted as a male, with clothing decorations, a heart, and the open jaws of the devouring earth on its head.

In his ethnography of the Tepehuas, Williams García includes two complete sets of paper images used in curing rituals. In typical fashion, these are arranged as a series of paper beds. One set is composed of figures 160a, b, 158a, b, plus two beds of the paper images of people *(hombre)*, not reproduced here. Of the total of fifteen beds comprising both sets, only four contain images of *malos aires* (Williams García 1963, pp. 148, 268). Thus it would appear that Tepehua shamans do not cut a large variety of these disease-causing spirits. This contrasts with Nahua and Otomí shamans, who cut a diversity of types of *malos aires* and who use great numbers of them in curing rituals. An additional distinction of Tepehua *malos aires* is that they are invariably cut in male-female pairs or in groups that contain at least specific male and female individuals. The Nahuas occasionally cut male-female pairs, but they do not seem to emphasize the practice.

These differences, however, should not obscure the fundamental similarities among the three cultures in their conceptions of the disease-causing spirits. In fact, the points of similarity far outnumber the differences. In the first place, the *malos aires* are the wandering spirits of people who died tragically. They cause disease, are associated with the air, and are headed by a spirit called Moctezuma, who is an aspect of the earth. In addition they are led by a spirit called the Devil (Diablo in Spanish).

Stylistically the Tepehua cutouts resemble the Nahua figures more than those cut by the San Pablito Otomís. But they share with both Nahuas and Otomís the upright stance with the hands placed close to the head, the attention to details of dress and anatomy, and the symbolic importance of the headdress. In short, as a category of spirits the *malos aires* are remarkably similar among all three cultures in how they fit into the various pantheons, how they behave, how they are manipulated by the shaman, and how they are depicted.

The Tepehuas, like the Nahuas and Otomís, accord to shamans a high degree of stylistic freedom in portraying the *malos aires*. We have representative works from two shamans, each with his own stylistic conventions. The Boilès collection, including figures 155a, b, c. 156a, b, 157a, b, and 159, were cut by a single shaman. They are fairly simple and can be identified by their blocklike appearance, the pattern of V cuts in the body, and characteristic pointed heads. Figures 158a, b, collected by Williams García, were cut by another shaman, whose work is clearly distinguishable in the figures presented below. His style is generally more elaborate, with a greater variety of shapes cut from the body of the figure and greater elaboration in headdresses. In addition the heads on his figures are usually more rounded.

A TEPEHUA RITUAL

We have selected a cleansing ritual recorded by Roberto Williams García in his ethnography *Los Tepehuas* (1963, pp. 164–68) to illustrate how paper images are used among the Tepehuas. The ritual is more complex than the Nahua and Otomí cleansings described previously because among the Tepehuas three specialists collaborate to conduct rituals of this type: the shaman *(adivino);* an *adivina* (in this case, his wife); and a midwife *(partera).* Each of them has his and her own ritual procedures, although only the shaman cuts the paper images.

The Setting

The patients are a man and his wife, both of whom have suffered from illness and bad dreams. A diviner called in earlier has determined that the couple is being molested by spirits of the dead in retaliation for a breach of conduct previously committed by the man's father. It seems that the father was implicated in a murder, and the dead kinsmen of the victim are now seeking revenge on the son and his wife. A ritual to cleanse the couple is first held on the patio and then inside their house.

The Cleansing

The ceremony begins at noon. The shaman, the *adivina*, and the midwife sit on the ground before their separate displays of ritual items. The displays are composed of paper images *(muñecos)*, the small brushlike *muñecas* used by the midwife and *adivina*, candles, bottles of *aguardiente*, braziers, unshelled ears of corn, corncobs, copal incense, flowers, leafy branches of *limonaria*, clods of earth, and bunches of grass. Each prays in a hushed voice, censing and sprinkling *aguardiente* over his display. The midwife prays to Señor Santasoma to remove the *malos vientos* that infect the couple. The midwife forms a bundle from the items in her display and moves it over and around the patients while continuing to pray.

The shaman now begins to act, first praying to the earth and then forming a bundle from paper figures, *limonaria* leaves, flowers, and a bottle of *aguardiente*. He holds this bundle over each of the patients' heads while chanting, then suddenly waves it left and right, taking care not to let it touch the couple. Next he holds the bundle in front of their faces and has them spit on it. The act of spitting on the paper images shames the spirits and causes them to vacate the area. The curer hands each patient paper images representing his own *sombra* as he picks up a live rooster and adds it to the bundle. He describes a horizontal arch over the patients with the bundle of ritual items and the rooster, after which he has the couple spit on the paper images a second time. He then wrenches the head off the rooster and sprinkles the blood around the patients "in order to give food to the Devil and bad winds."

Next, after placing their paper images on the ground before the shaman, the patients go to the midwife's display to ritually wash the dirt clods, ears of corn, and corncobs. The clumps of earth and ears of corn symbolize the field where the couple grows its food. These are washed to make amends to the earth and to cleanse away actions that have offended the dead spirits. They symbolically wash the corncobs to purify the food consumed by the spirits of the dead. Meanwhile the shaman stamps blood on each paper image with the severed head of the rooster. The three officiants next gather up their displays, forming three bundles. The shaman's bundle, along with the bunches of grass that represent the pasture, is suspended in the branches of a tree. The women's bundles are eventually thrown into the jungle along with ashes from the incense braziers. The ears of corn and corncobs, along with offerings of *aguardiente* and copal incense, are kept by the patients in a basket. These will continue to safeguard the couple against recurring spirit attack long after the ritual is over.

Inside the house the three officiants engage in separate ritual activities:

Shaman: The shaman cuts fresh paper images representing the Earth, Water, Wind, Maize, Cross, Shrine (Lakachínchin), and Star, and he lays them out on the ground in front of the house altar. (See figures 160–71 for examples of these seven and of some additional major spirits). At one side of his display he lays marigold blossoms and the clods of earth taken from the field.

He, too, invokes Señor Santasoma in his chants and then continues to pray as he censes the display and sprinkles it with *aguardiente*. Later he sacrifices two large roosters and douses the paper images with their blood. This blood constitutes the offering to Señor Santasoma.

Midwife: Nearby the midwife arranges her brushlike *muñecas de jonote*, flowers, and *limonaria* leaves on a wooden box she calls her table *(mesa)*. While chanting to the spirits, she arranges plates of food on her display and then dedicates the food by throwing pieces of it on the hot coals in the brazier. In her chant she addresses the dead relatives of the patients. She then has the couple exchange flowers and vows of mutual respect with the group of relatives who have gathered for the occasion. Afterward a third rooster is killed, and the midwife stamps blood on each one of the *muñecas* with the severed head. Finally she forms a bundle out of her display, which she discards deep in the jungle.

Adivina: The *adivina* arranges some *muñecas de jonote* on the earthen floor near the house altar. She ritually cleanses the area, kills a fourth rooster, and casts its body out the door "for the Devil." Next she takes a statue of the Virgin of Guadalupe and places it in the display along with flowers, *limonaria* leaves, and candles. She then takes paper images of farm animals and the *sombras* of the patients, all cut by her husband the shaman, and lays them out near the statue. This procedure enlists the Virgin in the protection of the patients and their animals.

Midwife: Meanwhile the midwife lays out additional *muñecos* cut by the shaman and dedicates offerings to them. The number of *muñecos* corresponds to the number of prayers recited. She enlists the aid of the beneficial spirits represented to guard over her patients.

Shaman: The shaman now arranges cups of coffee and bread on top of his display of paper images. He chants over them and occasionally pours coffee into a receptacle nearby. Apparently these offerings are dedicated to the shaman's intermediary spirit on the Golden Hill. Later on the coffee will be taken to the field and poured on the ground.

Midwife: At this point the midwife conducts a cleansing of the patients to liberate them from the influences of Santa Rosa (marijuana). After dedicating offerings and conducting several cleansings, she paints the *muñecas de jonote* with blood from one of the sacrificed roosters, using a feather as a brush. The bunches of flowers and *limonaria* leaves used in this sequence are placed by the doorway to repel any bad winds that try to enter the house.

Shaman: The shaman makes another offering over his display as a gift to Señor Santasoma, this time using two of the roosters sacrificed earlier.

Adivina: Meanwhile the *adivina* gathers up the paper images of farm animals and a smoking brazier and proceeds outside to cleanse the animals in the corral. She returns and, after dedicating offerings again to the *muñecas de jonote*, stamps each one with the bloody neck of a sacrificed rooster. Then she gathers up the items in her display and forms them into yet another bundle.

At this point the officiants place the remaining offerings and paper images on the house altar. The shaman has finished forming several small bundles using selected items that are put aside for later use. All of the items appearing on the house altar, including cigarettes and sacrificed roosters, are given to the three specialists as part of their payment.

It is 3:00 A.M., and the shaman is digging a hole in the ground in the house patio. At the bottom of the hole he arranges four pieces of copal incense into a "bed." He wraps a living rooster with paper images of the Earth and the Shrine, and, after holding them to the four cardinal points, he places the bird in the hole. He then fills in the hole, burying the rooster alive, and covers the burial site with a heavy stone to keep away rooting animals. At this point the shaman, *adivina*, and the midwife leave for home, carrying their payment goods in baskets.

At dawn the patients walk to their field carrying paper images, the little bundles prepared by the shaman, the container of coffee, bread, and other offerings. Near a spring in the field, the bread and coffee are poured onto the ground as an offering to the water. Another rooster is buried alive along with paper images of Water, Maize, Wind, Cross, Star, and the Shrine. This act protects the couple from accidents. Back in the patients' house, paper images of their *sombras* are displayed on the house altar to aid in their convalescence.

Paper Images and the Ritual

Although aspects of this ritual appear to be unique to the Tepehuas, in overall conception it is remarkably similar to the curings described in the previous two chapters. Structurally the cleansing of the *malos aires* precedes the offerings made to beneficial spirits, just as it does among the Nahuas and Otomís. The spirits addressed in the ritual are similar in conception to those addressed by the Nahuas and Otomís, such as *malos aires*, the Devil, Moctezuma, Water, and the Earth. Since the leading cause of the patients' mental and physical disturbances was diagnosed as the intruding spirits of a murder victim's kinsmen, it appears that the *malos aires* play a role in disease etiology that is similar to that played by polluting *ejecatl* spirits of the Nahuas. As is done with the other groups, harmful spirits are removed in three basic steps: arranging paper images, making offerings, and casting out or destroying the paper figures. The five ritual elements first noted among the Nahuas (paper images, altars, offerings, chanting, and overall strategy) are also found here, with the forms only slightly modified. But it is the use of cut-paper images that distinguishes the *costumbres* of this area of Mexico from other religious complexes. The description provided by Williams García clearly illustrates the central place of paper images in Tepehua rituals.

In addition to gross similarities, many of the smaller details also coincide. Offerings are made indirectly to the spirits of deceased ritual specialists who act as intermediaries. These appear to be equivalent in function to the witness spirits of the Nahuas. A bundle of sacralized herbs placed over the doorway performs the function of barring dangerous spirits, similar to the function of the large Otomí paper cutouts in figures 136–38. The striking offering to the earth in which a fowl is buried alive is also a reported practice among both Nahuas and Otomís. Underlying the main surface similarities is a layer of smaller correspondences, such as the liberal use of *aguardiente*, copal incense, flowers, sacred herbs, sacralized bundles, animal blood and cooked meat sacrifices, candles, and paid ritual specialists.

This Tepehua curing ritual has many features, however, that are not reported for the other groups. Probably the most notable difference is the special ritual functions performed by the midwife, female diviner, and shaman. As described above each of these ritual specialists has a separate set of procedures that, when added together, create the complete ritual. The midwife, with her *muñecas de jonote*, is concerned with the earth and the spirits of the dead. The *muñecas* apparently symbolize some unspecified beneficial spirits. The shaman, or male diviner, seems to address a broader range of spirits and to set the pace of the ritual. The role of the female diviner is less clear. She enlists the aid of the Virgin of Guadalupe and has responsibility for cleansing the farm animals belonging to the patients.

There are other differences as well. The procedure of spitting on the paper images to humiliate the *malos aires* is not reported for the other groups. The sequence of washing earth taken from the fields, as well as ears of corn and corncobs, does not appear to be part of the Nahua or Otomí curing rituals, although packets of earth are ritually cleansed in the Nahua-Otomí ritual described in chapter 2. The animal blessing has been reported among the Otomís but not among the Nahuas. Additional unique features include the use of the statue of the

Virgin of Guadalupe to aid in protecting the patients, the exchange of mutual vows of respect among the relatives of the patients, the protection from the adverse influence of Santa Rosa, and the formation of *mesas* (tables) symbolically recreating the structure of the Golden Hill.

Additional Tepehua rituals are listed in Table 8. As is the case with the other groups, a complete listing is impossible because the ritual specialists constantly innovate new rituals. The table gives an idea of the range of rituals practiced, along with the types of paper images associated with each one.

TABLE 8. Major Tepehua Rituals

Limpia: The basic curing-cleansing ritual. Paper images: *malos aires*, including the Devil, stars, spirit of the patient (Gessain 1938, pp. 356ff.; Williams García 1963, pp. 154-68; 1972, pp. 55-56).

Costumbrita: Curing ritual held by midwives directed to the earth and spirits of the dead. Paper images: *muñecos de jonote de hule* (Williams García 1963, pp. 149ff.).

Limpia para Traer la Sombra: Curing ritual to restore stolen spirit of the patient. Paper images: figure of the patient, figure of the spirit suspected of stealing the *sombra* (Williams García 1963, p. 137).

Ceremony for Barren Wives: Modified cleansing ritual used formerly to mark the physical maturity of girls. Paper images: figures of women who have committed infanticide and those who have not (Gessain 1938, p. 358; Williams García 1963, pp. 169-72).

Ritual to Prevent Epidemics: Ritual means of keeping disease out of the village. Paper images: guardian stars, shaman with brazier on his head, shaman dancing on the head of the Devil (Gessain 1938, p. 358; 1952-53, pp. 205-206).

Costumbre a las Semillas: Major seed ritual that may involve a pilgrimage to a sacred lake. Paper images: seed spirits (Williams García 1963, pp. 98ff., 200-203; 1972, pp. 56-57).

Fiesta de Elotes: Ritual celebrating the young ears of corn. Paper images: seed images, flowering maize plants, figure of man planting (Gessain 1938, p. 350; 1952-53, p. 206; Williams García 1963, 284-85; 1972, pp. 57-58).

Ritual for Rain: Pilgrimage made to a sacred lake to propitiate the

TABLE 8. *Continued*

siren who controls rainfall. Paper images: water siren, wind, thunder, stars, figure of man, male and female water carriers, red sun figure (Gessain 1938, pp. 355–56; 1952–53, p. 205; Williams García 1963, pp. 204ff.; 1972, pp. 56–57).

Ritual to Prevent Flooding: Offerings are cast into the river to cause the water to recede. Paper images: unidentified (Gessain 1938, p. 355; 1952–53, p. 205).

Costumbre para Enamorarse: Love magic rite. Paper images: spirits of lovers (Gessain 1938, p. 370).

Ritual for a New House: Offering made to placate the spirit of a newly built house. Paper images: house spirit (Gessain 1938, p. 350).

Ritual Initiation of a Shaman: Rite of passage for a shaman. Paper images: the sun (Gessain 1938, pp. 352ff.; 1952–53, p. 207).

Costumbre a Santa Rosa: Marijuana ritual held to communicate with spirits. Paper image: marijuana (Williams García 1963, pp. 215ff.).

Santorum: Ritual to feed the spirits of ancestors: syncretized with All Souls. Paper images: no information (Williams García 1963, pp. 225–27, 232–35, 285; 1972, pp. 41, 50–53).

Navidad: Syncretized with Christmas, this celebration includes processions, construction of altars and dancing. Paper images: no information (Gessain 1952–53, p. 202; Williams García 1963, pp. 228–32; 1972, pp. 53–54).

Año Nuevo: New Year's. Paper images: no published information on the content of this observance (Williams García 1963, p. 244).

Carnaval: Masked performers dance throughout the village, and the Devil is a prominent character; syncretized with the Christian celebration of Carnival. Paper images: no information (Gessain 1952–53, p. 202; Williams García 1963, pp. 244ff., 286; 1972, pp. 54–55).

Levantada de Cama: Ritual held by midwife to protect a newborn baby. Paper images: no information (Gessain, 1938, p. 358; Williams García 1963, pp. 140ff.; 1966b; 1967, pp. 302ff.; 1972, p. 47).

Funeral: Ritual held to prevent return of the dead person's spirit. Paper images: no information (Gessain 1938, pp. 359–60; Williams García 1963, pp. 222–25; 1972, pp. 48–50).

Ritual One Week after the Death: Continuation of funeral rite. Paper images: spirit of dead person, shaman dancing over cadaver (Gessain 1938, p. 361).

TEPEHUA MAJOR SPIRITS

The figures in this section represent powerful spirits of a somewhat more beneficent character. One cannot say that they are
totally salutary because they do have the power to steal a person's "soul" and cause sickness and death. However, the Tepehuas look to them for protection and to provide the conditions
necessary for growing their crops. Also, their role in curing is
significant, as illustrated in the ritual just described.

Figure 160a
Wilhcháan, Sol, Sun
Green
Approximately 10 × 3 cm
After Williams García
   (1963, p. 148)

Figure 160b
Wilhcháan, Sol, Sun
Red
Approximately 10 × 3 cm
After Williams García
   (1963, p. 148)

These two paper images of the Sun are identical except for
color. The headdress is a burst of sunrays, and a cross is cut
from the chest. The cross has lost its strictly Christian connotation among the Tepehuas and now represents the Sun-Christ,
a fusion of the two traditions. The diamond-shaped cuts are
apparently clothing decorations.

   These images were collected by Williams García as part of
a complete set used in the curing of a shaman. In fact the
image of the sun is cut only for the curing of a ritual specialist.

While the Sun is all powerful, seated as it is at the center of the Gran Mesa on the Golden Hill, the Tepehuas consider it to be somewhat remote from daily life. The meaning of the green and red colors is not known, but it is likely that they distinguish male and female aspects of the Sun.

Figure 161
Ishqatlmushu Abilcham, Sol Rojo,
    Red Sun
Blue on a red background sheet
Size of the original unknown
After Gessain (1938, following p. 366)

This cutting, collected by Gessain over forty-five years ago, is cut for a large ceremony held to save the crops from drought. The cutout is suspended by a thread tied to a stake in the center of an altar. A red sun is believed by the Tepehuas to be a sign of intense heat and to pose an extreme danger to the fields. At the center of the image is the sun, casting scorching rays. All around the sun are images of babies, women, and men who have died in the drought. Over the heads of several figures are the chevron-shaped crowns of death (see figure 182). Although the ritual in which this image is used had not been held for many years at the time Gessain lived among the Tepehuas, Tepehua shamans were still able to cut it.

Figure 162a
xapainín, meaning unknown
  (male)
White
23.5 × 8 cm
Boilès collection

Figure 162b
xapainín, meaning unknown
  (female)
White
23.5 × 8 cm
Boilès collection

The identification of this pair of spirits is uncertain, but we have included them because they present an interesting symbolic contradiction. The headdress has the appearance of a cross that is identified with the Sun (Jesus). The bare feet give further evidence that the spirit is salutary. However, cuts in the body represent ribs, thus linking it to spirits of the dead. The shaman who cut the figure said that this is the most important spirit of them all, the one that commands the rest. One likely explanation for this apparent contradiction is that the figure represents the sun during a period of drought, that is, at a time when its heat is a threat to life.

Figure 163a
Xalapanalakat'un, Señor de
 la Tierra, Lord of the
 Earth in the guise of
 Santasoma (from the
 Nahuatl Motecuhzoma,
 or Moctezuma)
White
Approximately 10 × 3 cm
After Williams García
 (1963, p. 187)

Figure 163b
Xalapanalakat'un, Señor de
 la Tierra, Lord of the
 Earth in the guise of
 Santasoma (from the
 Nahuatl Motecuhzoma,
 or Moctezuma)
White
Approximately 10 × 3 cm
After Williams García
 (1963, p. 187)

The Tepehuas share with the Nahuas and Otomís a complex view in which the earth is seen simultaneously as a provider of food and as a monster that devours the dead. Consequently paper images such as those in figures 163a, b are frequently cut as part of curing rituals, since the earth contains within it the spirits of the dead. They are also cut in rituals held to recompense the Spirit of the Earth for the numerous offenses committed against it, such as planting crops. Finally they are cut for use in rituals when the earth is thought to have stolen the patient's life-force.

The distinctive feature of these images is the comblike head-dress, which Williams García identifies as either plants that grow on the surface of the earth or, more likely, as the open, devouring jaws of the Earth monster. The ambiguous nature of the Earth spirit seems to be reflected in the fact that one of the pair is depicted wearing shoes (signifying outsider status) while the other is not. It appears likely that figure 163b is female because of the longer dresslike garment she wears.

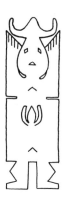

Figure 164
Xalapánaak Xkán, Señor del Agua,
    Lord of the Water
White
Approximately 10 × 3 cm
After Williams García (1963, p. 187)

Figure 164 represents one aspect of the Lord of the Water. The Tepehuas conceive of water, like the earth, as a spirit with both positive and negative aspects. It makes the crops grow, but it also robs "souls," drags people into the water, and threatens to flood the world. The following brief myth recorded by Williams García reveals the ambiguous nature of water: Jesus is old and tired and wants to flood the world. This would please the Muchacha del Agua, an aspect of Water, because then her underlings, the fish, would rule the earth. The Virgin Mary, however, stops Jesus from destroying the earth (1972, p. 36).

The headdress on figure 164 is really hair arranged in three lobes. The shaman who cut it said that the cut in the center of the body is "like a little well where water comes out" (Williams García 1963, p. 187).

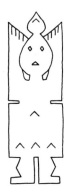

Figure 165
Xalapánaak Xkán, Señor del Agua,
    Lord of the Water
White
Approximately 10 × 3 cm
After Williams García (1963, p. 187)

The version of the Lord of the Water in figure 165 was cut by another shaman. The headdress is designed to represent a drop of water or a stylized water jar (Indian women carry water jars on their heads). The heart and clothing decorations are depicted in typical fashion.

Figure 166
An aspect of Xalapanak'un, Señor
   del Viento, Lord of the Wind
Green
Approximately 10 × 3 cm
After Williams García (1963, p. 187)

This cutting depicts Wind in the form of a birdlike figure. The headdress is a blowing tuft of hair, and at each side are wings. Between the legs is a bird's tail. The shape cut in the lower center of the figure is unidentified, but it may represent a drop of water or the bud of a growing plant. Wind in its positive aspect is identified with the coming of rain and, thus, indirectly with growing crops. Williams García sees a correspondence between this spirit and the Aztec deity Ehécatl-Quetzalcóatl.

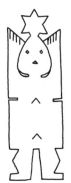

Figure 167
'Istakuní, Estrella, Star
Black
Approximately 10 × 3 cm
After Williams García (1963, p. 188)

The headdress in figure 167 clearly identifies the spirit as a star guardian. The black color represents the night, and the two cuts probably represent the heart and stomach or genitals.

Figure 168a
'Istakuní, Estrella, Star
   (female)
White
23 × 9 cm
Boilès collection

Figure 168b
'Istakuní, Estrella, Star
   (male)
White
23.5 × 8.5 cm
Boilès collection

The additional star guardians in figures 168a,b, in male and female aspect, watch over people during the night when the sun is absent. They are cut with hearts, winglike projections representing starlight, and clothing decorations.

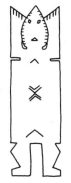

Figure 169
Fuego, Fire
White
Approximately 10 × 3 cm
After Williams García (1963, p. 190)

The Tepehuas consider the Spirit of Fire, portrayed as an old man, to come from the sky but to be a child of the Earth. The small cuts around the head are wrinkles, and the pattern in the body represents firewood. This hearth spirit has a long history among Middle American Indian cultures. The Aztecs propitiated a hearth deity named Huehueteotl (the Old God), who also was portrayed as an old man with a wrinkled face.

About a week following a funeral, the Tepehuas perform a ritual that consists of lighting and extinguishing a fire in the deceased person's fireplace. The ritual is performed to pay back the Earth for the times that the person burned it with fire during his lifetime. Failure to perform this ritual may cause the children of the dead person to sicken and die (Williams García 1963, p. 194).

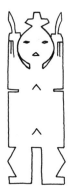

Figure 170
Cruz, Cross
White
Approximately 10 × 3 cm
After Williams García (1963, p. 188)

In figure 170 the Spirit of the Cross is cut as a separate figure. Just as it is among the Nahuas and Otomís, the cross for the Tepehuas has become a sacred object in its own right and is thought to possess great power. In addition to its innate power, the figure is also cut to represent the Sun-Christ in rituals. In its hands the figure holds swords that are shaped like crosses and that signify power. The headdress is a straightforward symbol for the cross.

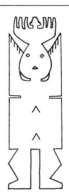

Figure 171
Cruz-Tierra, Earth-Cross
White
Approximately 10 × 3 cm
After Williams García (1963, p. 188)

This paper image represents a combination of the spirits of the Earth and the Cross. The Tepehuas occasionally plant a large wooden cross in the ground in front of the shrine to symbolize further the power of these combined spirits. The image is cut with an earth spirit headdress, except that the middle prong is shaped like a cross.

Taken as a group, Tepehua beneficial spirits reveal an animistic world view similar to that of the Nahuas and Otomís. Each important aspect of nature, such as the earth, water, and sun, has its corresponding spirit. Like the Otomís, the Tepehuas also cut images of everyday objects like houses and candles. Although generalization is difficult because of the lack of comparative field data from the region, it appears that the Tepehuas are more given to cutting images of major beneficent spirits than are the other groups. Images of Earth, Star, Wind, and Water, for example, are commonly cut for their rituals. One explanation for this practice is that even these spirits are believed to steal "souls," and thus images of them must be cut for curing rituals.

The cuttings of four shamans are represented in this section. We have included two specimens from the Boilès collection (figures 168a, b) that were cut by the same shaman whose figures are presented in the previous section of disease-causing spirits (figures 155–57 and 159). A quick glance at these series reveals that the style of the shaman carries over from disease-causing spirits to beneficent ones. Five specimens (figures 160a, b, 165–67) were cut by another shaman whose images are also presented in the previous section (figures 158a, b). Four additional images (figures 163a, b, 164, 169) were cut for Williams García by a third shaman, and figure 161 was cut for Gessain by a fourth.

TEPEHUA SEED SPIRITS

Images of seed spirits cut by Tepehua shamans are similar to those cut by the Nahuas in that they are restricted in variety, and the profile of the fruit or vegetable is cut from the interior of the body. These spirits are called Sombras de las Semillas (Shadows of the Seeds) or Antiguas (Ancient Ones) by the Tepehuas. They are cut by shamans either on top of a special hill or on the shore of a sacred lake. Although it is the shaman who cuts the paper images, the Tepehuas say that the Water Spirit actually gives the seed spirits to the village. The images of the seeds are dressed in tiny clothes, including hats and shoes, and are brought to the village in wooden boxes. After being placed on special altars in the traditional shrine, the boxes are attended by four young men and four young women. These specially appointed caretakers, along with members of the politicoreligious hierarchy in the village, are responsible for making periodic offerings to the seeds throughout the year and for conducting major crop-increase rituals. Failure to keep the seed spirits properly satisfied means that they might escape from the boxes and leave the village, resulting in famine (Williams García 1963, 202).

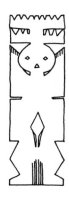

Figure 172a
Maíz, Maize (male)
White
Approximately 10 × 3 cm
After Williams García
   (1963, p. 189)

Figure 172b
Maíz, Maize (female)
White
Approximately 10 × 3 cm
After Williams García
   (1963, p. 189)

The most important single crop for the Tepehuas is maize, and these images accordingly play a central role in increase rituals. As is so often the case among the Tepehuas, the spirit is represented in both male and female form. The male figure has a headdress of leaves, an ear of corn cut from its body, and roots cut between the legs. The female figure has a head-dress of flowers and ears of corn on its chest and sides. The heels of its feet are represented as roots.

Figure 173
Maíz, Maize
Purple
Approximately 10 × 3 cm
After Williams García (1963, p. 214)

Figure 173 is another version of the Spirit of Maize, also cut with the double-tiered headdress of leaves, the ear of corn in the body, and the roots emerging from between the legs. This image is part of a large bundle of sacred paper cuttings used in various religious rituals. Figures 173 and 174 are used together to stand for all crops grown by the Tepehuas (Williams García 1963, p. 214).

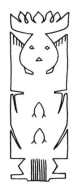

Figure 174
Chiltepín, Dios de Chile Rojo,
    Spirit of the Red Chile
Red
Approximately 10 × 3 cm
After Williams García (1963, p. 189)

The chile pepper is another important crop for the Tepehuas. This paper cutting represents the spirit of the small red chile, one of the numerous varieties grown. Peppers are cut in the headdress and body of the figure, and roots are symbolized by the fringe between the legs. Paper images of chile and maize are often used together in Tepehua rituals.

Figure 175
Plátano, Banana
Green
Approximately 10 × 3 cm
After Williams García (1963, p. 189)

Although the banana plant is of little economic importance

to most Tepehua families, this image of the banana seed spirit is highly significant. The reason given is that the banana is closely associated with the Spirit of Thunder and, thus, with Water. Williams García was not able to explain why this connection is made by the Tepehuas, however. According to informants, the Spirit of Thunder has the same appearance and color as the banana (Williams García 1963, p. 196). Although this figure has a human face, it is unusual in that it is not strictly anthropomorphic. Its main features are the leaves that surround the face and the roots that protrude from the base of the figure.

The very small number of Tepehua seed images presented here reflects their scarcity in the published literature and in private collections. Since ethnographers have been able to collect fairly large samples of paper images from the Tepehuas, it is puzzling why so few are seeds. A likely answer is that Tepehua shamans simply do not cut many seed spirit images. Like their Nahua counterparts, they limit their seed images to maize and chile peppers.

Another interesting parallel between the Tepehuas and Nahuas is the style of the seed spirits. In general, outlines of the crop are cut from the body of the figure. An exception is figure 174, in which the chile peppers are part of the headdress. This style of portrayal contrasts with that of the San Pablito Otomís in which the fruit or vegetable protrudes from the sides or head of the figure. The significance of these representational differences is not known.

TEPEHUA MISCELLANEOUS PAPER CUTTINGS

Like the Nahua and Otomí shamans, Tepehua shamans also cut paper images for special purposes. Figures 176–86 have been included as a sample of this category of cuttings.

Figure 176a
Ixtukuwín, Cera, Candle
  (female)
16.5 × 5.5 cm
Boilès collection

Figure 176b
Ixtukuwín, Cera, Candle
  (male)
White
16.5 × 5.5 cm
Boilès collection

Candles are an important component of ritual occasions and are used by all ritual specialists in the Huasteca region regardless of cultural affiliation. Portrayed here is the Tepehua Spirit of the Candle in its male and female aspects. The headdress of each figure represents a flame, and the uppermost inverted V cut is the heart. Other cuts are pockets or clothing decorations. The candle most commonly used in the region is made from locally produced beeswax. A second variety is made from tallow and is purchased at the market. Each type of candle is associated with a different part of the ritual.

   Shamans rub candles over a patient's body to remove harmful spirits. Lighted candles are also used to cleanse a house or ritual area of harmful spirits. Sacralized candles are often burned on the house altar to offer protection or to recall a curing ceremony held several days previously. They are always burned on altars during a ritual and in the area where paper figures are being cut. In sum, candles are a type of offering, but they also serve to mark out an area in which ritual activity is taking place.

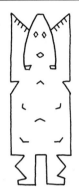

Figure 177a
Xtukuwí Lapának', Espiritu del
  Hombre, Spirit of a Man (male)
White
17 × 6 cm
Boilès collection

Figure 177b
Xtukuwí Lapának, Espiritu del
  Hombre, Spirit of a Man (female)
White
17 × 5 cm
Boilès collection

Portrayed in figures 177a, b are the male and female aspects of a person's life-force. The figures have no headdresses, and each is rendered with a heart and clothing decorations. In Tepehua thought a person may temporarily lose his life-force by being frightened or by having it captured. Any spirit in the Tepehua pantheon may steal it for any number of reasons. The victim is in a state of spiritual and physical decline until the life-force is returned, usually through the efforts of a shaman. Images such as these are often placed on the home altar to aid in convalescence. Sorcerers (*haxkayanán*) are known to cut figures like these and to use them in secret ceremonies to cause harm.

Figure 178
Lakatuhún Hatupas Diqalh, Tiene Siete
    Pensamientos, She Has Seven Thoughts,
    Sacred Rose (Saint Rose of Lima?), Marijuana
White
17 × 5.5 cm
Boilès collection

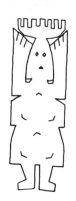

This rather plain figure represents a powerful spirit that can steal a person's soul or put him in contact with the spirit world. As among the Nahuas and Otomís, Santa Rosa is the Tepehuas' name for marijuana. In some villages it is eaten or mixed with *aguardiente* and drunk as a way of establishing communication with spirits. Ceremonial use of the plant is under the strict control of a shaman who insures that people use it with care. The Tepehuas say that Santa Rosa "is living, she is above all a piece of the heart of god" or that she is the "flower of god" (Williams García 1963, p. 221).

A paper image such as this one is cut during marijuana rituals. The meanings of the seven-pronged headdress and the name "She has Seven Thoughts" are uncertain (see Boilès 1967, pp. 269–70). Among the Nahuas and Otomís the spirit is associated with water but, according to Williams García, the Tepehuas apparently associate it with the earth (1963, pp. 215ff.; 1975).

Figure 179
Muñeco para enamorarse, "image to
    make someone fall in love"
White
Size of original unknown
After Gessain (1938, following p. 370)

Like the Nahuas and Otomís, the Tepehuas have developed magical means to make someone fall in love. Figure 179 is a large paper cutout used by wives to make their husbands lose interest in all other women and to prevent them from becoming jealous. In the center is a circle of female figures standing over reclining male figures. The images symbolize the dominance of the wife over her husband. The paper is folded and placed under the husband's sleeping mat (Gessain 1938, p. 370).

Figure 180
Muñeco para enamorarse, "image to
   make someone fall in love"
Color and size of original
   unknown
After Gessain (1938, following p. 370)

This figure is cut by the shaman to use in a ceremony that magically keeps a husband from falling in love with someone else. The double image of the husband illustrated here is folded together with a similar image of the jealous wife. They are then slipped under the husband's sleeping mat. If the magic works, the husband will lose interest in all other women, and he will remain faithful to his wife (Gessain 1938, p. 370).

Figure 181
Muñeco para enamorarse, "image
   to make someone fall in love"
Color and size of original
   unknown
After Gessain (1938, following
   p. 370)

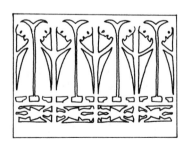

A variation of figure 179, this cutout is used by wives to ensure the fidelity of their husbands. It is also used to prevent the husband's striking the wife or becoming jealous. The female figures are doubled in number and size to increase the wife's influence over the husband, who lies beneath her feet. The image is hidden in the house by the woman so that her husband does not see it (Gessain 1938, p. 370).

Figure 182
Ish pukuka maqan kan alasani', "to go
    and get rid of the dead"
Black
Size of original unknown
After Gessain (1938, following p. 368)

Tepehua shamans cut figure 182 as part of a ceremony held one week after a death. The object of the ritual is to prevent the deceased's spirit from returning and causing harm. In this cutout the shaman is shown dancing over skeleton images representing the dead "soul." The image symbolically represents the dominance of the shaman over the dead. The small chevrons over each skeleton are the "crowns of death." Twelve of these images are cut for the death of a woman, 24 for a man, and 100 for a shaman. After the ritual the images are placed under a rock at the bottom of a river (Gessain 1963, p. 369).

Figure 183
Shaman with copal incense
    brazier on his head
Color and size of original
    unknown
After Gessain (1938, following p. 366)

This figure is cut as part of a ceremony to prevent epidemics from entering the village. During the ceremony the shaman performs a dance wearing a circular paper headdress called the "crown of the sorcerer" while simultaneously balancing a brazier on his head. After the ceremony a paper image is cut depicting the shaman with the brazier on his head. The figure is placed along with paper images of guardian stars on the trails leading to the village. Any epidemic diseases trying to enter the village will be turned away by the sacralized paper images (Gessain 1938, p. 368).

Figure 184
Shaman dancing on the head
    of a devil
Color and size of original
    unknown
After Gessain (1938, following p. 366)

This figure is cut by Tepehua shamans to prevent the spread of epidemic diseases. The figure is hung over the doorway of each house to prevent the disease from entering. It represents the spirit of a shaman dancing on the head of a devil or, in other words, the conquest of disease (Gessain 1938, pp. 367–68).

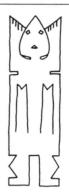

Figure 185
Casa, House
White
Approximately 10 × 3 cm
After Williams García (1963, p. 190)

For all Indian groups in the region the house has a kind of spiritual presence. This paper image of the House spirit is depicted with support beams cut out of the body. When a dwelling is built, certain ritual procedures are always followed to prevent the House spirit from becoming angry. If the proper offerings are made, the spirit will protect household members from harm. Like virtually all spirits, the House spirit has both beneficial and harmful sides. If disease spreads within a family or if a patient does not respond to treatment, the shaman often cuts a figure similar to the House Spirit and makes offerings to it.

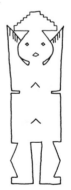

Figure 186
Lakachínchin, Sun Place or
    House of Antiguas (Ancient Ones)
Black
Approximately 10 × 3 cm
After Williams García (1963, p. 188)

Figure 186 depicts the Spirit of the Shrine in which traditional rituals are held. The headdress is cut in the image of a pyramid that represents the Golden Hill—the residence of the Sun, the Stars, and the other important spirits in the Tepehua pantheon. What is remarkable about this figure is its similarity to the pyramids built by the pre-Hispanic civilizations of Middle America as shrines to the various deities. Roofed structures built on top of them housed images of the deities. They were, in short, like Tepehua "Golden Hills," the residences of the spirits. Tepehua shamans unknowingly recall these ancient monuments in their contemporary paper images. The syncretic nature of Tepehua religion is clearly illustrated in this paper figure. The Golden Hill is the image of a pre-Hispanic pyramid, and on the Golden Hill reside the Sun-Christ and his entourage seated around a table, a re-creation of the Last Supper. Tepehua shamans use this paper image during rituals held in the village shrine when they want to symbolize all of the spirits who occupy the Golden Hill.

We have enough information on Tepehua religion to be able to demonstrate remarkable similarities to the Nahua and Otomí religions. As with the other groups, the Tepehuas have a multiplicity of spirits. In fact it seems that the list of manifestations and alter egos of any single spirit could be expanded almost indefinitely. For example, rain is thought to be caused by the Water Spirit, the Old Ones, San Juan, the female Water Bearers, the male Siren, Jesus, Thunder, and so on. These are separate spirits in a sense, and yet they are tied together in the myth system. To this paradoxical aspect of the *costumbre* complex is added the apparent contradictory roles of some of the spirits. For example, Jesus is identified with the Sun and at the same time with San Juan, the "Negro" who lives in the sea and who sends rain. The Sun is a protector spirit, and yet Jesus threatens to flood the world because he is bored with it. Only the Virgin Mary stops this primary Tepehua guardian spirit from destroying the earth.

The levels of apparent contradictions multiply when the beneficial spirits are examined. The Earth, Sun, and Water conjoin to produce Maize, which sustains the Tepehuas. These major spirits are thought to underly all of life, and they are the subjects of numerous offerings to repay their bounty. Yet they are precisely those spirits most likely to steal a person's "soul," causing sickness and possibly death. Difficulties in categorizing Tepehua spirits result partly from the lack of information on their cosmology. It is, however, apparent from what we do know that they share with the Nahuas and Otomís a degree of ambiguity and amorphousness in how their pantheon is organized. These problems in understanding the larger picture of the *costumbre* system are discussed in the concluding chapter.

Stylistically it appears that Tepehua paper images are easily distinguishable from those cut by the Nahuas and Otomís. Until more research is conducted in the region, however, we cannot tell if these distinctions represent real differences in style or if they are simply an artifact of the sample of specimens we have available for study. As indicated above, differences exist in how shamans portray spirits. Shamans in a given area, however, seem to have certain limits to how innovative they can be. The most unusual cuttings compared to the bulk presented in this chapter are those collected by Gessain. What would be called altar mats among the Nahuas and Otomís serve here as individual images. The more naturalistic, curvilinear appearance of some of these cuttings may be because all of them represent the spirits of human beings rather than spirit entities.

CHAPTER 7

THE PAPER FIGURE
AS ART AND CULTURAL ARTIFACT

If the red slayer think he slays,
    Or if the slain think he is slain,
They know not well the subtle ways
    I keep, and pass, and turn again.

Far or forgot to me is near;
    Shadow and sunlight are the same;
The vanished gods to me appear;
    And one to me are shame and fame.

They reckon ill who leave me out;
    When me they fly, I am the wings;
I am the doubter and the doubt,
    And I the hymn the Brahmin sings.

The strong gods pine for my abode,
    And pine in vain the sacred Seven;
But thou, meek lover of the good!
    Find me and turn thy back on heaven.

—"Brahma," by Ralph Waldo Emerson

EMERSON's well-known poem about the principle of unity that underlies many Eastern religions offers a profound insight into the nature of the religious systems discussed in this work. To the first travelers and ethnographers who entered the region of papermaking, Indian religious beliefs and practices appeared to be straightforward and as "simple" as the villages in which they lived. There was worship of idols and ceremonies to cure diseases and to ensure that the crops flourished. Paper images cut by Indian shamans were further proof of the "superstitious" and simple nature of *costumbre* religions. As information ac-

cumulated on the paper images and their rituals, contradictions
and complications became evident. Spirits appeared in varying,
sometimes inconsistent guises, and there seemed to be no clear
hierarchically arranged pantheon of deities. Interestingly, scholars engaged in analyzing the great pre-Hispanic urban religions have faced the same apparent contradictions. Part of the
problem in both areas of research is the persistent tendency to
underestimate the sophistication and subtlety of thought that
characterizes these religious systems. We will return to the concept of unity after reviewing some initial responses to the *costumbre* complex and after examining in some detail the paper
images that contribute so much to its character.

The responses of earlier researchers to Nahua, Otomí, and
Tepehua religion were a mixture of disdain and condescension.
Frederick Starr, who reflected the ethnocentric anthropology
of the nineteenth century, wrote of the papermaking region,
"There is no better place in all Mexico for study of super-
stition than this district of mingled population" (Starr 1901,
p. 80). The disparaging remarks of Dard Hunter and V. W.
Von Hagen are on record (see chapter 1), and Bodil Christensen, who was generally sympathetic to the Indians, still wrote
about them as living "in a world full of spirits," a statement
implying a childlike fatalism they do not possess (Christensen
1971, p. 26). Hans Lenz titles his chapter on the contemporary
uses of paper "El papel y las supersticiones" (Paper and Super-
stitions), and he states that "in many regions it was not possible
to eliminate all of the vestiges of idolatry that even now exist in
the aboriginal mentality" (Lenz 1973 [1948], p. 120).[1] As late
as 1969, Leonardo Manrique referred to the religion practiced
in San Pablito as "paganism" (1969, p. 715; see chapter 5),
a term with negative connotations usually rejected by anthropologists.

Modern ethnographers who have worked in the area generally
avoid ethnocentric judgments, but they do express a degree of
perplexity over the apparent lack of structure in the religious
systems. Information gathered from one native informant is invariably contradicted by another. An added problem is the ad-

mixture of Christian and pre-Hispanic beliefs among the Indians, giving outsiders the impression of an incompatible mélange of traditions.

Four major reasons can be given for the evident confusion. First, the Mexican Indians have been the victims of one of the most brutal colonial policies in history, and they have, by necessity, developed means of hiding traditional beliefs behind a façade of Christian trappings. Second, in level of sociocultural integration, these are peasant or perhaps tribal societies that do not have full-time theologians to systematize all elements of their religious systems. Third, there is an extreme particularism in the region such that differences in ritual performance and religious belief occur not only between villages but also among groups within a single village. Finally, much of the research in the region has been conducted in Spanish, which is a second language for the Indians and is thus inadequate for eliciting information on complicated philosophical or cosmological questions. Each of these reasons has validity, and, taken together, they help explain the difficulties that ethnographers face in understanding the *costumbre* complex. One additional reason, rarely mentioned by ethnographers, is that the religions of this region are indeed highly sophisticated and are not, therefore, amenable to simplistic analyses.

SIMILARITIES OF NAHUA, OTOMÍ, AND TEPEHUA RELIGIONS

Up to this point we have been talking about the Nahua, Otomí, and Tepehua religions as though they are separate, each standing on its own. Each religious system is discussed in its own chapter. The ethnographic research on these three groups has not produced totally comparable religious data to date. Even with the available information, however, the casual reader cannot help but notice the remarkable similarities among the three. A comparison of tables 2, 5, and 7 reveals striking correspondences in the three pantheons. Each group has developed an important celestial spirit complex involving the stars, Moon, fire, Christian saints, the Virgin Mary, and especially the Sun, which has been syncretized with Jesus Christ. In the beliefs of each group, the stars protect people while the Sun is absent, and the Moon is either ambivalent or negative in its effect on human beings. The fire spirit, also associated with the sky, lives in the stones surrounding the family hearth and protects household members from harm. In addition each culture views the earth as a complex entity with multiple manifestations of a positive and negative character. The earth is conceived as a living being whose fertility makes the crops grow. Life-giving seed and rain spirits live in earthly caves, but at the same time it is the earth that devours bodies of the dead. Even the names of important earth-related spirits such as the Antiguas or Moctezuma are shared among the three groups. Other names, such as Lord of the Mountain and Mother Earth, are shared by at least two groups, and it is possible they will be shown to exist in the third when more information becomes available.

Each group has an underworld in which the spirits of the dead and the *malos aires* reside, ruled by malevolent spirits associated, at least in name, with the Christian Devil. The *malos aires* are polluting agents associated with the wind that cause disease and misfortune. Shamans from each culture endeavor to control the *malos aires* through rituals termed cleansings. In addition each group propitiates a complex of water spirits including the Lady of the Water. Water spirits are ambivalent in that they provide water and rain but also drown people and demand offerings. Finally all three groups conceive of intermediary spirits that act as messengers between the human and spirit realms. The Nahuas have their witnesses, the Otomís their mountain spirits, and the Tepehuas the divine ritual specialists on the Golden Hill. Similarities extend to the residences of their spirits: the hills, caves, and lakes that are visited by processions bearing offerings. It is possible that many apparent differences among the three cultures, such as the Tepehua association of Santa Rosa with the earth rather than water, are the result of mistakes made by ethnographers or their informants.

Further similarities emerge when we examine the concept of "spirit" or "soul" among the three groups. It is clear from the brief summaries we have presented that the Indian conceptions are intricate and probably not fully understood by most outsiders. The concept of spirit or soul is always one of the most difficult to translate from one culture to another. In fact, even in our own society people are not in agreement about the nature of either spirit or soul. The Nahuas have the *noyolo* and *notonal,* both of which appear to mean "life-force." We have not been able to clarify the differences between these concepts among the Nahuas of the region despite our numerous attempts while in the field. The Otomís have at least two terms, *zaki* and *na xudi,* which mean "life-force" and "shadow," respectively. For the Tepehuas, the term *tukuwín* has been reported and translated as "shadow." The *nagual,* which some scholars identify as a type of soul (see, for example, Adams and Rubel 1967, p. 336) is instead considered to be a transforming sorcerer. The spirits listed in tables 2, 5, and 7 and their paper images are really animating principles or forces rather than incorporeal beings—ethereal shadows of energy possessed by both human beings and other aspects of existence. They are abstractions that become specific spirits during rituals or when they are cut from paper, but which generally remain amorphous in day-to-day life. As will be seen, it is this generalized concept of spirit or shadow shared by all three groups that lies behind the multiple manifestations of specific spirit entities.

The four rituals we describe also reveal remarkable similarities among Nahua, Otomí, and Tepehua religious practices. Undoubtedly the most obvious correspondence is in the way paper images are used to depict the various spirits. In addition there are the shared ritual elements, which are discussed in the analyses following each description, and the shared sequences of ritual episodes (cleansings followed by offerings to major spirits). Besides common overall ritual strategy, the groups also share specific procedures and props. These include copal incense, candles, *aguardiente,* sacred guitar and violin music, tobacco, burying of live fowl for the earth, bloody animal sacri-

fice, palm and marigold adornments, sacred cabinets containing dressed paper images of seed spirits, and many others. But
the real test of compatibility of belief among the three groups
is that they are willing to accept each others' shamans to perform rituals.

Similarities extend to Nahua, Otomí, and Tepehua ritual
calendars. For the most part the three groups have taken over
the Christian liturgical calendar (see chapter 3). They have
added many saints' days to their lists of celebrations. Even observances that clearly have a pre-Hispanic base, such as All
Souls and Carnival, are syncretized with the Christian celebration of similar character. The more strictly traditional rituals
are less tied to the calendar. All groups have planting and
harvest rituals involving seed spirits sometime in early spring
and early fall respectively. The other traditional rituals vary as
to when they are held or are linked to specific "crisis" situ-
ations, such as completion of a house, birth, disease, or death.

We wish to note similarities among the three groups, but do
not mean to assert that they are identical. Throughout the
previous chapters we have discussed differences in ritual performance and religious belief as well as correspondences. The
differences, however, remain unpatterned, and it is impossible,
with the available information to classify traits according to
whether they are strictly Nahua, Otomí, or Tepehua. The
Nahuas among whom we worked did not appear to identify
with other Nahua villages particularly, except to note that
they spoke the same language. They hold stereotypes of the
Otomís and Tepehuas, but they hold similar stereotypes of
Nahuas in other villages. This lack of clearly stated ethnic
identity has led one researcher to ask whether or not there
exists a distinct Otomí culture at all (see Galinier 1977). Of
course a clear distinction is made by everyone in the area between their local Indian culture and *mestizo* culture, but the
question remains as to the degrees of similarities and differences among the local Indian groups.

We suggest that the religious systems of the three groups
are quite similar for three major reasons. For one thing the

Indians do not live in isolated enclaves; Nahua, Otomí, and Tepehua villages are found in the same area. Starr noticed this fact when he wrote: "Where the states of Hidalgo, Puebla, and Veracruz come together we find the strangest interminglings. There Aztecs, Otomís, Tepehuas, and Totonacs are surprisingly sprinkled" (Starr 1901, p. 79). As reported earlier this is the core region in which the *costumbre* complex survives. A second reason is that this particular area of Mexico has suffered devastating upheavals in pre-Hispanic as well as colonial times. The Aztecs invaded the region several times and Spanish colonial policies were particularly harsh in and around the Huasteca. Slavery, disease, forced migration, and outright murder reduced the population by as much as 90 percent within a few years of the Spanish Conquest, and the survivors must have experienced a high amount of stress (see chapter 3). In the process of reconstituting their cultures, the Indians undoubtedly borrowed heavily from one another. Finally, all three contemporary Indian groups are heirs to a common Mesoamerican cultural tradition that was and still is influential in virtually every society throughout the region.

THE PRE-HISPANIC BASIS OF THE PAPER CULT RELIGIONS

The pre-Hispanic basis of the beliefs and practices of contemporary Indians must be proven and not assumed. Some ethnographers have a tendency to make uncritical connections between pre-Hispanic and modern beliefs. For example, contemporary water spirits are presumed to be modern versions of the Aztec Tlaloc, or a spirit that rules in the underworld is automatically equated with the Aztec Mictlantecutli. These individual connections may or may not be valid. Often the modern village spirit differs markedly in character from what is known of its ancient Aztec counterpart. To demonstrate an historical link between the ancient civilizations and modern Indians, whole patterns of symbols and spirit types must be shown to be similar or identical. Attempts to achieve this include Reyes García (1960, pp. 39–40), who shows some correspondences between

the ancient Aztec and modern Nahua ritual calendars; and
Monnich (1976), who lists over twenty-five specific correspondences between ancient Aztec and modern Nahua religious
beliefs and folk tales. Because of the similarities among Nahuas,
Otomís, and Tepehuas, many of these Aztec-Nahua correspondences apply to the latter two groups as well. Recent work
by the late Eva Hunt, however, provides a general framework
for the comparison of pre-Hispanic and contemporary Indian
sacred symbol systems.

Hunt argues that pre-Hispanic religion was virtually identical all over Mesoamerica:

> At the time of the Spanish conquest, the whole of Mesoamerica
> shared a distinct religion, unique in its basic armature and gross
> cryptographic detail. The dominant divine images, the calendar,
> the ritual cycles, the iconographic materials from which the deities
> were made up and identified, the myths of their origins, travels,
> doings, and powers, were pan-Mesoamerican. [Hunt 1977, p. 46]

She isolates forty-five coded taxonomies or classes of symbols
out of which pre-Hispanic deities were created. These symbol
classes constituted the raw material from which clusters of symbols were formed. "Each [pre-Hispanic] deity was defined by
one of these unique clusters of cross-class, cross-taxonomy symbols" (Hunt 1977, p. 54). But the process of creating deities
from this reservoir of symbols was continuous, so that by the
time of the Conquest each had multiple identities, alter egos,
or manifestations. It follows that if the religious systems of the
modern Indians are pre-Hispanic in nature, they too should
contain spirits formed from these common symbol classes.

Table 9 itemizes the pre-Hispanic symbol classes discussed
by Hunt so that they can be compared with the symbol classes
among modern Nahuas, Otomís, and Tepehuas. (Explanations
of the symbol classes and specific examples of the symbols
derived from each culture are contained in the Appendix.) A
plus sign (+) under the group name indicates that the symbol
class listed on the left has been reported in the modern religion. A question mark (?) indicates not absence but a lack of
conclusive ethnographic data on that particular symbol class.

TABLE 9. Symbol Classes of Contemporary Nahua, Otomí, and Tepehua Indians Compared with Symbol Classes of Pre-Hispanic Mesoamerican Indians

Pre-Hispanic Symbol Classes*	Nahua	Otomí	Tepehua
Animal Taxonomies			
1. Volatiles	+	+	+
2. Crawlers and swimmers	+	+	+
3. Four-legged walkers	+	+	+
4. Mankind	+	+	+
Symbolic Plant Taxonomies			
1. Domestic plants	+	+	+
2. Powerful plants and plant parts	+	+	+
3. Flowers	+	+	+
4. Trees and bushes	?	?	?
Corporeal Taxonomies or Classes			
1. Sex	+	+	+
2. Stages of growth and ages of man	+	+	+
3. Parts of the body	+	+	+
4. Sickness	+	+	+
Natural Phenomena—The Elements			
1. Winds	+	+	+
2. Falling water	+	+	+
3. Surface water	+	+	+
4. Fire	+	+	+
5. The Earth	+	+	+
6. Geographic aspects of the earth	+	+	+
Celestial Bodies			
1. The sun	+	+	+
2. The inner planets	?	?	?
3. The moon	+	+	+
4. Venus	?	?	?
5. Mercury	?	?	?
6. The outer planets	?	?	?
7. Mars	?	?	?
8. Jupiter and Saturn	?	?	?
9. The stars and constellations	?	?	?
The Visible Spectrum	+	+	+
Minerals	?	?	?
Cultural Orders—Material Culture			
1. Tools and weapons	+	+	+

TABLE 9. *Continued*

2. Household equipment and furniture	+	+	+
3. Clothing	+	+	+
4. Face-painting and masks	+	+	+
Social Structure and Stratification			
1. Professions	+	+	+
2. Food as a marker of social status	+	?	?
3. Historical culture heroes	?	?	?
4. Ethnic groups	?	?	?
Kinship	+	+	+
Names and Language Transformations	?	?	?
Ethos	+	+	+
Mathematical Orders	?	?	?
Direction	?	+	?
Space-Time Continuum			
1. Geometric designs	+	+	+
2. Numerology and signs	?	?	?
Human Settlements and Numerology	?	?	?

*Categories after Hunt (1977).

Half of the question marks appear under the heading "Celestial Bodies," and this is obviously an area where we lack substantive information on the contemporary cultures. It is possible that complex astronomical observations and numerology, both of which were prominent in the pre-Hispanic religion, have not survived among modern villagers. Fully two-thirds of Hunt's pre-Hispanic symbol classes are present in the modern religions, however, which clearly suggests an historical connection between contemporary and pre-Hispanic religions.

The paper images themselves are a means of expressing these symbols and thus are a part of the greater Mesoamerican pre-Hispanic pattern. However, as mentioned, we have only indirect evidence that paper images of spirits were actually cut before the Conquest. Fitl conducted a detailed examination of several of the codices and found images of vegetative deities that bear a remarkable resemblance to the seed images of modern Indians (1975, pp. 210ff.). In several of the codex paintings, for example, plant parts emerge from the figures' heads and sides. This suggests that the design of the contemporary seed images traces to the pre-Hispanic period. In another study Klein examined all of the known examples of pre-Hispanic two-dimensional art in which the figure is front-faced. This form of representation is rare, and Klein wished to determine whether or not there is a symbolic basis for it. She finds that frontally portrayed figures are associated with western, southern, or central world directions; the female earth; fertility; death; and darkness, which stand for completed spatiotemporal cycles (1976, pp. 257–58). She concludes that "frontality itself therefore had an inherent meaning and function distinct from that of the [more common] profile form" (1976, p. 258). Since the overwhelming majority of paper images are *en face* and relate to one or more of these pre-Hispanic categories, it seems likely that frontality is another design feature carried over from pre-Hispanic times.

STYLISTIC FEATURES OF THE PAPER IMAGES

The modern paper images are ritual objects, but they are also works of art that reflect something of the world view and aesthetic principles of the cultures in which they are created. Individual images are judged by shaman and layman alike according to how well they are cut and whether they properly incorporate the religious symbols. No shaman can establish a positive reputation without first becoming a master paper cutter. But perhaps more important, the paper images represent an attempt to express the deepest concerns and most complex philosophical and theological concepts of a culture in an aesthetic manner. The paper images are intellectual achievements because they are visual images of what people think about nature and humanity's place within it. The images break the flow of consciousness and events into analytical units such as sun, earth, water, seeds, germination, growth, love, lust, jealousy, disease, and death. These are symbolically depicted in paper and laid out in an organized pattern during rituals so that they form a meaningful whole. The paper images are strikingly dramatic aesthetic forms that work in rituals and work as art because they express the world view of the people who produce them.

The Indian shaman-artist must strike a balance between repetition and innovation. Shamans learn to cut paper during their apprenticeships and are inclined to repeat the form taught by the master. But each shaman must establish his or her own style in order to attract a clientele. One way to do this is to cut the paper images a little differently from everyone else. Shamans thus become ritual entrepreneurs who innovate to survive. This explains much of the variation in the portrayal of spirits exhibited throughout the culture area. If they want to be successful, however, shamans are not free to create at will. They are constrained by the expectations of the people they serve and by the logical requirements of the philosophical and theological system in which they operate.

These factors have led to the development of regional subtraditions in paper cutting. A renowned shaman, for example, may train a dozen neophytes during his lifetime who then carry on variations of his particular style of cutting. The villagers in the area soon become habituated to the new style, and over time a regional variation emerges. Evidence suggests that these subtraditions cover large areas and that they cross cultural boundaries. Thus the particular location of a village may be as important in understanding its paper images as the cultural affiliation of the people. Images collected among Otomís (figures 150–53) and Tepehuas (figures 160, 163–65, 167, 169–71, 178, 185–86) of northern Veracruz, for example, are closer in form to some Nahua images from the same area (figures 38–47) than they are to Otomí and Tepehua images from some distance away (for example, Otomí figures 60–149 and Tepehua figures 161, 179–84). Additional systematic collection of paper images will make possible a description of the various papercutting subtraditions, as well as the determination of their genealogical relationships to one another.

Several stylistic features of the paper images are shared widely throughout the culture area. As the catalog demonstrates, most of the spirits portrayed are anthropomorphic and have the characteristic front-faced stance with the hands raised by the sides of the head. The Otomís of San Pablito, however, typically portray disease-causing spirits *(judíos)* with two heads in profile, looking left and right, and, in most instances, sharing a common front-faced body. All forms are bilaterally symmetrical, although some of the altar adornments cut by all three groups exhibit radial symmetry as well. These characteristics are related to the fact that the paper is always folded before being cut. The faces, for the most part, are similar from culture to culture. With the exception of the *judíos* cut by the San Pablito Otomís, the spirits are portrayed with benign expressions that reveal little of their characters. Most figures are cut with small diamond-shaped eyes and either a triangular- or a diamond-shaped mouth. These shapes are formed when the flap of paper in the aperture is either folded back, creating a triangle, or entirely cut out, forming a diamond. Sometimes the eyes and mouth are formed by cutting a V-shaped slash, without folding back the flap, giving the spirit the appearance of being asleep. The Otomí *judíos,* by contrast, have hideous expressions that communicate their dangerous characters. Except for these figures cut in profile, none of the images is depicted with a nose. Ears also do not generally seem an important anatomical feature since only Otomí seed spirits are cut with them.

The head shape of the paper images is an important feature shared throughout the culture area. Once again with the exception of the Otomís of San Pablito, heads are portrayed either as circular or, more commonly, as rounded, with the top of the head approaching a point. Cutting the heads in this way gives the paper images an otherworldly appearance and serves to emphasize the nonhuman character of the spirits. Also, the head shape possibly may be a survival, in artistic representation, of the pre-Hispanic practice of occipital cranial skull deformation. In this practice the skull was artificially flattened by strapping small boards to the front and back of a baby's head. The result was a characteristic shape similar to that seen in the paper images. Among the San Pablito Otomís,

head shape is somewhat more naturalistic. The *judíos* are cut
with more humanlike heads, although facial features are grossly
exaggerated and have a threatening appearance. Seed spirits
in San Pablito are cut with a bulging cranium that is con-
stricted above the ears. This gives them a babylike appearance
that we feel may relate symbolically to the fact that seeds are
considered children of more powerful spirits.

Probably the most critical feature of any paper image is its
headdress. In pre-Hispanic times headgear and hair style were
important symbols of a person's rank in society, and now the
headdress of each paper image is an important identification
marker. A common head ornament is a crown composed of
three or more prongs—sometimes so many that the crown resembles a tuft of hair. In fact when Frederick Starr first saw
paper images he described them as having hair on their heads
(see chapter 1). In some cases the crowns are multitiered, while
in others they have a rakelike appearance. Harmful spirits may
wear hats or headdresses made of animal horns or the crescent
moon. Seed spirits often have a crown that includes an image
of the ripened crop they represent; sometimes this is a representation of a bud or flower, signifying the growing plant.
These vegetative headdresses are among the most elaborate
features of all the paper images. The San Pablito Otomís sometimes include small spirit helpers in the headdress, and the
Tepehuas use a chevron-shaped crown to signify that the image
is associated with death. In general the dangerous spirits tend
to have spiky or hornlike headdresses.

Nahua, Otomí, and Tepehua shamans share additional aesthetic and symbolic conventions. All of the anthropomorphic
images are portrayed wearing clothes, although some, concur-
rently, have a small V cut representing the spirit's genitals.
The portrayal of genitals is an interesting feature Klein also
found in pre-Hispanic frontally portrayed figures (Klein 1976,
p. 242). Even the male and female figures placed together in
a lovemaking position for love magic are fully clothed. Often,
in fact, great attention is paid to making cuts in the paper to
represent pockets or clothing decorations. Another shared char-

acteristic of paper images is that even among the less elaborate examples great attention is always paid to certain details. For example, all images are cut with fingers and toes; frequently five digits can be counted. When images are portrayed with shoes or boots, these too are usually clearly indicated. In most of the seed-spirit images care is taken to portray the roots of the plant. If a root crop is depicted, the San Pablito Otomís sometimes even show the vegetable protruding from the figure's feet. Finally, in all seed images great care is taken to represent in a naturalistic manner the shape of the desired vegetable or fruit.

Although generalizations about the paper images must remain provisional because of the absence of representative collections, there are some observed differences in portrayal based on cultural affiliation. The Nahuas seem to be the only group to cut multiple identical images. These are cut in groups of four or eight and are typically images of disease-causing spirits. In addition only Nahuas cut images side by side like the chains of paper dolls made by children in Western European cultures. The Nahuas express the powerful character of spirits by duplicating their images in paper and by highlighting the garments they wear. Dangerous spirits are cut wearing suits of hair, shells, spines, and so on—a symbolic mode not found among the Otomís or Tepehuas. The altar adornments or "tortilla napkins" of the Nahuas rely far more on geometric designs than do those produced by the Otomís or Tepehuas. These latter groups, by contrast, incorporate anthropomorphic and theriomorphic motifs to a far greater extent. Finally, Nahua shamans, like their Tepehua counterparts, focus on the paper image's interior configuration. For example, they portray internal organs such as ribs, hearts, genitals, and stomachs. In addition Nahua and Tepehua seed spirits are cut so that the crops appear as internal organs.

The Otomís of San Pablito, by contrast, pay very little attention to the internal parts of paper images. Crops protrude from the sides of the figures or sprout from their headdresses. Unlike the Nahuas, their portrayal of dangerous spirits is graphic and highly descriptive. The *judíos* are cut with machetes and malicious faces. Malevolence exudes from these figures far more than it does from the Nahua *ejecatl* spirits with their multiple images, benign expressions, and spiny suits of clothes. In fact, it is often difficult to distinguish the harmful from the salutary spirits among the Nahuas based on the appearance of the paper image. The Otomís often associate the spirit class of *judíos* with animals and cut their images with animal tails and heads. This is not usually the case with the Nahuas and Tepehuas, who generally prefer anthropomorphic figures, although we do have an example of the Tepehuas cutting a bird spirit associated with the wind. Similarly, the intermediary spirits among the Otomís are portrayed as small birds rather than as the anthropomorphic cutouts associated with the Nahuas (compare figures 75–80 to figures 27–37).

In contrast to the Otomí cuttings, Tepehua paper images are far less ornate. With the exception of figures 161 and 179–84, which were collected in the 1930s, Tepehua cutouts are basically rectangular in outline, with symmetrically patterned details composed of straight lines of varying lengths. Like the Nahua examples, these paper images have somewhat simplified headdresses. Tepehua shamans are unique in the degree to which they cut dualistic representations of the spirits. Many of their paper figures come in pairs, one image representing the male aspect of the spirit and the other representing the female aspect. The images collected in the 1930s differ markedly from those collected more recently. The earlier figures are highly elaborate and consist of curvilinear anthropomorphic forms. While they do retain the Tepehua emphasis on dualism, they are stylistically distinct from other images in the catalog. They appear so different that it seems likely they are the conception of a single shaman.

The paper images cut in San Pablito stand apart stylistically from those cut among the Nahuas and Tepehuas. In fact the San Pablito images differ even from the cuttings of other Otomí groups (see figures 149–54). Since the Otomís of San Pablito are apparently among the last people to manufacture bark paper, it seems logical that the images they produce must also be the most ancient. The evidence, however, does not support this supposition. More than any other group, the Otomís of San Pablito have incorporated elements from Western European culture in their cuttings. The *judíos*, for instance, carry machetes, often have beards, and wear heavy boots. They have names like President of Hell, Lord Devil, and Lord Jew, all of which are based on alien concepts. The Otomís of San Pablito also have increased the number of seed images cut to include the many crops introduced by the Spaniards. For example they cut figures of the apple, pineapple, and pomegranate spirits. Certain seed images are cut with remarkably elaborate headdresses, far out of proportion to the economic importance of the particular crop. The most likely explanation for these innovations and for the generally more flamboyant style of the San Pablito images is that shamans have been influenced by the demands of the tourist trade. As the Indians have come into contact with outsiders and as they have begun to appreciate which design features attract tourists, they have incorporated appropriate foreign ideas into their paper cuttings.

The historical pattern followed by the Otomí craftsmen of San Pablito has been repeated in many areas of Mexico. Over the past several decades Mexico has developed into an important center of tourism, drawing visitors from all over the world. Tourists flood local marketplaces and have created a demand for the "authentic" folk crafts of various Indian groups in Mexico. Small-scale village craft industries have been transformed virtually overnight into profitable businesses. Thus, in addition to farming, many Indians are also engaged in producing traditional clothes, pottery, wool blankets, straw sculptures, yarn paintings, musical instruments, straw hats, sandals, and so on. As mentioned in chapter 1, one of the most successful new ventures for the Indians has been the production of colorful bark-paper paintings by Nahuas of the state of Guerrero. Since it was the Otomís of San Pablito who supplied the paper, they too were drawn into the burgeoning tourist market. Although historical information is lacking, it seems likely that the creation of new forms and the elaboration of existing ones accelerated as the paper images began to sell. Thus, one effect of the tourist industry has been to revitalize an ancient craft and to promote the innovation and creativity that characterize a vital, living tradition.

THE PLACE OF PAPER IMAGES IN INDIAN THOUGHT AND CULTURE

Anthropologists are not yet able to provide a universal, all-encompassing theory to explain the place of religion and ritual in culture. Religion is a multidimensional phenomenon that has implications for all aspects of human behavior. It must be understood on multiple levels, including the psychological, sociological, cultural, and ecological. The paper images as key elements in Indian religion likewise have broad implications for native thought, culture, and social organization.

In order for people in a society to behave in a coherent manner, they must to some extent share a world view that assumes a fundamental regularity or predictability of events. As previously indicated, all religions select from the biological, social, and natural world elements that become metaphors for the underlying order of the universe (see the Appendix for a list of major symbol classes used by the Indians of Mesoamerica based on this type of metaphor). These elements are cloaked in sacred mysteries and are revealed during ritual observances. They act to focus the minds and center the emotions of the ritual participants, and they impress upon each person in the strongest way that his shared social life is in harmony with the basic hidden structure of the world. Religion in this sense is a reflection of what people think is ultimately real and important. In this view, then, religious symbols stand for the organizing principles of reality and provide people with an explanation for why things happen the way they do.

The Nahuas, Otomís, and Tepehuas have a view of the world in which invisible spirits or forces are held responsible for important events. Paper images are the tangible representations of spirits that can be manipulated by the ritual specialist. They are palpable demonstrations of how and why people get sick. The pathogens are cut from paper, given offerings, and physically removed from the patient. The crucial reproductive power of plants is visualized in the paper images of the seeds, which are also given periodic offerings. Sun, water, and earth have an important place in rituals and are symbolically tied to crop growth. Misery and misfortune are explained as products of dangerous underworld spirits associated with the dead. The power of lovemaking, music, or good and bad people is represented as a kind of spiritual force depicted in paper. Even fear, hatred, or jealousy are seen as kinds of spirit presences that lead to negative consequences. All of these forces and many more make an impact on human life, and their portrayal in paper gives people an explanation of why they exist and how they operate.

The paper images are a mnemonic device by which people can label aspects of natural and social reality. They represent a type of analytical thought, similar to that employed by scientists, in which complex processes are broken down to their component parts. The fact that the Indians attribute occurrences to spirits in no way reduces their ability to use this form of thought in a reasonable, rational way. In Western culture, some diseases are attributed to bacterial invasion of the body tissue. For the Indians, disease is attributed to invasion of the patient's body by one or more spirits. Both concepts of disease explain the illness and both lead to appropriate remedial action. Although quantified information is not available, personal communications with a number of field workers strongly indicate that the cure rate using traditional procedures among the Indians is quite high. Should a child begin to disobey his parents, a shaman will be called in to cut an image of the spirit of disrespect. The paper image symbolizes the complex psychosocial factors that lead the child to misbehave, and during the ritual the image is eliminated. The powerful message carried by the paper images in the context of an emotionally charged ritual can produce a far more profound effect on people than a verbal analysis of the misbehaviour.

It is precisely this analytical quality of the spirit pantheons that allows people of differing degrees of belief to participate in the religious rituals. To some people the spirits are as real as the paper used to portray them. These people may actively support rituals in order to please or placate the spirits. To others the spirits and paper images are highly symbolic and have no literal existence. Their significance lies not only in the processes they represent — processes that underlie all human existence — but also in their ability to provide explanations of complex psychosocial and natural phenomena. The fact is that seeds, sun, earth, and water are important elements of nature, whether or not people are dependent upon horticulture. Individuals are free to participate fully in the highly symbolic rituals simply as a kind of celebration of life.

Ritual specialists cut paper images for the purpose of exercising influence over the spirits that intrude into human affairs. Nahua, Otomí, and Tepehua religions are pragmatic in orientation, and all rituals are held with a definite end in mind. This is particularly apparent in rites of increase, cleansing, and propitiation. But relations between human desire and the spirit world are complex. First, the strategy of obligating spirits by making offerings to them is an attempt to influence or persuade the spirits rather than strictly to control them. Second, there is a clear idea among the Indians that spirits more or less act according to their nature and cause trouble only if they are offended by human shortcomings. Thus, while the Indians recognize disease-causing spirits as troublesome and on the prowl, they believe that the spirits are released in the village only when people fight, gossip, show disrespect, or behave greedily. Similarly, the earth, water, and seed spirits are basically benign entities that withhold crops only when people abuse them or fail to compensate them. Even the most dangerous spirits can be mollified by making offerings to them. Thus, the role of shaman is as much to reestablish balance or harmony between the spirit and human domains as it is mechanically to control spirits. A shaman's reputation, however, depends on how often the rituals he or she performs achieve their goals.

A third way of analyzing the paper images is to view them as a means of communicating messages to people. As already indicated, many of the spirits and concepts represented in paper are quite ancient. In a sense the pantheon of spirits is an accumulation of knowledge about the world in symbolic form, communicated from one generation to the next. Each spirit is a bit of information distilled from hundreds or thousands of years of human experience. For example, speaking badly of others, an action that often has negative consequences in real life, is discouraged in the symbolic realm by the belief that gossip and slander cause spirit attack. The paper images also impart crucial attitudes and orientations to people. For example, the sun, water, and seeds will provide food so long as a balance is maintained and people do not become greedy. The idea of a tenuous balance between humans and the forces of nature is of critical importance to slash-and-burn horticulturalists. Growing crops in the traditional way requires that large sections of land be left fallow for long periods in order to regenerate the soil. The system works well so long as individual farmers do not try to increase production too radically by cutting larger areas of the forest or by substantially reducing fallowing time.

The paper images are also an important communication link between segments of contemporary Indian society. When a person becomes ill, a curing ritual is held. The shaman portrays the pathogenic spirits and then symbolically removes them in front of the patient's eyes. Here the message is straightforward: identify the cause, destroy it, and the disease will vanish. The patient is also receiving an indirect message of support, not only from close kin who sponsor the cure, but also from the entire community whose traditions provide the means of diagnosing and treating disease. In similar fashion a pregnant woman can have her apprehension symbolically portrayed in paper and then ritually banished. The powerful, emotionally charged rituals communicate to sufferers that the community stands behind them and that everything is under control. Community-wide increase rituals directed to the seeds, water, and earth help to define, clarify, and focus the concerns of villagers. In addition the witnessing of offerings spread on images of seeds, water sirens, or malevolent earth spirits impresses on people the complex interchange between human groups and their social and natural environment. Paper images of dead souls provide people with information about the relationship between the living and the dead. Kin who die become potentially dangerous spirits that must be controlled and kept at a distance. The fact that images of dead souls are given form in paper, dealt with, and then destroyed seems to communicate that the world is for the living and that people should not become obsessed with memories of the dead. In sum, paper images can transmit information that links the past and present, the individual and community, and family members and deceased kin.

The use of paper images in rituals distinguishes the traditional Indians of the southern Huasteca from non-Indian *mestizos* in the region. Thus, the religious system, although syncretized with Christianity, provides the Indians with an aspect of common identity. Within particular Indian populations the different regional subtraditions of paper cutting represent a basis of somewhat smaller group identification. Although stylistic subtraditions cross cultural boundaries in a given region, there is also some basis for identifying cutting styles with specific cultures. Thus, for example, Nahua Indians from one area can sometimes identify Nahua paper images from a different region even though the styles may vary considerably. As further anthropological research among Indians of this culture area is carried out, we will be better able to determine how they accomplish this and the degree to which paper images are used as symbols of cultural identity.

In some instances a particular style of paper image becomes associated with a political faction in a village, thus serving as a symbol of that faction's group identity. The crop fertility ritual described in chapter 2 is an excellent case in point. In a struggle over land distribution policy, two factions developed in the village. Each group was united in its opposition to the other, and the most powerful faction began to sponsor rituals under the direction of a shaman of another culture. Local people even apprenticed themselves to the alien shaman, and in a short time both the style of paper images and ritual performances of the faction became unique in the village. Thus the one faction developed a distinctive style of both ritual performance and paper images to create solidarity and an esprit de corps in its members in opposition to the other faction.

Another example involves the use of rituals and associated paper images to produce cohesion in kinship groups. Often an extended family sponsors a seed ritual to increase crops grown by its members. Preparations for the ritual unite family members in a goal-directed activity, which undoubtedly produces feelings of unity and identification with the group. In some cases large extended families even keep a cabinet filled with their own private paper images of the seeds. The cabinet becomes a focus of kinship activity and identity.

All social systems must exercise some degree of control over the behavior of their members in order to operate successfully. Social control may be achieved in a variety of ways, but the religious system of a group often plays an important role. As previously implied, there is little idea in this culture area that bad behavior will result in punishment in the afterlife. The consequences of antisocial behavior are felt immediately, usually by the imposition of disease and misfortune. Bad people are thought to attract dangerous spirits; therefore, such people pose a double threat to the community. First, their behavior—whether it is fighting, gossiping, showing lack of respect, or engaging in sorcery—is a direct danger to the people around them. Second, their behavior attracts dangerous spirits that are likely to attack the weaker members of the community, such as babies or the aged. Equally antisocial is the behavior that upsets the delicate balance between the human community and the spirit world. A person who takes water from a spring or wood from the forest without making the proper show of respect may anger normally beneficent spirits. The importance of social control in Nahua, Otomí and Tepehua religious systems is reflected in their inventory of paper images. A large number of figures portray dangerous spirits associated with bad deeds, and each beneficent spirit has a paper image of its wrathful alter ego.

PAPER IMAGES AS VISUAL REPRESENTATIONS

A somewhat deeper level of analysis is possible if we focus on design elements of the paper images themselves. Since we cannot consistently link specific design elements with specific cultural groups, we will treat the *costumbre* complex of the entire area as a single system in the following discussion. Nancy Munn (1966) has suggested that culturally standardized visual representations can be analyzed by isolating constituent visual elements and then showing how these are assembled into meaningful images. Thus we can break each paper figure down into its design elements and show how the shaman puts these together to arrive at the final product. The purpose of this procedure is not only to reveal the aesthetic principles of paper image design but also to gain insight into the nature of the religious system of which the figures are a part. As Munn states, ". . . systems of visual representation, like other sorts of cultural codes, function as mechanisms for ordering experience and segmenting it into manageable categories" (1966, p. 936). Analysis of the paper images, then, illuminates something of the world view and cosmological principles that underly the *costumbre* complex.

Each paper image is a combined visual element composed of irreducible single visual elements. These elements, whether single or in combination, convey meaning to the people in the culture. The kinds of visual elements used in the paper images are "iconic" in that there is a direct correspondence between the visual image and the item represented. An example of a single visual element is the fruit or vegetable cut as a part of seed spirits. The paper crop in silhouette is an "icon" in that it resembles the actual crop in the field. This differs from a "symbol," where there is no similarity in appearance between the representation and the item represented. An example of an icon composed of a combination of elements is the paper image of the Spirit of the Chile. The cutout is an assemblage of single visual elements including the anthropomorphic figure with a head, arms, legs, images of chile peppers, and roots. In this case, if any element is left out (with the possible exception of the roots), the image would have no meaning.

The meanings represented by a single visual element or by a unitary combination of elements are called a "visual category." Categories of meanings represented by a single visual element, such as the particular paper fruit or vegetable item, are called "elementary categories." Categories of meanings represented by a combination of elements, such as the complete, assembled paper image of the chile spirit, are called "composite categories." For example, the visual element "shoes" is an elementary category that means either "travel," as among the Nahua witness spirits, or "outsider," as among the Otomí *judíos*. Which of these meanings is actually assigned will be determined by the context of other elements of the paper images or by verbal cues given by the shaman. The single element has both of these meanings, and perhaps more that we are unaware of, and these constitute an "elementary category." A paper image of a seed spirit, on the other hand, contains many single elements, each contributing to the total meaning or meanings, and these together constitute a "composite category."

Munn has studied Australian tribes, and in her analysis she notes that the Walbiri of central Australia attribute whole ranges of different meanings to individual visual elements. For example, the circle stands for "circular path," "waterhole," "fruit," "fire," "yam," "tree," "buttocks," and the like (Munn 1966, pp. 938, 945). She calls meaning ranges of this type "discontinuous" because they include many different classes of items. In any specific visual representation, however, only one meaning applies at a time. On the other hand, some cultures employ largely "continuous" meaning ranges in their visual representations. A specific visual element stands for one particular thing or class of things and not for a range of different things. The paper images appear to be examples of the continuous type of meaning range since each visual element has a restricted number of meanings. In cases where more than one meaning is attached to an element, the images are often of the same class or at least closely related. For example, many of the seed images are portrayed with branches, leaves, and roots.

The same visual representation is used for the many different species of plants depicted.

In sum, visual categories are the meanings attached to visual representations (icons). The meanings attached to single elements are called elementary categories, and the meanings attached to elements in combination are called composite categories. If the range of meanings comprising these categories is heterogeneous and covers many different classes of phenomena, it is called "discontinuous." If on the other hand, the range of meanings is homogeneous, restricted to a single type or class of phenomena, it is called "continuous."

Societies tend to employ one or the other type of visual representation, although it is not known why one form—continuous or discontinuous—is selected over the other. Representational systems that are continuous must operate with a larger number of elements since the meanings attached to any single element are limited. We believe that this analysis helps to explain why so many different paper images are cut. For the Indians, each iconic element has a restricted meaning range; thus many images are needed to portray the variety of spirits in the pantheon. If the range of meanings was discontinuous among these cultures, one generalized image could have been used to stand for all spirits. In the case of seed images, the Nahuas as well as the Tepehuas have circumvented the necessity of cutting a separate figure of each crop. Nahua shamans say they cut images of only the most important crops because if these do well in the fields, they assume the other crops will also prosper.

The literal way that the shamans represent the spirits gives additional insights into this religious complex. Paper images share a "core-adjunct" method of composition (Munn 1966, p. 943). At the center of each image is a core element: the human figure set in its characteristic stance. The only real exceptions to this are the Otomí animal companion spirits and the bird messengers of the Lord of the Mountain. Even in these cases, however, an animal or bird body is simply substituted for the human form. Added to the core are a series of iconic markers that define the character of the spirit being depicted. These markers are called "adjuncts" when they are essential parts of the composition of the core and "emblems" when they are additions to the core. Examples of adjuncts include crowns, clothing, shoes, hair, facial features, fruits and vegetables, and hats. Examples of emblems include attached machetes, swords, leaf-covered arches, and spirit helpers.

The core-adjunct method of depiction allows the viewer to distinguish individuals in a group of spirits while seeing continuity among them at the same time. Adjuncts and emblems are contrastive from one image to another, but the common core element reveals a structural similarity among almost all of the paper images. The anthropomorphic core element is an invariable feature of paper images regardless of which shaman cut them. Therefore, the core element must reflect something important about the way Nahuas, Otomís, and Tepehuas conceive of their spirits. As Munn asserts, "To the extent that the design structure conveys an organization inherent in the cosmology, the designs function as visible models that present these principles, as it were, directly for inspection" (Munn 1966, p. 946). We believe that the paper images, and particularly their common core elements, reveal the organizational principle of the Indians' cosmology. Contrary to the impression given by the numbers of spirits in the pantheons and the numbers of paper images cut for rituals, this principle is one of unity rather than diversity.

THE PRINCIPLE OF UNITY AND THE NATURE OF DEITY

The religions practiced by the people in great cities of ancient Mesoamerica as well as in the small rural villages in present-day Mexico are neither polytheistic nor monotheistic. Polytheism is based on belief in a number of individual spirits, each with a name, personality, range of power, and specific domain. Monotheism is based on belief in one individual spirit that rules over the universe. Mesoamerican religions were, and still are, pantheistic. In this conception the divinity is expressed in the workings of the universe as a whole, including the sun, the earth, water, growing crops, and human beings. Although she was speaking about the pre-Hispanic people, Hunt could have been describing modern Indians when she wrote:

> In their view, as in those of all pantheistic cultures, reality, nature, and experience were nothing but multiple manifestations of a single unity of being. God was *both* the one and the many. Thus the deities were but his multiple personifications, his partial unfoldings into perceptible experience. The partition of this experience into discrete units such as god A or god B is an artifice of iconography and analysis, not part of the core conception of the divinity. Since the divine reality was multiple, fluid, encompassing the whole, its aspects were changing images, dynamic, never frozen, but constantly being recreated, redefined. This fluidity was a culturally defined mystery of the nature of divinity itself. Therefore, it was expressed in the dynamic, ever-changing aspects of the multiple "deities" that embodied it. For didactic, artistic, and ritual purposes, however, these fluid images were carved in stone, painted into frescoes, described in prayer. It is here, at this reduced level of visualization, that the transient images of a sacralized universe became "gods," with names attached to them, with anthropomorphic attributes, and so on. [Hunt 1977, p. 55]

In pantheism the universe itself is deified, and the spirits in a pantheistic religion are nothing more than temporary manifestations of a great unity. The nature of the unity is such that everything is related, and what appears to be separate and even opposite is actually the same thing. It is this quality of interrelatedness that Emerson captures in the poem that introduces this chapter. By assuming that the *costumbre* complex is polytheistic and that the paper images are pictures of multitudes of living spirits, early ethnographers have seriously underrated the sophistication and subtlety of this religion. The view that Indian beliefs are polytheistic has also created much of the confusion that plagues our understanding of their religious concepts. The earth, for example, is not a unitary spirit that makes crops grow; rather it is an aspect of a deified universe that is connected to everything else and that contains within it all of the complexity and contradictions of the universe at large.

The earth exists in unity with everything else, but it temporarily becomes a separate spirit when it is being addressed in a ritual or when a shaman cuts its image from paper. When they are asked about this spirit, people will obviously describe its nature as it appears in that particular context. Thus we have reports of the earth as being a beneficent provider, a bringer of rain, a devouring monster, and a leader of dangerous spirits. These characteristics become contradictory only if the Indian religion is viewed as polytheistic.

To carry the analysis further, in a pantheistic world view no real distinction exists between the earth and the water or between any other fundamental elements. The Indians, in fact, consistently link seemingly unrelated elements in their myths. For example, they connect the earth and water by saying that rain comes from deep underground caves. Spirits of the dead are associated with the earth, which is associated with the water, which, in turn, is linked to the sky, which is ruled by the sun. Thus we have a paper image of the life-giving sun surrounded by dead souls, two seemingly opposite concepts. Corn is a conjunction of earth, water, and sun; thus, the corn spirit incorporates the powers of the earth and water. It, too, can kill a person by stealing his "soul." All other aspects of the universe can be connected at higher and higher levels until all parts are subsumed into a totality. In sum, the multitudes of paper images portray the same spirit in different guises.

PROCESS OF CREATION OUT OF THE UNITY

Shamans create their rituals and paper images out of this unity, but they do so using a common reservoir of symbols and icons. They temporarily break the unity into manageable segments in order to restore harmony and balance between humans and the powers in the universe. Not surprisingly, they partition the unity into the constituent parts, such as the earth, water, seeds, and disease-causing agents, that express the concerns of horticulturalists. Shamans are constrained in their inventiveness by the common world view of the people and by the symbols and icons available for them to use in their rituals. Most of the creativity takes place in how the various symbols are manipulated; in the manifestations or aspects of the earth, water, and other elements that shamans select to emphasize; and in the adjunct elements and emblems chosen to modify the paper images. The anthropomorphic core element of the paper figure is not changed significantly, and it is always recognizable. This core element is the visible representation of the unity out of which all of the apparent diversity emerges.

This viewpoint helps to clarify one of the great puzzles of present-day studies of Mesoamerican Indian religion: how is it that the Indians came to accept Christianity and at the same time continued their pre-Hispanic beliefs and practices? We have already examined many examples of Christian and traditional beliefs that have been syncretized into the religious systems we find today. But this is not a simple reconciliation of colliding world views. The very process of syncretism is built into a pantheistic religion. "Syncretism, in this context, is simply the technical name of a process already inherent in the nature of the pantheon before the influence of Christianity was ever felt" (Hunt 1977, p. 234). The core of the pantheistic world view has remained intact among contemporary Indians, and for this reason the introduction of new spirits by the Spaniards, in the form of saints, the Trinity, and the Devil, poses no problem for them. The new pantheon simply "expands the repertoire of sacred 'words' that can be fitted into the divine 'sentence matrix'" (Hunt 1977, p. 56). Thus San Juan becomes an aspect of the water pantheon, and Santa Rosa, a saint renowned for her visions, becomes associated with the traditional marijuana spirit. This form of syncretism is problematic only to people used to thinking in terms of monotheism and polytheism. From the Indian perspective, the most puzzling aspect of colonial rule was the Spaniards' insistence on complete uniformity of thought and the exclusion of all spirits and conceptions but their own.

We know very little about the nature of the unity that lies at the heart of Indian religious conceptions. It is a profound mystery that reveals itself only partially amid the color and diversity of ritual practices, complex pantheons, and stacks of paper images. As a guide to future interpretations of the *costumbre* religion, however, we would like to suggest a possible definition of the unity that underlies this diversity. One key, we believe, lies in the central place occupied by the sun in all three pantheons. The sun, frequently deified in militaristic societies around the world, embodies the principles of action, movement, force, and power. Thus, the unity, as exemplified by the sun, is the principle of animation itself—that which imbues objects, animals, and people with a life-force. One Nahua concept of spirit or "soul" discussed in chapter 4 is based on a view of the sun as the source of the animating principle. As an additional clue, one researcher reports that the Tepehua word for their own religion is Halakiltúnti, which means Moving of the Things (Boilès 1967, p. 267). Finally, the pre-Hispanic Aztecs conceived of our current era as the fifth in the history of the cosmos. They called it Naui Ollin, or Four-Movement. This name, usually linked to their idea that our era will end in earthquakes, may also underscore that activity is the organizing principle of our age. The unifying principle in the Indian cosmos, as revealed by the small human figure with the hands by the head, is a kind of dance of life that animates the universe.

The analysis of visual representations such as the paper images can point to fruitful avenues for future research, can confirm or deny findings, or suggest interpretations of religious systems. Manufactured items always reveal much about their makers. Ritual objects in particular are concrete expressions of a people's world-view and deepest concerns. In order to understand the *costumbre* complex more fully however, we need extensive information of the native cosmology. We require systematic observation and decoding of rituals and collection and analysis of the myth systems that are operating. In addition, we need to know how the shamans generate the transformations that result in the cutting of specific paper images. Much work remains. The focus of our research must be on the process by which spirits are created from the unity and called into play during rituals and upon how the creations of individual shamans become socially shared. The purpose of anthropology is to explain cultural phenomena. Thus the work on the *costumbre* complex will not be complete until we can isolate the factors, ecological, social, historical, and psychological, that explain why a complex pantheistic religion develops in the first place.

APPENDIX

Listed below are explanations of the pre-Hispanic symbol classes developed by Eva Hunt (1977), with specific examples of the symbols derived from contemporary Nahua, Otomí, and Tepehua culture. Corresponding paper images are noted by figure number, where information is available.

Volatiles

This class of symbols is composed of "fliers" of different types, mainly birds. "Each flier [usually] represented a god or gods, in the role of alter ego 'messenger' between the earth and upper sky levels" (Hunt 1977, p. 58). The owl and eagle, among other birds, appear recurrently in Middle American symbolism. The owl is associated with darkness, the underworld, and death (Hunt 1977, p. 59).

Nahua: Tlacatecolotl (Owl Man) is chief of the underworld.
  Teyolcuahetl is a blood-sucking buzzard.
  Nagual is a blood-sucking night bird.

Otomí: Eagles are spirit companions of shamans.
  Owls are spirit companions of sorcerers.
  Nagual is a blood-sucking night bird (figure 70).
  Messengers of Lord of the Mountain are birds (figures 75–80).
  The watching-bird motif is used in many paper images (figures 136, 138, 140–42).

Tepehua: Lord of the Wind has wings and a bird's tail (figure 166).
  La Serena has feet like a duck.
  Nagual is a blood-sucking night bird (probable).
  Owls are harbingers of death (Williams García 1972, p. 121).

281

Crawlers and Swimmers

Reptiles, worms, and aquatic animals are included in this symbol class (Hunt 1977, p. 74).

Nahua: Lady of the Water controls aquatic animals.
    Snakes are associated with the earth and the underworld (see Montoya Briones 1977).
    Figure 16 is an *ejecatl* spirit with mollusk-shell clothes.

Otomí: Queen of the Bad Earth (figure 60) has snake spirit helpers.
    Lady of the Water controls aquatic animals.

Tepehua: Girl of the Water controls fish

Four-legged Walkers or Mammals

In pre-Hispanic times animals used as symbols were all wild except for the domesticated dog. When the Spaniards introduced domesticated animals, such as cattle, horses, and mules, these animals were incorporated into Indian symbol systems (Hunt 1977, p. 80).

Nahua: The Devil leads all animals.
    People become animals when they die (Williams García 1957, p. 62).
    Figures 14, 16, 17, 19, 23, 24 are portrayed with animal horns as a sign of their animallike temperament.

Otomí: Jaguars and cougars are animal companion spirits of shamans (figure 148).
    Foxes are animal companion spirits of sorcerers.
    Figures 61-68, 70-73 have tails or heads of animals.

Tepehua: El Sereno is patron of animals.
    Deer is the father of the maize spirit.

Mankind

Human beings as part of the natural order were considered by pre-Hispanic peoples to be a transformational category. Human spirits are partly animal spirit *(nahual)* and partly other cosmic elements, such as heat from the sun *(tona)*. The living orders are arranged in a "phagohierarchy": animals eat each other and plants; man eats all lower orders; and the gods eat man. Man was created by the sun and is one step below the ancestors (Hunt 1977, pp. 88-89).

Nahua: Humans have animal companion spirits.
Humans were created by the Sun (Toteotsi).
One name for "soul" is *tonal* (heat).
Humans eat the earth's products and are eaten by the earth in turn.
Shamans cut anthropomorphic paper images.

Otomí: Humans have animal companion spirits *(rogi)* (figure 148).
Humans were created by the sun (figure 150).
Humans eat the earth's products and are eaten by the earth in turn (figure 67).
Shamans cut anthropomorphic paper images.

Tepehua: Humans were created by the sun (figures 160a, b).
Humans eat the earth's products and are eaten by the earth in turn (figures 163a, b).
Shamans cut anthropomorphic paper images.

SYMBOLIC PLANT TAXONOMIES

Domestic Plants

Maize was a major cultigen of symbolic importance. It was considered to be the offspring of earth and sun. Many domestic plants had internal subdivisions based on the growth cycle. Corn was distinguished as flowering corn, ripening corn, dry corn cob, etc. (Hunt 1977, pp. 89ff.).

Nahua: Seed images represent crop spirits (figures 38-51).
Maize is the most important seed image (Chicomexochitl, Seven-Flower).
Growth stages of maize are distinguished (figures 38-40).
Crops are considered to be the products of earth, water, and sun.

Otomí: Seed images represent crop spirits (figures 81-135).
Crops are considered to be the products of the earth, water, and sun.

Tepehua: Seed images represent crop spirits (figures 172-75).

Maize is the most important seed image (figures 172a, 172b, 173). Crops are considered to be the products of the earth, water, and sun.

Powerful Plants and Plant Parts

This class of plants used symbolically by pre-Hispanic peoples includes hallucinogens such as tobacco, alcohol, and, presumably, marijuana. It also includes copal incense, which is made from a tree resin, and sacred herbs. Since colonial times *aguardiente* has been added to this class (Hunt 1977, pp. 91–92).

Nahua: Marijuana, copal, tobacco, *aguardiente,* and sacred herbs are all used in rituals.

Otomí: Marijuana (figure 153), copal, tobacco, *aguardiente,* and sacred herbs are all used in rituals.

Tepehua: Copal, tobacco, *aguardiente,* sacred herbs, and marijuana (figure 178) are used in rituals.

Flowers

Many different kinds of flowers were used in ritual contexts in pre-European Middle America. Flowers stood for ornaments, poetry, beauty, vegetable nature, sophisticated thinking, love, sexual pleasure, and the like. Several deities were named for flowers, such as Macuilxochitl (Five-Flower) and Xochipilli (Flower Prince). Special flowers were often identified with single ideas. For instance, marigolds were considered to be flowers of the dead (Hunt 1977, p. 92).

Nahua: Many flowers are used in rituals.
    Several spirits or spirit classes contain "flower" in their names, such as Macuilxochitl, "Five-Flower" (see Sandstrom 1982); Chicomexochitl, "Seven-Flower"; and Xochiejecatl, "Flowery Wind."
    The marigold is known as the "death flower."

Otomí: Many flowers are used in rituals.
    The marigold is known as the "death flower."

Tepehua: Many flowers are used in rituals.
    The marigold is known as the "death flower."

Trees and Bushes

Trees and bushes are used as sacred symbols based on their special attributes (Hunt 1977, p. 94).

Nahua: Tropical cedar, *teocuauitl* (sacred wood), is used for support beams in houses and to make the box containing the seed images.

Otomí: No information.

Tepehua: No information.

CORPOREAL TAXONOMIES OR CLASSES

Sex

All classes of the natural orders were distinguished by sex. "Mountains, caves, and other features of the landscape were personified and defined as having a specific sex." Manifestations of deities were either male or female and many were married couples. This class of symbols includes sexual anomalies and deified women who died in childbirth (Hunt 1977, pp. 95ff.).

Nahua: Many spirits are identified by sex and are conceptualized as male-female pairs (figures 1, 7).
  Features of the landscape are given sexual identities.
  Women who die in childbirth become dangerous spirits.
  There is a sexual division of labor among ritual specialists.

Otomí: Many spirits are identified by sex and are conceptualized as male-female pairs.
  Sexual jealousy exists among spirits (figure 60).
  Features of the landscape are given sexual identities.
  Women who die in childbirth become dangerous spirits (figure 69).
  Paper images are cut for love magic (figures 154a–c).

Tepehua: Many spirits are identified by sex and are conceptualized as male-female pairs.
  Many spirits have male-female unities as "parents."
  Women who die in childbirth become water carriers.
  Paper images are cut for love magic (figures 179–81).
  There is a sexual division of labor among ritual specialists.

Stages of Growth and Ages of Man

"Stages of the life cycle were recognized in all things." Pre-Hispanic peoples used stages of growth and junior-senior relations in religious symbols. In addition, the ritual calendar was arranged so that rituals of aging and death were observed in the winter months and rituals of fertility and growth were held near the end of the winter solstice period or at the onset of the rainy season (Hunt 1977, pp. 109ff.).

Nahua: Witness spirits have senior rank (figures 27–31).
   Seeds are thought of as children.
   The maize seed spirit is expressed as a series of growth stages (figures 38–40).
   The Tonantsi myth concerns the birth and maturation of four sons.
   Antiguas are old spirits.
   The ritual calendar reflects stages of the year.

Otomí: Figures 71–72 are the spirits of disrespectful children (juniors).
   Figures 136–39 are Child of the Mountain spirits.
   Antiguas are old spirits.
   The ritual calendar reflects stages of the year.

Tepehua: Spirits are usually in a parent-child relationship.
   Seed spirits are thought of as children.
   Rain spirits are "Old Ones."
   Antiguas are old spirits.
   The ritual calendar reflects stages of the year.

Parts of the Body

Body parts were used as elements of symbolic classification in pre-Hispanic religions (Hunt 1977, pp. 112ff.).

Nahua: Earth's body, blood, and bones are soil, water, and rocks, respectively.
   Shamans use anthropomorphic paper images.
   Bones signify death (figure 12).
   Many paper images are cut with hearts, stomachs, and genitals (e.g., figures 1–7, 42–44, 47).
   Paper images with toes are identified with the Indian world (e.g., figures 43, 44, 47).
   The pointed head shape of paper images may indicate the other worldly nature of spirits (figures 1–59).

Otomí: Spirits undergo transformation of human into animal body parts (figures 71-72).

Spirits have multiple heads and legs along with exaggerated teeth, tongues, stomachs, noses, and beards, all to convey danger (figures 61-63).

Shamans use anthropomorphic paper images.

Paper images cut with toes are identified with the Indian world (e.g., figures 81-135).

The seed images have babylike head shapes to signify immaturity (figures 81-135).

Tepehua: Heads are used to represent the spirits of the dead (figure 182).

Shamans use anthropomorphic paper images.

Bones signify death (figures 155a, b).

Many paper images are cut with hearts, stomachs, and genitals (e.g., figures 155a-59, 162a-65, 167-71, 176a-78).

Midwives include a copal "heart" in each one of their brushlike *muñecas.*

Sickness

"From the religious point of view, sickness was utilized in a trans-formational subsystem, which had associations with cardinal direc-tionality and with the gods" (Hunt 1977, pp. 114-15). For example, water diseases or drowning were associated with the water gods. In general the pre-Hispanic system for dealing with disease is bound up with religious and cosmic symbolism.

Nahua: Illness is a sign of imbalance between humans and spirits or of spirit attack.

Certain diseases are associated with specific spirits.

Death by certain diseases can determine the fate of the "soul."

Drowning is associated with the water spirit.

Disease is cured mostly through ritual means.

Otomí: Illness is a sign of imbalance between humans and spirits or of spirit attack.

The water spirit (figure 68) drowns people, controls disease-causing spirits, and can cause illness by capturing a person's "soul."

Disease is cured mostly through ritual means.

Tepehua: Illness is a sign of imbalance between humans and spirits or of spirit attack.

The moon is associated with disease-causing spirits.

Illness can be caused when spirits steal a person's "soul."

Disease is cured mostly through ritual means.

NATURAL PHENOMENA—THE ELEMENTS

Wind

Wind was an important symbol in pre-Hispanic religion, and it was subdivided according to origin, season of the year, velocity "and such other variables as [winds'] beneficial or harmful quality for man and his habitat." Among these were the small winds *(aires)* that brought disease and the stronger winds that brought storms and hurricanes. Waterspouts and whirlwinds were key images of major deities (Hunt 1977, pp. 116–17).

Nahua: Wind spirits cause disease (Flowery Wind, Seven-Wind, Polychrome Winds of Cultivation) (figures 1–26).

Otomí: Wind spirits cause disease (figures 60–73).

Tepehua: Tamoswilhi'untín is a whirlwind that carries off people's spirits.

Maxkai'un (wind spirits) cause disease (figures 155a–59)

Lord of the Wind (figure 166).

Falling Water

Falling water or rain is associated with the god Tlaloc, one of the most ancient in the pre-Hispanic pantheon. Rain was thought to come from caves in the earth, from whence it went up to the sky and then fell back to earth. Minor deities associated with Tlaloc were called *tlaloques* or water goblins. Rains that watered the crops were distinguished from rains producing floods (Hunt 1977, pp. 123–24).

Nahua: Thunder and Lightning, which are conceived of as dwarflike spirits that live in caves, transport water from the sea before they release it as rain (see also chapter 2).

Old Ones are spirits who live in stone ruins and send rain.

Lady of the Water controls the amount of rainfall.

Otomí: The spirit "Two-Shrine" lives in a cave and sends rain.
Lady of the Water brings rain to the fields.

Tepehua: The spirits of women who die in childbirth are water carriers.
Lord of the Wind foretells of coming rain (figure 166).
Female water spirit (La Serena) sends rain.
Small humanoid spirits, Old Ones, actually produce the rain.
San Juan lives in the ocean and initiates the rainy season each year.

Surface Water

"The springs, lagoons, rivers, waterholes, lakes, irrigation canals and other bodies of water on the earth's surface were conceptualized as female and [were] represented by a set of deities" (Hunt 1977, p. 125).

Nahua: Santa Rosa (marijuana) is a water-related spirit.
The Lady of the Water lives in springs and rivers.
San Juan is a water spirit possibly associated with the ocean.

Otomí: Lady of the Water, Siren of the Lake, and Spirit of the Well are all spirits associated with bodies of water.
Wicked Siren and Santa Rosa are water-related spirits (figures 68, 153).

Tepehua: Lord of the Water is one of the most important spirits.
El Sereno and La Serena (the sirens) are parents of the Lord of the Water, and they control animals, food production, etc.
San Juan lives in the ocean and initiates the rainy season.
Girl of the Water and Halapanaxkán are water-related spirits.

Fire

Fire had complex symbolic associations in pre-Hispanic Middle America. A distinction was made between manmade fire, which included the fire used in the slash-and-burn horticultural cycle and for cooking, and natural fire, which included lightning, the sun, stars, volcanoes, etc. It was associated with light and heat and was linked to the life forces of people and animals (Hunt 1977, pp. 125–26).

Nahua: The fire spirit Tlixauantsi guards household members from its home in the three fireplace stones and is propitiated in rituals.

Otomí: The fire spirit Maka Xita Sibi accompanies the sun but lives in the three stones surrounding the household fireplace, from which it guards family members.

Tepehua: Sacred Fire lives in the sky when it is not guarding families from the three stones around the household fireplace (figure 169).

Earth

"The earth played an interface role in the taxonomical system of natural and sacred orders. The religious representations of earth in the symbolism of prehispanic Mesoamericans embody some of the most complicated, diversified, and exotic of their ideas." Some symbolic associations include the earth as mother to domestic plants and as womb, mouth, tomb, and house of the universal deities. Fire and water were also elements of earth. "All the deities which symbolized aspects of reproduction, birth, and death had earthly aspects. . . . It was loving and destructive, nurturant mother and carnivorous monster . . . human and animal, male and female, a dead and living thing" (Hunt 1977, pp. 129–31).

Nahua (see chapter 4 for a more detailed list):
Tlaltepactli is the spirit of the earth's surface, which includes the sacred hills and caves that are the spirits' residences.
Tlaltetata and Tlaltenana are male-female aspects of the earth which are propitiated in rituals.
Moctezuma is the devouring aspect of the earth.
The earth is a tomb in that it contains Mictlan, the realm of the dead.
The earth is mother to the seeds, related to fire and water, consumer of dead bodies, and viewed by the Nahuas with ambivalence.

Otomí (see chapter 5 for a more detailed list):
The beneficient spirit Earth Mother or Queen of the Good Earth is balanced by the malevolent Queen of the Bad Earth (figure 60) and Moctezuma (figure 67).
The earth is a tomb in that it contains the underworld in which live disease-causing spirits of the dead.
The earth has the caves and hills on its surface that serve as the residences of many spirits.
The earth is strongly linked to Maka Me (Sacred Lady), who

controls fertility; Ma Yoho Nija (Two-Shrine), who controls rain; and many other spirits.

The earth is conceived of as the mother of seeds, and it is viewed with ambivalence.

Tepehua (see chapter 6 for a more detailed list):

The Lord of the Earth (Xalapanalakat'un) is the major earth spirit and is accompanied by a unitary male-female parental couple (Ixpayixnatilakat'un).

The earth is mother of the seeds, but it is ambivalent because in the guise of Moctezuma/Santasoma it devours corpses (figures 163a, b).

The earth contains the underworld (Lak'nín) with the spirits of the dead, which can cause disease among the living.

Devil (Tlakakikuru) is a fearsome earth spirit that causes disease and death.

The earth has the caves and hills on its surface that serve as the residences of many spirits.

Santa Rosa (figure 178) among the Tepehuas is apparently associated with the earth.

Geographic Aspects of the Earth

". . . many features of the earthly landscape were systematically associated with features of prehispanic religion." The include mountains, deserts, rivers, forests, lakes, waterholes, caves, etc. (Hunt 1977, p. 134).

Nahua, Otomí, Tepehua: Among these groups, mountains, lakes, springs, caves, and additional geographic features such as crossroads are all important aspects of religious symbolism.

CELESTIAL BODIES

The Sun

"If for Western culture 'the measure of all things' is man, for prehispanic Mesoamerican peoples it was the deified planets. And among the planets, there ruled, victorious and unchallenged, the sun" (Hunt 1977, p. 138).

Nahua: The Sun (Toteotsi) is syncretized with Jesus and is the paramount spirit.

Sun symbols are included in many rituals (figure 59).

Otomí: The Sun (Maka Hyadi) is syncretized with Jesus and is the paramount spirit.

The Sun may be equivalent to Dios de Antigua (Ancient Lord).

Tepehua: The Sun (Wilhcháan) (figures 160a, b) is syncretized with Jesus and is the paramount spirit.

The Sun rules over the universe from the Golden Hill.

The Inner Planets

See Hunt 1977, p. 139. No published information exists on this symbol class for the Nahuas, Otomís, and Tepehuas.

The Moon

For the people of pre-Hispanic Middle America the moon was a "complex deity subsystem." Some of its images were male, others were female, some were human, and others were animal (Hunt 1977, p. 139). The moon was often conceived of in conjunction with or in opposition to the sun. ". . . the moon-fire takes an ambivalent role, at times an enemy of the sun at times neutral between [the sun and stars, i.e. day and night]. Obviously, the moon which is sometimes lighted like a minor sun, at other times absent, leaving the sky to be ruled only by the stars, fitted this metaphor with great economy and beauty" (Hunt 1977, p. 152). The phases of the moon were believed to have an effect on events; for example, a full moon was felt to cause increased sap flow in trees.

Nahua: The moon (Metstli) is associated with Tonantsi and fertility, but it is also ambivalent in nature.

Otomí: The moon is associated both with fertility and dangerous spirits of the night.

Tepehua: The moon (Malhkuyú') is associated with the Devil and *malos aires.*

Paper images of dangerous moon spirits have crescent-shaped headdresses (figures 155a, b, 157a, b).

Aspects of the moon are linked to the menstrual cycle.

Venus

Mercury

The Outer Planets

Mars

Jupiter and Saturn

The Stars and Constellations

See Hunt 1977, pp. 140ff.

Nahua, Otomí, and Tepehua: Each of these celestial bodies played an important role in the religious symbolism of pre-Hispanic peoples. We do not have information on their importance among contemporary people in the region except that the Nahuas have a name for Venus (Tonquetl) and for the Pleiades (Chicome Citlali, Seven-Star).

THE VISIBLE SPECTRUM

The symbolic meanings assigned to different colors in pre-Hispanic Middle America are not completely understood. "For religious and sacred purposes, however, five colors were dominant: black, white, red, yellow, and blue-green (turquoise)" (Hunt 1977, p. 154).

Nahua, Otomí, Tepehua: The three contemporary groups symbolically link these same five colors to the paper images. Among the Nahuas the colors identify the cosmological origin of the spirit. Otomí and Tepehua color symbolism is also clearly important, but additional field studies are required before it can be clarified.

MINERALS

In pre-Hispanic religions certain minerals had symbolic significance (Hunt 1977, pp. 155–56).

Nahua, Otomí, Tepehua: Little is known about the symbolic significance of minerals in these groups. In all three cultures, rock crystals are placed on altars and have some link to the religious systems. The Nahuas view them as mirrors *(tezcatl),* which shamans can use to peer into the future.

CULTURAL ORDERS — MATERIAL CULTURE

Tools and Weapons

In pre-Hispanic times, "Implements of work and war were symbols of human activities that were attributed to the gods." Some of the items in this category include knives, arrows, household implements, paper fans in different shapes, and staffs (Hunt 1977, p. 157).

Nahua: Walking sticks or staffs *(bastones)* used in rituals identify thunder and lightning spirits (see chapter 2).

Otomí: Many of the paper images carry machetes (figures 62, 63–64, 67, 71–73).
    Grandfather Fire carries a walking stick.
    The spirit of the patient is depicted with a blanket (figure 149).
    Paper images of musical instruments are cut (figures 151–52).
    Walking sticks or staffs *(bastones)* used in rituals identify thunder and lightning spirits (see chapter 2).

Tepehua: Guardian stars shoot arrows at stones that threaten to become jaguars.
    Spirits of the dead pass through a sugarcane press.
    Old Ones carry walking sticks that produce thunder and lightning.
    San Juan has a walking stick.
    The paper image of the cross spirit holds swords (figure 170).
    A paper image is cut of a shaman with a brazier on his head (figure 183).

Household Equipment and Furniture

"Household goods were also attached to the gods to indicate their sex, status, activity and the domains of life they controlled." Kitchen spirits were symbolized by the three stones surrounding the cooking fire (Hunt 1977, pp. 157–58).

Nahua: Shamans cut paper images of "tortilla napkins," which serve as spirit beds (figures 52–58).
    Miniature furnishings are included in the box containing the seed images.
    The three fireplace stones represent the hearth spirit.

Otomí: Shamans cut paper "beds" or "seats" for paper images (figures 144–45).

Miniature furnishings are included in the box containing the seed images.

The three fireplace stones represent the hearth spirit.

Tepehua: Shamans cut paper "beds" for paper images.

Miniature furnishings are included in the box containing the seed images.

The three fireplace stones represent the hearth spirit.

Clothing

"Clothing had enormous social importance among prehispanic peoples. It was the major symbol in the presentation of the self as a social being, identifying age and sex status, social class, ethnic group, profession, and special privileges. . . . Elaborate variations in clothing details . . . formed a complex sartorial language of divine identifications" (Hunt 1977, p. 159).

Nahua: Dancers wear headdresses during Tlacatelilis.

Seed images are clothed (figures 45–46).

Complex elaboration of clothing is associated with paper images: *jorongos* (figures 4, 8, 28–30, 38, 40–41); dresses which indicate sex (figures 7, 13, 15); mollusk shells (figure 16), hair (figure 18), spines (figure 10), etc., all of which indicate the disease-bearing nature of the spirit.

Paper images are cut with hats (e.g., figures 8, 14, 40) and crowns (figures 1, 7, 10, 11, 43, 45–47).

Paper images are cut with shoes as a symbol of outsider status and travel (e.g., figures 1, 5, 8, 10–11, 14).

Paper images are cut with elaborate designs in clothing, including pockets (e.g., figures 2, 4–7, 27–30).

Otomí: Seed images are clothed.

Complex elaboration of clothing is associated with paper images: dresses that may indicate sex (e.g., figures 60, 68, 69, 136–38, 146, 154b); pants that may indicate sex (e.g., figures 136–38, 147, 154a); thunderclaps (figures 65–66, 69); *jorongos* (e.g., figures 74, 81–135).

Paper images are cut with crowns (e.g., figures 65–66, 69, 73–74, 81–135, 76–79).

Paper images are cut with shoes as a likely symbol of outsider status (e.g., figures 60–73, 146, 154a–c).

Tepehua: Seed images are clothed.

The spirits on the Golden Hill are conceived of as being lavishly dressed.

Complex elaboration of clothing associated with paper images: *jorongos* (e.g., figures 155a, 156b, c, 157b, 159, 166, 172a, b–174); clear distinction between male pants (e.g., figures 155a, 156b, c, 157b, 159, 162a, 163a, 176b, 177a) and female dresses (e.g., figures 155b, 156a, 157a, 162b, 176a, 177b).

Paper images are cut with crowns (e.g., figures 155a, b–159, 161–67, 170–74, 176a, b, 178, 182).

Paper images are cut with designs in clothing (figures 155a, b–160b, 162a, b, 168a, b, 176a, b–177a, b).

Face Painting and Masks

"Prehispanic peoples used face painting or ornamentation to indicate their status . . . in the same manner in which they used clothing. . . . All the gods had special colors and designs over their faces" (Hunt 1977, p. 160).

Nahua, Otomí, Tepehua: The Nahuas impersonate underworld spirits by painting their faces and bodies and wearing masks during the observance of Nanauatili (Carnaval) (see Reyes García 1960). The Otomís and Tepehuas also wear masks during Carnaval, and the Tepehuas cover their faces during All Souls (Todos Santos). Otomí shamans use charcoal to blacken the facial features of the *malos aires* paper images (see chapter 2).

SOCIAL STRUCTURE AND STRATIFICATION

Professions

"The gods mapped out the social order according to the division of labor in the society." Each professional group had a tutelary deity, such as Huitzilopochtli for warriors and Teteoinnan (Mother of Gods) for midwives (Hunt 1977, p. 161).

Nahua: Spirits associated with natural phenomena are called *dueños* in Spanish, meaning "owner" or "lord"; for example, Apanchane (Lady of the Water) is owner of the water, and Tlaltetata and Tlaltenana rule the earth.

Spirits are arranged hierarchically, to some extent; for example,

Tonantsi is master of the seeds, the Devil (Tlauelilo) leads the *ejecatl* spirits, etc.

Christian saints are often tutelary spirits of occupations; for example, San Jose is patron of carpenters, and San Isidro is the patron of farmers (Reyes García 1960, p. 35).

Otomí: Spirits associated with natural phenomena are called *dueños* or "owners"; for example, Maka Xumpö Dehe is owner of the water, and Earth Mother rules the earth.

Spirits are arranged hierarchically, to some extent; for example, the Devil (figure 62) and Moctezuma (figure 67) lead the *malos aires,* and Lord of the Mountain (figure 74) leads his helpers (figures 75–80).

Christian saints are probably tutelary spirits of occupations.

The President of Hell (figure 61) is a spirit named after a modern political office.

Tepehua: Spirits associated with natural phenomena are called *dueños* or "owners"; for example, Xalapánaak Xkán (Lord of the Water, figure 164) is owner of the water, and Xalapanalakat'un (Lord of the Earth, figures 163a, b) rules the earth.

The underworld is organized like a *municipio* with a *presidente.*

Spirits are arranged hierarchically to some extent; for example, the Devil (Tlakakikuru, figures 157a, b, 158a, b) leads the *malos aires,* and the Lord of Water (figure 164) leads the Old Ones (Papanín).

The Golden Hill is arranged hierarchically into two "tables."

Christian saints are probably tutelary spirits of occupations.

Deceased ritual specialists are tutelary spirits of living specialists.

Food as a Marker of Social Status

"Since each god had his own place in the calendrical rituals, he also had his special food. These foods were cooked and eaten by the participants in specified rituals, as offerings to the deity" (Hunt 1977, p. 161). Some were luxury foods; others were seasonal.

Nahua, Otomí, Tepehua: Little information has been published on this aspect of the contemporary systems of symbolic classification. Special foods, including tamales and *mole,* a sauce made with chocolate, are served during Todos Santos (All Souls). Young ears of corn, called *elotes,* have a ritual connotation and are eaten in the early fall. The

Nahuas eat a special cornbread called *piki* during the winter solstice ritual of Tlacatelilis. Finally, each ritual offering contains foods and beverages, including cornmeal, chicken or turkey meat soup, tortillas, coffee, bread, *aguardiente,* and blood, which are considered appropriate to feed the spirits. This is an important area of symbolic classification since all spirits related to plant growth and fishing are, in a sense, linked to specific food types.

Historical Culture Heroes

"Many of the prehispanic deities had apparently been living beings who were deified after their deaths. Others were historically real culture heroes who for some reason had become identified with an already existing deity" (Hunt 1977, p. 163).

Nahua, Otomí, Tepehua: Like most other contemporary Middle American Indians, the Nahuas, Otomís, and Tepehuas have syncretized their culture heroes with sacred personages from Christianity. Very little published material exists on the myth systems of these groups.

Ethnic Groups

This class includes tutelary deities of ethnic groups (Hunt 1977, p. 163).

Nahua, Otomí, Tepehua: No published information exists on this symbol class.

KINSHIP

"The gods, like man, had intricate genealogical relationships with each other." The entire sacred kinship system contained contradictions, however, and an overall genealogy was never worked out by the theologians. "However, when the gods are taken in small mythical sets of two or three, they form genealogical constellations of primary lineal relatives" (Hunt 1977, p. 164).

Nahua: Tonantsi is the mother of four important spirits: Tlauelilo, San Juan, Moctezuma, and Jesus.
  Tonantsi is also the mother of the seed spirits.
  The earth, sun, and water are also the parents of the seeds.
  The sun is father to all humans (Tata Sol).

Several spirits are conceived of as married couples (e.g., figures 1 and 7).

Otomí: Queen of the Good Earth and Queen of the Bad Earth (figure 60) are sisters.

Queen of the Good Earth and Dios Antigua are married.

The Sacred Lady (Maka Me) is probably the mother of the seeds.

Tepehua: Most major deities have a unitary, male-female parental pair; for example, Ixpayixnatikinpaydios, parents of the sun, and Ixpayixnati Malhkuyú', parents of the moon.

Many paper images are cut in male-female, husband-wife pairs (e.g., figures 155a, b, 157a, b, 162a, b, 176a, b).

Seed spirits are children of the Lord of the Water (Xalapánaak Xkán).

NAMES AND LANGUAGE TRANSFORMATIONS

"Prehispanic Mesoamerican religion, based as it was in complex games of a mytho-poetic nature, reached one of its most developed forms in its imaginative, elegant, creative use of language. Hence it is not surprising that in ideas about the divinity, plays on words . . . had a most important role" (Hunt 1977, p. 167).

Nahua, Otomí, Tepehua: No published information is available on this aspect of the contemporary religion.

ETHOS

"The Mesoamerican peoples of the past mapped out, in their conceptions of the gods, their ambivalences about the social, moral and psychic domain. . . . None of the deities were without ambivalent images, none of them were pure metaphors for good or bad, wholly beneficial or destructive" (Hunt 1977, p. 170). "To obtain [the gods'] favor requires constant cajoling and gifts. They simultaneously bind burdens of sickness and fear upon man and feed him with precious corn" (Hunt 1977, p. 171).

Nahua, Otomí, Tepehua: This characterization clearly applies to the three contemporary cultures. For example, the earth is conceived of as a provider of sustenance and a consumer of the dead. It gives life and then takes it away by sending spirits of the dead to attack people. Water spirits, the sun, ancestor spirits, etc., all have positive and negative qualities. The Tepehuas seem the most explicit about this ambivalence in their statements that even crop spirits can steal a "soul." The sequence of ritual obligations met by each culture also indicates that the spirits require constant gifts. Activities of humans annoy the spirits, who demand a continuous compensation because of this.

MATHEMATICAL ORDERS

"Prehispanic peoples used mathematics in accounting and astronomy, and for other practical needs; they also raised it to the status of an esoteric art" (Hunt 1977, p. 172).

Nahua, Otomí, Tepehua: Sophisticated mathematical systems undoubtedly were found in the urban centers in pre-Hispanic Mesoamerica and not in the smaller villages. Thus, little has survived today. No information is published on this aspect of the religious symbol system of these three cultures.

DIRECTIONS

"Prehispanic peoples conceived of the cosmos as having a number of dimensions and directions which corresponded with several alternate models, all of which are basic mathematical-typological constructs" (Hunt 1977, p. 177).

Nahua, Otomí, Tepehua: No information exists on this aspect of the religious system for the Nahuas and Tepehuas. Galinier (1979a) has written a brief article on directionality among the Otomís.

SPACE-TIME CONTINUUM

Geometric Designs

"Stereotyped geometric shapes with a religious symbolic value—circles, eye shapes, undulant lines, squares, and many other figures—abound in prehispanic architecture, painting, and writing" (Hunt 1977, p. 180).

Nahua, Otomí, Tepehua: While we will not assert that the cut paper designs of contemporary peoples are equivalent to those produced in pre-Hispanic times by painters, sculptors, or architects, it is clear that the paper images share in the general tradition of using geometric designs to convey and express religious symbols.

Numerology and Signs

"Clearly, sign and number names as well as other esoteric combinations were transformationally derived from all the taxonomic orders combined: natural, cultural, divine, and logical-mathematical" (Hunt 1977, pp. 202–203).

Nahua, Otomí, Tepehua: The complex numerological system that characterized pre-Hispanic religion does not appear among these modern groups. Aspects of the system undoubtedly remain. The ritual calendars of the modern Indians still reflect their pre-Hispanic roots (Hunt 1977, p. 186; Reyes García 1960, pp. 39–40), although the Christian influence is significant. No detailed study of this aspect of the religious symbol system has been published.

HUMAN SETTLEMENTS AND NUMEROLOGY

"The numerology of the space-time directions had a practical application in the planning of prehispanic cities and towns, and certainly in the arrangements of temples and other public places" (Hunt 1977, p. 203).

Nahua, Otomí, Tepehua: No published information exists on this topic.

NOTES

CHAPTER 1

1. The Mazatec Indians of Oaxaca manufacture a clothlike substance from the inner bark of trees for use during rituals (Lenz 1973 [1948], pp. 101-104; Weitlaner and Hoppe 1969, p. 520). This substance is called paper, but it more closely resembles bark cloth. Also, the Totonac Indians just south of the Huasteca proper make some use of cut paper figures in their rituals, but the idea was probably borrowed from Otomís or Tepehuas farther north. In any case, the paper figures are apparently not important aspects of Totonac ritual (Ichon 1969, pp. 235-36).

2. "Había entre estos naturales cinco libros, como dije de figuras y caracteres: el primero hablada de los años y tiempos: el secundo de los días y fiestas que tenían en todo el año: el tercero que habla de los sueños y de los agueros, embaimientos y vanidades en que creían: el cuarto era del bautismo y nombres que daban a los niños: el quinto es de los ritos, cerimonias y agueros que tenían en los matrimonios. . . . mucha orden y manera tenían de contar los mesmos tiempos y años, fiestas y dias. . . . Ansimismo escribían y figuraban las hazañas e historias de guerra (y tambien) del subceso de los principales señores, de los temporales y pestilencias, y en qué tiempo y de qué señor acontecían, y todos los qué subjetaron principalmente este tierra e se enseñorearon hasta que lo españoles entraron. Todo esto tienen escrito por caracteres e figuras.

"Este libro que digo se llama en lengua de estos indios *xihutonal amatl*, que quiere decir libro de la cuenta de los anos" (Motolinía 1971 [1536-41?], p. 5).

3. "Usaba tambien este gente de ciertos caracteres o letras con las cuales escribían en sus libros sus cosas antiguas y sus ciencias, y con estas figuras y algunas señales des las mismas, entendían sus cosas y las daban a entender y enseñaban. Hallámosles gran número de libros de estas sus letras, y porque no tenían cosa en que no hubiese superstición y falsedades del demonio, se los quemamos todos, lo cual sintieron a maravilla y les dío mucha pena" (Landa 1938 [1566?], p. 207).

4. Those mentioning tree bark include Anghiera 1912 [1530?], 2:40; Díaz del Castillo 1944 [1568-84], 3:242; Landa 1938 [1566?], p. 75; Sahagún 1950-69 [1575-80?], pt. 12, bk. 9, p. 111. Those mentioning maguey leaves

302

include Gómara 1943 [1544?], p. 292; Boturini Benaduci 1933 [1746], p. 95; Humboldt 1822, 2:480; Prescott 1843, 1:89. Those mentioning both sources include Hernández 1959 [1571-76?], 1:83, 348; Motolinía 1971 [1536-41?], p. 365.

5. "Las echaban à podrir, y lavaban el hilo de ellas, el que ha viendose ablandado estendian, para componer su papel gruesso, ò delgado, que despues bruñian para pintar en èl" (Boturini Benaduci 1933 [1746], pp. 95-96).

6. "Nace en lose montes de *Tepoztlan*, donde con frequencia se mira hormiguear una multitud de obreros que fabrican de este árbol un papel no muy a propósito para escribir o trazar lineas, aunque no se corre en él la tinta, pero propio para envolturas y muy adecuado y útil entre estos indios occidentales para celebrar las fiestas de los dioses, confeccionar las vestiduras sagradas, y para adornos funerarios. Se cortan sólo las ramas gruesas de los árboles, dejando los renuevos; se maceran con agua y se dejan remojar durants la noche en los arroyos o ríos. Al día siguiente se les arranca la corteza, y, después de limpiarla de la cutícula exterior, se extiende a golpes con una piedra plana pero surcada de algunas estrías, y que se sujeta con una vara be mimbre sin pulir doblada en círculo a manera de mango. Cede aquella madera flexible; se corta luego en trozos que, golpeados de nuevo con otra piedra más plana, se unen fácilmente entre sí y se alisan; se dividen por último en hojas de los palmos de largo y palmo y medio aproximadamente de ancho, que imitan nuestro papel más grueso y corriente, pero son más compactas y más blancas, aunque muy inferiores a nuestro papel más terso" (Hernández 1959 [1571-76?], 1:83-84).

BIBLIOGRAPHY

Adams, Richard N., and Arthur J. Rubel. 1967. "Sickness and Social Relations." In Manning Nash, ed. *Social Anthropology*, pp. 333–56. Vol. 6 in Robert Wauchope, gen. ed. *Handbook of Middle American Indians*. Austin: University of Texas Press.

Anders, Ferdinand. 1976. *Mexikanische Zauberfiguren: Eine Sonderausstelung des Niederoesterreichischen Landesmuseums* [Schloss Riegersburg, N.Oe. Juni bis Oktober 1976]. Katalog des Niederoesterreichischen Landesmuseums Neue Folge Nr. 68. Vienna: Amt der Niederoesterreichischen Landesregierung, Kulturabteilung.

———. 1980. "Mexikanische Zauberfiguren: Zur Sonderausstellung anlaesslich des Kolloquiums ueber Mexiko in Erlangen im Dezember 1977." In *Wirtschaft und gesellschaftliches Bewusstsein in Mexiko seit de Kolonialzeit*. Lateinamerika Studien, no. 6. Munich: Wilhelm Fink Verlag.

Anghiera, Pietro Martire d'. 1912 [1530?]. *De Orbe Novo: The Eight Decades of Peter Martyr d'Anghera*. Trans. Francis A. MacNutt. New York: G. P. Putnam's Sons.

Anonymous. 1900. "Exploration in Mexico." *American Anthropologist*, n.s. 2:400.

Barlow, Robert H. 1979 [1949]. *The Extent of the Empire of the Culhua Mexica*. Iberoamericano, no. 28. Berkeley: University of California Press; reprint, New York: AMS Press.

Berdan, Francis. 1982. *The Aztecs of Central Mexico: An Imperial Society*. New York: Holt, Rinehart and Winston.

Bernal, Ignacio, and Eusebio Davalos Hurtado, eds. 1952–53. "Huastecos, totonacos, y sus vecinos." *Revista mexicana de estudios antropológicos*, 13 (2–3): 1–567.

Beutler, Gisela. 1976. "Bemerkungen zum literarischen und volkskundlichen Hintergrund der Nahua-Texte = Comentarios respecto al fondo literario y folklórico de los textos Nawas." *Quellenwerke zur alten Geschichte Amerikas* (Stuttgart), 12:35–41 (Spanish translation pp. 145–50).

Boilès, Charles L. 1967. "Tepehua Thought-Song: A Case of Semantic Signaling." *Ethnomusicology*, 11(3): 267–92.

———. 1969. "Cognitive Process in Otomí Cult Music." Ph.D. diss., Tulane University, New Orleans.

———. 1971. "Síntesis y sincretismo en el carnaval otomí." *América Indígena*, 31 (3): 555–63.

Boturini Benaduci, Lorenzo. 1933 [1746]. "Catálogo del Museo histórico indiano del cavallero Lorenzo Boturini Benaduci." In *Idea de una nueva historia general de la América Septentrional*, pp. 1–96. facsim., Paris: Les Éditions Genet.

Bower, Bethel. 1946. "Notes on Shamanism among the Tepehua Indians." *American Anthropologist*, n.s. 48:680–83.

Butler, Alban. 1956. *Lives of the Saints*. Complete ed. New York: Kenedy.

Chamoux, Marie-Noelle. 1981. *Indiens de la Sierra: la comunauté paysanne au Mexique*. Paris: L'Harmattan.

Chipman, Donald E. 1967. *Nuño de Guzman and the Province of Pánuco in New Spain, 1518–1533*. Glendale, Calif.: Arthur H. Clark, Co.

Christensen, Bodil. 1942. "Notas sobre la fabricación del papel indígena y su empleo para 'brujerías' en la Sierra Norte de Puebla, México." *Revista mexicana de estudios antropológicos*, 6(1–2):109–24.

———. 1946. "La fabricación del papel entre los Aztecas y los Mayas." *Cuadernos americanos* (México, D.F.), 2:217–21.

———. 1952. "Los Otomís del estado de Puebla." *Revista mexicana de estudios antropológicos*, 13(2–3):259–68.

———. 1963. "Bark Paper and Witchcraft in Indian Mexico." *Economic Botany*, 17:360–67.

———. 1971. "Bark Paper and Witchcraft." In Bodil Christensen and Samuel Martí. *Brujerías y papel precolombino = Witchcraft and Pre-Columbian Paper*, pp. 9–45. México, D.F.: Ediciones Euroamericanas.

Christensen, Dieter. 1976. "Zur Musik der Nahua = Acerca de la música de los Nawas." *Quellenwerke zur alten Geschichte Amerikas* (Stuttgart), 12:27–28 (Spanish translation pp. 137–38).

Cook, Sherburne F. and Lesley Byrd Simpson. 1948. *The Population of Central Mexico in the Sixteenth Century*. Iberoamericano, vol. 31. Berkeley: University of California.

Cook de Leonard, Carmen. 1971. "Minor Arts of the Classic Period eds. *Archaeology of Northern Mesoamerica*, pt. 1. pp. 206–27. Vol.

10 in Robert Wauchope, gen. ed. *Handbook of Middle American Indians*. Austin: University of Texas Press.

Davies, Nigel. 1982. *The Ancient Kingdoms of Mexico*. London: Allen Lane.

Dávila Garibi, José Ignacio Paulino. 1942. *Toponimias nahuas*. Instituto Panamericano de Geografía e Historia. Publicación no. 63. México, D.F.: Editorial Stylo.

Díaz del Castillo, Bernal. 1944 [1568-84]. *Historia verdadera de la conquista de la Nueva España*. 3 vols. Nueve edición corregeda y aumentada. Introducción y notas por Joachín Ramírez Cabañas. México, D.F.: Editorial Pedro Robredo.

Dibble, Charles E. 1947. "Commentary on the Codex Hall, Aztec Paper and Papermaking." In Charles E. Dibble, ed. *Codex Hall: An Ancient Mexican Hieroglyphic Picture Manuscript*, pp. 3-4. Monographs of the School of American Research, no. 11. Santa Fe, N.M.: School of American Research.

Douglas, Mary. 1968. "Pollution." In David Sills, ed. *International Encyclopedia of the Social Sciences*, Vol. 12, pp. 336-42. New York: MacMillan.

Dow, James W. 1973. "Saints and Survival: The Functions of Religion in a Central Mexican Indian Society." Ph.D. diss., Brandeis University, Waltham, Massachusetts.

————. 1974. *Santos y supervivencias: funciones de la religión en una comunidad Otomí, México*. Colección SEP-INI, no. 33. México, D.F.: Instituto Nacional Indigenista y Secretaría de Educación Pública.

————. 1975. *The Otomí of the Northern Sierra de Puebla, Mexico: An Ethnographic Outline*. Latin American Studies Center Monograph Series, no. 12. East Lansing: Michigan State University.

————. 1976. "The Effectiveness of Magical Symbols: Paper Dolls in Otomí Shamanism" (unpublished ms.).

————. 1982. "Las figuras de papel y el concepto del alma entre los Otomís de la Sierra." *América Indígena* 42(4):629-50.

Dykerhoff, Ursula. 1984. "La historia de curación antigua de San Pablito, Pahuatlan, Puebla: Autor Antonio López M." *Indiana* (Berlin) 9(1): 69-85.

Eshelman, Catherine Good. 1981. "Arte y comercio nahua: el amate pintado de Guerrero." *América Indígena* 41(2):245-63.

Fitl, Regina. 1975. "Die 'Muñecos' von San Pablito: ein Beitrag zur Kenntnis der 'Brujería' in der Sierra de Puebla, Mexiko." Ph.D. diss., University of Vienna, Austria.

G. B. (unidentified contributor). 1938. "Rapport préliminaire de la mission du Dr. Robert Gessain au Mexique, 1937-1938." *Journal de la Société des Américanistes* (Paris), n.s. 30:381-84.

Galinier, Jacques. 1976a. "Les frontières culturelles actuelles des Otomís de la Huasteca méridionale." *Sociedad Mexicana de Antropología*, Mesa redonda 14:185-90.

————. 1976b. "La grande vie: représentation de la mort et practiques funéraires chez les indiens Otomís (Mexique)." *Cahiers du Centre d'Etudes et de Recherches Ethnologiques*, Université de Bordeaux 2(4):2-27.

————. 1976c. "Oratories otomís de la région de Tulancingo." *Actas de XLI Congreso Internacional de Americanistas* (México, 1974) 41(3):158-71.

————. 1977. "Mutaciones sociales y particularismos ideologicos entre los Otomís del sur de la Huasteca." *Sociedad Mexicana de Antropología*, Mesa redonda 15, 3:345-50.

————. 1979a. "La Huasteca (espace et temps) dans la religion des indiens Otomís." *Actes du XLIIe Congrès International des Américanistes* (Paris, 1976) 9B:129-40.

————. 1979b. *N'yūhū, les indiens Otomís: hiérarchie sociale et tradition dans le sud de la Huasteca.* Estudios mesoamericanos—Serie 2, no. 2. México, D.F.: Misión Arqueológica y Etnológica Francesca en México.

————. 1979c. "La peau, la pourriture et le sacré champ sémantique et motivation dans un exemple otomí (Mexique)." *Journal de la Société des Américanistes* (Paris), n.s. 66:205-18.

————. 1980a. "Indian Ideology, Conservatism, and Development in the Otomí Communities." *Mexicon* (Berlin) 1(6):83-85.

————. 1980b. "Inversion et prédiction dans les reves otomís." *Cahiers ethnologiques*, Université de Bordeaux II, Centre d'Etudes Ethnologiques (Talence, France) no. 1:14-33.

Gerhard, Peter. 1972. *A Guide to the Historical Geography of New Spain.* Cambridge Latin American Studies, Vol. 14. Cambridge: Cambridge University Press.

Gessain, Robert. 1938. "Contribution a l'étude des cultes et des cérémonies indigènes de la région de Huehuetla (Hidalgo)." *Journal de la Société des Américanistes* (Paris), n.s. 30:343-71.

————. 1939. "Magic in Mexico." *Nature*, 144:1033-36.

————. 1952-53. "Les indiens tepehuas de Huehuetla." *Revista mexicana de estudios antropológicos*, 13(2-3):187-211.

Gillow, D. Eulogio G. 1889. *Apuntes historicos.* México: Imprenta del Sagrado Corazon de Jesus.

Gómara, Francisco López de. 1943 [1554?]. *Historia de la conquista de México.* Introducción y notas por Joachín Ramírez Cabañas. México, D.F.: Editorial Pedro Robredo.

Harnapp, Vern R. 1972. "The Mexican Huasteca: A Region in Formation." Ph.D. diss., University of Kansas, Lawrence.

Hernández, Francisco. 1959 [1571–76?]. *Historia natural de Nueva España,* Vol. 1. México, D.F.: Universidad Nacional de México.

Heyden, Doris. 1975. "La supervivencia del uso mágico de las figurillas y miniaturas arqueológicos." *Sociedad Mexicana de Antropología,* Mesa redonda 13:341–49.

Hough, Walter. 1899. "Material of the Mexican Codices." *American Anthropologist,* n.s. 1:789–90.

Humboldt, Alexander von. 1822. *Political Essay on the Kingdom of New Spain.* Trans. John Black. 3rd ed. London: Longman, Hurst, Rees, Orme and Brown.

Hunt, Eva. 1977. *The Transformation of the Hummingbird: Cultural Roots of a Zinacantecan Mythical Poem.* Ithaca, N.Y.: Cornell University Press.

Hunter, Dard. 1927. *Primitive Papermaking.* Chillicothe, Ohio: Mountain House Press.

———. 1957. *Papermaking: The History and Technique of an Ancient Craft.* 2nd ed. New York: Alfred A. Knopf.

Ichon, Alain. 1969. *La religion de Totonaques de la Sierra.* Paris: Editions du Centre National de la Recherche Scientifique.

Jansen, Maarten E. R. G. N., and Th. J. J. Leyenaar. 1975. *De Amate-geesten van San Pablito.* Leiden: Verre Naasten Naderbij.

Johnson, Irmgard Weitlaner. 1971. "Basketry and Textiles." In Gordon F. Ekholm and Ignacio Bernal, eds. *Archaeology of Northern Mesoamerica,* pt. 1. pp. 297–321. Vol. 10 in Robert Wauchope, gen. ed. *Handbook of Middle American Indians.* Austin: University of Texas Press.

Kaupp, Robert. 1975. "The Basis of Political Power of the Political Middlemen of San Pablito de la Sierra de Puebla, Mexico." Ph.D. diss., University of Massachusetts, Amherst.

Kelly, Isabel, and Angel Palerm. 1952. *The Tajín Totonac. Part 1: History, Subsistence, Shelter and Technology.* Smithsonian Institution, Institute for Social Anthropology, Publication No. 13. Washington, D.C.: Smithsonian Institution.

Klein, Cecelia F. 1976. *The Face of the Earth: Frontality in Two-*

Dimensional Mesoamerican Art. New York: Garland Publishing Co.

Knab, Tim. 1979a. "Talocan Talmanic: Supernatural Beings of the Sierra de Puebla." *Actes du XLIIe Congrès International des Américanistes* (Paris, 1976) 42(6):127–36.

―――. 1979b. "Uso ritual de la cannabis en México." Simposio internacional sobre actualización mariguana (SIAM). Cuadernos cientificos CEMESAM, Centro mexicano de estudios en salud mental (México, D.F.) 10:221–37.

Knecht, Sigrid. 1966. "Mexikanische Zauberpapiere: Ihre Herstellung und magische Verwendung bei den Otomí-Indianern in Mexico." *Tribus* (Stuttgart) (NF) no. 15:131–48.

Landa, Diego de. 1938 [1566?]. *Relación de las cosas de Yucatán.* Introduction and notes by Héctor Péres Martínez. 7a ed. México, D.F.: Editorial Pedro Robredo.

Lannik, William, Raymond L. Palm, and Marsha P. Tatkon. 1969. *Paper Figures and Folk Medicine among the San Pablito Otomí.* Indian Notes and Monographs Miscellaneous Series, no. 57. New York: Museum of the American Indian, Heye Foundation.

Laughlin, Robert M. 1969. "The Huastec." In Evon Z. Vogt, ed. *Ethnology*, pt. 1, pp. 298–311. Vol. 7 in Robert Wauchope, gen. ed. *Handbook of Middle American Indians.* Austin: University of Texas Press.

Leander, Birgitta. 1972. *Herencia cultural del mundo náhuatl.* SepSetentas, no. 35. México, D.F.: Secretaría de Educación Pública.

Lenz, Hans. 1946. "El papel precortesiano." In Jorgé A. Vivó, ed. *México prehispánico.* pp. 694–701. México, D.F.: Editorial Emma Hurtado.

―――. 1949. "Las fibras y las plantas del papel indígena mexicano." *Cuadernos Americanos* (México, D.F.) 8(3):157–69.

―――. 1959. "La elaboración del papel indígena." In *Esplendor del México antiguo*, Vol. 1, pp. 355–60. México, D.F.: Centro de Investigaciones Antropológicos de México.

―――. 1969. "El papel y los supersticiones." In *Mitos, ritos y hechicerias. Artes de México*, no. 124, pp. 84–96. México, D.F.: Artes de México.

―――. 1973 [1948]. *El papel indígena mexicano.* SepSetentas, no. 65. México, D.F.: Secretaría de Educación Pública. (1st ed. Editorial Cultura 1950, c1948; 1st English ed. Editorial Libros de México 1961).

―――. 1984. *Cosas del papel en Mesoamerica.* México, D.F.

Lenz, Hans, and Federico Gómez de Orozco. 1940. *La industria papelera en México; bosquejo histórico.* México, D.F.: Editorial Cultura.

León, Nicolás. 1924. "La industria indígena del papel en México, en los tiempos precolombinos y actuales." *Boletín del Museo Nacional* (México, D.F.), Epoca 4, 2(5):101–105.

Manrique C., Leonardo. 1969. "The Otomí." In Evon Z. Vogt, ed. *Ethnology*, pt. 2, pp. 682–722. Vol. 8 in Robert Wauchope, gen. ed. *Handbook of Middle American Indians.* Austin: University of Texas Press.

Martí, Samuel. 1965. "Precolombian Paper Paintings." *Ethnos* (Stockholm) 30:144–62.

———. 1971. "Pre-Columbian Bark Paper." In Bodil Christensen and Samuel Martí. *Brujerías y papel precolombino = Witchcraft and Pre-Columbian Paper*, pp. 47–85. Mexico, D.F.: Ediciones Euroamericanas.

Martínez Cortés, Fernando. 1974. *Pegamentos, gomas y resinas en el México prehispanico.* SepSetentas, no. 124. México, D.F.: Secretaría de Educación Pública.

Martínez H., Librado. 1960. "Costumbres y creencias en el municipio del Ixhuatlán de Madero, Veracruz." *Boletín del Centro de Investigaciones Antropológicas de México* no. 8:9–13.

McBride, George McCutchen. 1923. *The Land Systems of Mexico.* American Geographical Society, Research Series, no. 12. New York: American Geographical Society.

Meade, Joaquín. 1942. *La Huasteca, época antigua.* México, D.F.: Editorial Cossio.

———. 1962–63. *La Huasteca veracruzana.* México, D.F.: Editorial Citlatépetl.

Medellín Zenil, Alfonso. 1979. "Muestrario ceremonial de la région de Chicontepec, Veracruz." *Actes du XLIIe Congrès International des Américanistes* (Paris, 1976), 9B:113–20.

Meggars, Betty J. 1975. "The Transpacific Origin of Mesoamerican Civilization: A Preliminary Review of the Evidence and Its Theoretical Implications." *American Anthropologist*, 77(1):1–27.

Melgarejo Vivanco, José Luis. 1960. *Breve historia de Veracruz.* Xalapa: Universidad Veracruzana.

Miranda, Faustino. 1946. "Algunos comentarios botánicos acerca de la fabricación del papel por los Aztecas." *Cuadernos Americanos* (México, D.F.), 29(5):196–204.

Molina, Alfonso de. 1944 [1571]. *Vocabulario en lengua castellana y mexicana.* Madrid: Ediciones Cultura Hispanica.

Monnich, Anneliese. 1976. "Zum Fortleben altindianischer Vorstellungen in der Volksreligion der Nahua von Veracruz und Puebla = La supervivencia de antiguas representaciones indígenas en la religión popular de los Nawas de Veracruz y Puebla." *Quellenwerke zur alten Geschichte Amerikas* (Stuttgart), 12:29–34 (Spanish translation pp.139–44).

Montoya Briones, José de Jesús. 1961. *Aspectos generales de la brujería en San Pablito.* México, D.F.: Instituto Nacional de Antropología e Historia.

———. 1964. *Atla: etnografía de un puebla nahuatl.* Departmento de Investigaciones Antropológicas, Publicaciones, no. 14. México, D.F.: Instituto Nacional de Antropología e Historia.

———. 1977. "El hombre y la serpiente en la Huasteca serrana hidalguense." *Sociedad Mexicana de Antropología*, Mesa redonda 15, 1:293–303.

———. 1981. *Significado de los aires en la cultural indígena.* Cuadernos del Museos Nacional de Antropología, no. 13. México, D.F.: Instituto Nacional de Antropología e Historia.

Motolinía, Toribio. 1971 [1536–41?]. *Memoriales; o, Libro de las cosas de la Nueva España y de los naturales de ella.* Edmundo O'Gorman, ed. 2d ed. Serie de historiadores y cronistas de Indias, no. 2. México, D.F.: Universidad Nacional Autónoma de México, Instituto de Investigaciones Históricas.

Munn, Nancy D. 1966. "Visual Categories: An Approach to the Study of Representational Systems." *American Anthropologist*, n.s. 68(4):936–50.

Ochoa, Lorenzo. 1979. *Historia prehispánica de la Huasteca.* Serie antropológica, no. 26. México, D.F.: Instituto de Investigaciones Antropológicos.

Peón Góngora, Nelia Elena. 1963. "Notas sobre el uso del papel entre los Mayas actuales de Yucatán." *Revista mexicana de estudios antropológicos*, 19:75–80.

Peterson, Frederick A. 1962 [1959]. *Ancient Mexico: An Introduction to the Prehispanic Cultures.* New York: Capricorn Books.

Prescott, William H. 1843. *History of the Conquest of Mexico, with a Preliminary View of the Ancient Mexican Civilization and the Life of the Conqueror Hernando Cortés.* New York: American Publishers Corp.

Provost, Paul Jean. 1975. "Culture and Anti-Culture Among the Eastern Nahua of Northern Veracruz, Mexico." Ph.D. diss., Indiana University, Bloomington.

————. 1981. "The Fate of the Soul in Modern Aztec Religious Thought." *Proceedings of the Indiana Academy of Science* (1980), 90:80–85.

Provost, Paul Jean, and Alan R. Sandstrom. 1977. *Sacred Guitar and Violin Music of the Modern Aztecs.* Ethnic Folkways Records, FE 4358. New York: Folkways Records.

Puig, Henri. 1976. *Vegetation de la Huasteca, Mexique: étude phyto-géographique et écologique.* Etudes Mésoaméricaines, Vol. 5. México, D.F.: Mission archéologique et ethnologique francaise au Mexique.

Reko, Blas Pablo. 1947. "El árbol del papel en el México antiguo." *Boletín de la Sociedad Botánica de México,* 5:12–19.

Reko, Victor A. 1934a. "Altmexikanisches Papier." *Wockenblatt fuer Papierfabrikation* Nr. 22:386–88.

————. 1934b. "Altmexikanisches Papier [Schluss zu Nr. 22]." *Wockenblatt fuer Papierfabrikation* Nr. 23:408–10.

Reyes García, Luis. 1960. *Pasión y muerte del Cristo sol; carnaval y cuaresma en Ichcatepec.* Xalapa: Universidad Veracruzana.

————. 1976. "Einleitung: die heutingen Nahua Mexicos = Introducción: los Nawas actuales de México." *Quellenwerke zur alten Geschichte Amerikas* (Stuttgart), 12:11–25 (Spanish translation pp. 123–35).

Sahagún, Bernardino de. 1932 [1575–80?]. *A History of Ancient Mexico.* Translated by Fanny R. Bandelier from the Spanish version of Carlos María de Bustamente. Nashville: Fisk University Press.

————. 1950–69 [1575–80?]. *Florentine Codex: General History of the Things of New Spain.* Translated from the Aztec into English by Arthur J. O. Anderson and Charles E. Dibble. Monographs of the School of American Research, no. 14. Santa Fe, N.M.: School of American Research.

Samoyoa-Chinchilla, Carlos. 1969. "Le papier chez les Mayas." *Arqueología* (Paris), 26:16–17.

Sandermann, Von W. 1968. "Ueber das altmexikanische Papier-herstellungsverfahren der Otomis im norden des Staates Puebla." In *Das Mexiko-Projekt der Deutschen Forschungsgemeinschaft: Eine Deutsch-Mexikanische interdisziplinaere Regionalforschung im Becken von Puebla-Tlaxcala.* Vol. 1. Weisbaden: Franz Steiner Verlag GMBH.

Sanders, William. 1952–53. "The Anthropogeography of Central Veracruz." In *Huastecos, totonacos, y sus vecinos.* Revista mexicana de estudios antropológicos, 13(2–3):27–78.

――. 1971. "Cultural Ecology and Settlement Patterns of the Gulf Coast." In Gordon F. Ekholm and Ignacio Bernal, eds. *Archaeology of Northern Mesoamerica*, pt. 2, pp. 543-57. Vol. 11 in Robert Wauchope, gen. ed. *Handbook of Middle American Indians.* Austin: University of Texas Press.

Sandstrom, Alan R. 1975. "Ecology, Economy and the Realm of the Sacred: An Interpretation of Ritual in a Nahua Community of the Southern Huasteca, Mexico. Ph.D. diss., Indiana University, Bloomington.

――. 1978a. *The Image of Disease: Medical Practices of Nahua Indians of the Huasteca.* University of Missouri Monographs in Anthropology, no. 3. Columbia: University of Missouri.

――. 1978b. "Sacred Paper Figurines of the Otomí Indians of the Sierra de Puebla, Mexico." In *Annual Report of the Museum of Anthropology*, pp. 41-62. Columbia: Museum of Anthropology, University of Missouri.

――. 1981. *Traditional Curing and Crop Fertility Rituals Among Otomí Indians of the Sierra de Puebla, Mexico: The Lopez Manuscripts.* Indiana University Museum Occasional Papers and Monographs, no. 3. Bloomington: Indiana University Museum.

――. 1982. "The Tonantsi Cult of the Eastern Nahua." In James Preston, ed. *Mother Worship*, pp. 25-50. Chapel Hill: University of North Carolina Press.

――. 1983. "Paper Dolls and Symbolic Sequence: An Analysis of a Modern Aztec Curing Ritual." *Folklore americano* (Mexico), no. 36:109-26.

――, and Paul Jean Provost. 1979. "Carnival in the Huasteca: Guitar and Violin Huapangos of the Modern Aztecs." *Ethnodisc Journal of Recorded Sound* (Tucson), 11:1-19 (and cassette).

Schneider, Harold K. 1977. "Prehistoric Transpacific Contact and the Theory of Culture Change." *American Anthropologist*, 79(1):9-25.

Schwede, Rudolf. 1912. *Über das Papier der Maya-Codices u. eininger altmexikanischer Bilderhandschriften.* Dresden: R. Bertling.

――. 1916. "Ein weiterer Beitrag zur Geschichte des altamerikanischen Papiers." *Jahresbericht der Vereinigung für angewandte Botanik* (Berlin), 13:35-55.

Simpson, Lesley Byrd. 1952. *Exploitation of Land in Central Mexico in the Sixteenth Century.* Iberoamericana, Vol. 36. Berkeley: University of California Press.

――. 1967. *Many Mexicos.* Berkeley: University of California Press.

Soustelle, Jacques. 1970. *Daily Life of the Aztecs on the Eve of the Spanish Conquest.* Stanford, Calif.: Stanford University Press.

Spranz, Bodo. 1961. "Zauberei und Krankenheilung im Brauchtum der Gegenwart bei Otomí-Indianern in Mexiko." *Zeitschrift für Ethnologie* (Berlin), 86(1):51–68.

Standley, Paul. 1977 [1944]. "American Fig Tree." In Victor W. Von Hagen, *The Aztec and Maya Papermakers*, pp. 94–101. New York: Hacker Art Books.

Starr, Frederick. 1900. "Mexican Paper." *American Antiquarian and Occidental Journal (Chicago)*, 22:301–309.

———. *1901.* "Notes upon the Ethnography of Southern Mexico." *Proceedings of the Davenport Academy of Sciences* (Davenport, Iowa), 8:102–98.

———. 1978 [1908]. *In Indian Mexico: A Narrative of Travel and Labor.* Chicago: Forbes and Co.; reprint, New York: AMS Press.

Stresser-Péan, Guy. 1952–53. "Les nahuas du sud de la Huasteca et l'ancienne extensión méridionale des Huastéques." *Revista mexicana de estudios antropológicos*, 13(2–3):287–90.

———. 1971. "Ancient Sources on the Huasteca." In Gordon F. Ekholm and Ignacio Bernal, eds., *Archaeology of Northern Mesoamerica*, pt. 2, pp. 582–602. Vol. 11 in Robert Wauchope, gen. ed. *Handbook of Middle American Indians.* Austin: University of Texas Press.

———, ed. 1979. "La Huasteca et la Frontière nord-est de la Mesoamérique." *Actes du XLIIe Congrès International des Américanistes* (Paris, 1976), 9B:1–157.

Stromberg, Gobi. 1976. "Amate Bark-Paper Paintings of Xalitla." In Nelson H. H. Graburn, ed. *Ethnic and Tourist Arts: Cultural Expressions from the Fourth World*, pp. 149–62. Berkeley: University of California Press.

Thompson, J. Eric. 1941. *Mexico Before Cortez: An Account of the Daily Life, Religion, and Ritual of the Aztecs and Kindred Peoples.* New York: Charles Scribner's Sons.

———. 1972. *A Commentary on the Dresden Codex, a Maya Hieroglyphic Book.* American Philosophical Society Memoirs, Vol. 93. Philadelphia: American Philosophical Society.

Tolentino, Serafin, and James Dow. n.d. "The Art of the Shaman." Unpublished preliminary ms.

Tolstoy, Paul. 1963. "Cultural Parallels Between Southeast Asia and Mesoamerica in the Manufacture of Bark Cloth." *Transactions of the New York Academy of Sciences* (Series 2), 25(6):646–62.

———. 1971. "Utilitarian Artifacts of Central Mexico." In Gordon
F. Ekholm and Ignacio Bernal, eds. *Archaeology of Northern Mesoamerica*, pt. 1, pp. 270-96. Vol. 10 in Robert Wauchope, gen.
ed., *Handbook of Middle American Indians*. Austin: University of
Texas Press.

Tyrakowski, Konrad. 1980. "Magie und Markt: Anmerkungen zur
Kommerzialisierung von 'Brujería' aus San Pablito/Puebla,
Mexiko." *Ethnología Americana* (Leiden), 17(2):965-68.

Valentini, Philipp J. J. 1880. "Mexican Paper." *Proceedings of the
American Antiquarian Society* n.s., 1:58-81.

Vivó Escoto, Jorge A. 1964. "Weather and Climate of Mexico and
Central America." In Robert C. West, ed. *Natural Environment
and Early Cultures*, pp. 187-215. Vol. 1 in Robert Wauchope,
gen. ed. *Handbook of Middle American Indians*. Austin: University
of Texas Press.

Von Hagen, Victor W. 1943a. "Mexican Paper-Making Plants."
Journal of the New York Botanical Garden, 44(517):1-10.

———. 1943b. "Paper and Civilization." *Scientific Monthly*, 57:301-14.

———. 1977 [1944]. *The Aztec and Maya Papermakers*. New York:
Hacker Art Books. (1st ed. 1944; 1st Spanish ed. Editorial Nuevo
Mundo, 1945).

Weitlaner, Roberto J., and Walter E. Hoppe. 1969. "The Mazatec."
In Evon Z. Vogt, ed. *Ethnology*. pt. 1, pp. 516-22. Vol. 7 in
Robert Wauchope, gen. ed. *Handbook of Middle American Indians*.
Austin: University of Texas Press.

West, Robert C. 1964. "The Natural Regions of Middle America."
In Robert C. West, ed. *Natural Environment and Early Cultures*,
pp. 363-83. Vol. 1 in Robert Wauchope, gen. ed. *Handbook of
Middle American Indians*. Austin: University of Texas Press.

Whettan, Nathan. 1948. *Rural Mexico*. Chicago: University of Chicago
Press.

Williams García, Roberto. 1955. "Ichcacuatitla: vida en una comunidad indígena de Chicontepec." Unpublished ms., Instituto de
Antropología, Universidad Veracruzana, Xalapa, Ver., México.

———. 1957. "Ichcacuatitla." *La palabra y el hombre* (Xalapa, Ver.),
no. 3:51-63.

———. 1960. "Carnaval en la Huasteca veracruzana." *La palabra y
el hombre* (Xalapa, Ver.), no. 15:37-45.

———. 1961. "Los Huastecos." Unpublished ms., Instituto de Antropología, Universidad Veracruzana, Xalapa, Ver., México.

———. 1963. *Los Tepehuas*. Xalapa: Universidad Veracruzana, Instituto de Antropología.

―――. 1966a. "Ofrenda al maíz." *La palabra y el hombre* (Xalapa, Ver.), no. 39:343–54.

―――. 1966b. "Plegarias para el fruto . . . la flor . . . ." *La palabra y el hombre* (Xalapa, Ver.), no. 40:653–98.

―――. 1967. "Algunos rezos tepehuas." *Revista mexicana de estudios antropológicos*, 21:287–315.

―――. 1970. *El mito en una comunidad indígena: Pisaflores, Veracruz.* Sondeos: una colección de estudios sobre el fenómeno religioso en América Latina, no. 61. Cuernavaca, México: CIDOC, Centro Intercultural de Documentación.

―――. 1972. *Mitos tepehuas.* SepSetentas, no. 27. México, D.F.: Secretaría de Educación Pública.

―――. 1975. "The Ritual Use of Cannabis in Mexico." In Vera Rubin, ed. *Cannabis and Culture*, pp. 133–45. The Hague: Mouton.

―――. 1979. "Una visión del mundo totonaquense." *Actes du XLIIe Congrès International des Américanistes* (Paris, 1976), 9B:121–28.

Wolf, Eric R. 1958. "The Virgin of Guadalupe: A Mexican National Symbol." *Journal of American Folklore*, 71:34–39.

INDEX

317